AMERICAN ETHICS
and
THE VIRTUOUS CITIZEN

Basic Principles

AMERICAN ETHICS
and
THE VIRTUOUS CITIZEN
Basic Principles

by

Robert Grant

HUMANIST PRESS
AMHERST, NEW YORK 14226

Published by Humanist Press
A division of the American Humanist Association
P.O. Box 1188, Amherst, New York, 14226-7188.

Printed and bound in the United States of America.

Library of Congress Catalog Card Number: 99-73508

ISBN 0-931779-11-1 Paperback

Cover photo taken from the painting *Declaration of Independence,* 1819, by John Trumbull.
Reprinted with permission of the Architect of the Capitol.

The publishers have generously given permission to use
extended quotations from the following copyrighted works:

From *America: A Narrative History*, by George Brown Tindall. Copyright © 1984 by W. W. Norton and Company, Inc. Reprinted by permission of W. W. Norton and Company, Inc.

From *American Scripture,* by Pauline Maier. Copyright © 1997 by Pauline Maier. Reprinted by permission of Alfred A. Knopf, Inc.

From *The Bill of Rights: Creation and Reconstruction,* by Akhil Reed Amar. Copyright © 1998 by Yale University. Reprinted by permission of Yale University Press.

From *A Brief Narrative of the Case and Trial of John Peter Zenger*, ed. James Alexander, Cambridge, Mass.: The Belknap Press of Harvard University Press. Copyright © 1963, 1972 by the President and Fellows of the University of Harvard College. Reprinted by permission of the publisher.

From *The Crime of Gallileo,* by Giorgio de Santillana. Copyright © 1955 by the University of Chicago, (copyright 1955 under the International Copyright Union, published 1955, third impression 1958). Reprinted by permission of The University of Chicago Press.

From *Democracy in America,* by Alexis de Tocqueville. Copyright © 1945 and renewed 1973 by Alfred A. Knopf Inc. Reprinted by permission of the publisher.

From *The Moral Animal,* by Robert Wright. Copyright © 1994 by Robert Wright. Reprinted by permission of Pantheon Books, a division of Random House, Inc.

From *Promoting Moral Growth*, by Joseph Reimer, Diana Pritchard Paolitto, and Richard H. Hersh. Copyright © 1983, 1979 by Joseph Reimer, Diana Pritchard Paolitto, and Richard H. Hersh, and reissued 1990 by Waveland Press, Prospect Heights, IL. Reprinted by permission of Waveland Press, Inc.

From *Social and Political Philosophy,* by John Arthur and William H. Shaw. Copyright © 1992 by Prentice Hall. Reprinted by permission of Prentice-Hall, Inc., Upper Saddle River, NJ.

From *The Story of Philosophy*, by Will Durant. Copyright © 1926, 1927, 1933 by Will Durant. Reprinted by permission of Simon and Schuster.

From *A Theory of Justice* by John Rawls, Cambridge, Mass.: The Belknap Press of Harvard University Press. Copyright © 1971 by the President and Fellows of Harvard College. Reprinted by permission of the publisher.

This book is lovingly dedicated to

my children
Robert John and Gema Marina Noemi
Thomas Joseph
Mary Elizabeth and Henry Charles
John Waldron
Kathleen Marie and Guy

and their children
Charlotte Elizabeth
Samantha Bridget
Jack Grant

and their children's children
whom I hope to see

and my beautiful Saralyn

Table of Contents

II. Equality   17

Foreword

What is the nature of man?

What is justice?

What is right and wrong, virtuous and illicit?

Is there a difference between public and private morality?

What role should the state, or the church, play in regulating conduct of the individual?

What is the proper balance between the good of society and individual freedom?

Great moral issues such as these have occupied the thoughts and writings of philosophers, kings, warriors, prophets, religious leaders, political, social and economic theorists and ordinary men and women throughout human history. And for good reasons! The structure and rules of societies and the relationships among people and between the individual and institutions depend upon the answers to these questions. And how radically different the answers have been over the centuries of humankind's recorded strivings. Even today, on the eve of a new millennium, in a world shrunken in time and space by technology and reduced to the interdependence of a neighborhood by instant communication and next-day transportation to virtually any point on the globe, we share the Earth with a vast diversity of peoples who do not necessarily share our answers to the great questions.

In this day and age, most of us are not equipped with the time, energy or scholarly resources to ponder the answers to the great questions of ethics and morality that shape our own culture and political system, let alone those of other peoples. Necessarily, we pass through our lives in the relatively parochial settings of city, town or village where we attend schools, find our jobs, make our homes and raise our families without too much reflection on the fundamental beliefs and institutions which shape the lives and opportunities of our ancestors, ourselves and our children.

To help us fill that gap, Robert Grant has made a valuable contribution in his book *American Ethics and the Virtuous Citizen—Basic Principles*. As he states succinctly in the Preface, "This is the study of the public morality of the American people." Concededly not written for philosophy professors or graduate students, this is a book for you and me written by a man of broad scholarship, great humanity and a keen understanding of American history and the American experience. Mr. Grant has drawn from a broad spectrum of philosophical, political, literary, legal, and historical sources to distill for us the great concepts of equality, the social contract, human rights and the relationships of the individual to institutions of society. To these he adds his own personal imperatives of obligation and virtue. The work is a remarkable combination of sophistication and simplicity.

This compact volume provides a wonderful tool for learning and teaching. It enriched my understanding, and it will yours too.

Adlai S. Hardin Jr.
New York, NY
September 1, 1999

Adlai Hardin, a practicing trial lawyer for 32 years, has been a Federal bankruptcy judge since 1995. While in private practice he served for three years as Secretary and three more years as Chairman of the Committee on Professional and Judicial Ethics of the Association of the Bar of the City of New York and for a number of years as a member of the Ethics Committee of the New York State Bar Association.

Preface

This book is aimed at a general audience, not philosophy professors or students. No special training is needed to understand and enjoy this work. A glossary is provided at the back of the book to clarify definitions of the more technical, legal, ethical, and philosophical terms used in this work.

The first purpose of this book is to explore the ethical values that Americans cherish. The ethical relationships that this book explores are not the sectarian values of a particular religion or sectarian community but, rather, those secular principles that extend to every member of American society. This is the study of the public morality of the American people. This unique expression of ethical values I call American ethics. It has developed over the course of our history and arises out of our historical experiences, our culture, traditions, and our political philosophy. American ethics focuses on acts that affect the common good, on conduct that affects others. Conduct that is exclusively personal in nature, that is, an act that does not hurt others, is the province of each one's religious beliefs or philosophical values.

Americans find our ethical values in the writings and speeches of the great leaders and thinkers of American colonial history, the founding fathers as well as the leaders, politicians, philosophers, and teachers of today. Americans turn to their history, their fundamental documents, the organic laws of the United States, especially the Declaration of Independence and the Federal Constitution. We look to the constitutions of the several states as well as their state and federal statutes. We look to the cases of the state and federal courts, especially the United States Supreme Court. We give a moral reading to these documents and writings in order to identify our underlying ethical values.

> The moral reading helps us to identify and explain not only these large-scale patterns, moreover, but also more fine-grained differences in constitutional interpretation that cut across the conventional liberal-conservative divide...
>
> ...the moral reading is not revolutionary in practice. Lawyers and judges, in their day-to-day work, instinctively treat the Constitution as expressing abstract moral requirements that can only be applied to concrete cases through fresh moral judgments... History is crucial to that project, because we must know something about

the circumstances in which a person spoke to have any good idea of what he meant to say in speaking as he did....[1]

American ethics are those values and principles that have been accepted by most of the American people and not just some sectarian groups. The duties and rights of American ethics form the basis of many of the criminal laws (as well as certain other laws) that guide our conduct. The rights arising from those principles are protected and the corresponding duties enforced by the federal and State governments. This is not a minimalist ethics but an attempt to develop those values that are at the heart of our American heritage and that have a broad consensus among most Americans.

Some of the ethical principles and dilemmas that we shall raise have long since been resolved, such as slavery. However, these subjects are included to give a rounded and complete view of American ethics as well as an historical background that will be useful in analyzing current ethical problems. For example, understanding the history and background of slavery will help us understand the reasons for today's Affirmative Action programs. On the other hand, this is not intended to be a complete description of every possible good or bad deed of which human beings are capable. Of necessity, we will explore only the more basic human rights, duties and virtues that can offer some practical and relevant guidance for current ethical problems.

At the end of each chapter, there are additional readings that explore the subject of the chapter in greater depth or give more detailed historical background. Also at the end of each chapter, there are landmark cases, generally Supreme Court cases that have particular ethical importance in our history and that interpret and apply the legal principles that constitute American ethics.

This book discusses some fundamental principles and is only an introduction to American ethics. Later works, yet to be written, shall explore our basic human rights to life, liberty and the pursuit of happiness. We shall add the right to acquire and own property, as well as the right to economic justice, to our list of basic human rights. To round out our subject, we will also discuss the growing ethical problems in protecting the environment. Finally, we will give perspective to American Ethics by discussing urgent ethical problems at the global level.

The second purpose of this book is to offer you help and guidance to know the right course of conduct when faced with a personal ethical dilemma. This book is to assist you in reaching and strengthening your ethical center by helping you to develop a strong personal code of morality and be what the founding fathers referred to as a virtuous citizen. Each of us has and lives by a basic set of core values; some of these we may know, some we may not know or fully understand, and some we may deny. These core values define our char-

---

[1] Ronald Dworkin, "The Moral Reading of the Constitution," *The New York Review*, 21 March 1996, pp. 46-50.

acter and what kind of a human being we are.

Understanding our core values gives us great strength and confidence in making ethical decisions and makes us much more effective in our various roles in life as student, spouse, parent, employee, employer or teacher. Business consultant Stephen R. Covey teaches that effective people are proactive people who have explored their inner selves—their centers—and have based their core values on ethical principles.

> Principles are deep, fundamental truths, classic truths, generic common denominators. They are tightly interwoven threads running with exactness, consistency, beauty, and strength through the fabric of life.

> Even in the midst of people or circumstances that seem to ignore the principles, we can be secure in the knowledge that principles are bigger than people or circumstances, and that thousands of years of history have seen them triumph, time and time again. Even more important, we can be secure in the knowledge that we can validate them in our own lives, by our own experience....

> We are limited, but we can push back the borders of our limitations. An understanding of the principle of our own growth enables us to search out correct principles with the confidence that the more we learn, the more clearly we can focus the lens through which we see the world. The principles don't change; our understanding of them does.

> The wisdom and guidance that accompany principle-centered living come from correct maps, from the way things really are, have been, and will be. Correct maps enable us to clearly see where we want to go and how to get there. We can make our decisions using the correct data that will make their implementation possible and meaningful.

> The personal power that comes from principle-centered living is the power of a self-aware, knowledgeable, proactive individual, unrestricted by the attitudes, behaviors, and actions of others or by many of the circumstances and environmental influences that limit other people....[2]

This book is to help you develop a principle-centered life by urging you to affirm your obligations and to develop virtuous habits. At the end of each chapter, there is a discussion of those ethical obligations and virtues which flow from that subject matter. We should incorporate these ethical values into our lives as part of our personal ethical development. I would observe that these obligations and virtues, although relevant to a particular discussion, have general application to the whole of ethical conduct and you will see how many of these obligations and virtues could be assigned to other chapters. The result will be that you will become a more self-confident individual who has attained a higher level of inner peace. And you will be a more effective person and a more ethical and virtuous student, spouse, parent, employee, employer, teacher, citizen and human being. Hopefully, the relationships with the others in your life will be happier and more satisfying.

---

[2] Stephen R. Covey, *The Seven Habits of Highly Effective People* (Simon and Schuster, New York, 1989), p. 122-3.

Acknowledgements

I need to acknowledge the help that many people have given to me in the preparation of this work.

I thank the members of the Ethical Culture Society of Westchester who suffered through the seminar based on this book.

A special thanks to Beth Lamont and the Half Moon Foundation that helped me to publish this work.

Many thanks to Fred Edwords, executive director of the American Humanist Association, who published this book, and Mira Poudrier, who was my patient editor.

Thanks to Paul Weimer, Director of the Georgia Center for Character Development, for his help and encouragement.

Thanks to United States Bankruptcy Judge Adlai S. Hardin, Jr., who wrote the foreword to this book, a scholar, a friend, and an expert in legal ethics.

I thank my children who patiently read my manuscript and gave me meaningful advice.

And I thank my Saralyn who listened and listened and listened to my pontificating.

And to the many others who have read the manuscript and have given me constructive suggestions. They know who they are.

Prologue

Socrates asked, "What is man and what can he become?"

So he went about prying into the human soul uncovering assumptions and questioning certainties. If men discoursed too readily of justice, he asked them, quietly, "to ti?"— "what is it?" What do you mean by these abstract words with which you so easily settle the problems of life and death? What do you mean by honor, virtue, morality, patriotism? What do you mean by yourself? It was with such moral and psychological questions that Socrates loved to deal. Some who suffered from this 'Socratic method,' this demand for accurate definitions, and clear thinking, and exact analysis, objected that he asked more than he answered, and left men's minds more confused than before. Nevertheless he bequeathed to philosophy two very definite answers to two of our most difficult problems—What is the meaning of virtue: and What is the best state?...

It was his reply to these questions that gave Socrates death and immortality. The older citizens would have honored him had he tried to restore the ancient polytheistic faith; if he had led his band of emancipated souls to the temples and the sacred groves, and bade them sacrifice again to the gods of their fathers. But he felt that that was a hopeless and suicidal policy, a progress backward, into and not 'over the tombs.' He had his own religious faith: he believed in one God, and hoped in his modest way that death would not quite destroy him, but he knew that a lasting moral code could not be based upon so uncertain a theology. If one could build a system of morality absolutely independent of religious doctrine, as valid for the atheist as for the pietist, then theologies might come and go without loosening the moral cement that makes of wilful individuals the peaceful citizens of a community.[3]

---

[3] Will Durant, *The Story of Philosophy, The Lives and Opinions of the Greater Philosophers* (Simon and Schuster, New York, Second Edition, 1953), pp. 9-10.

CHAPTER I

Introduction

> ***Ethics***....*the discipline dealing with what is good and bad and with moral duty and obligation...   2. a set of moral principles or values...   3. theory or system of moral values...*
>
> —Webster's New Collegiate Dictionary

> *A man's conscience and his judgement is the same thing, and as the judgement, so also the conscience, may be erroneous.*
>
> —Thomas Hobbes
Leviathan, Part ii, ch. 29

> *Labour to keep alive in your breast that little spark of celestial fire, called conscience.*
>
> —George Washington
Rules of Civility and Decent Behaviour
(Spark, Life of Washington, Vol. ii)

On Sunday, July 12, 1998, France played Brazil for the World Cup of Soccer in St. Denis, a suburb of Paris. About 80,000 spectators jammed the Stade de France, built for these games. It was reported that 1.7 billion people around the world watched the game on television, making it one of the largest audiences for any event in human history.

What is most interesting and instructive about the event is not that France won the championship by trouncing the reigning champion, Brazil, but that almost one out of every three people on the planet knew the rules of the game and were committed to play the game by those rules. So when Laurent Blanc, France's star defender, received a "red card" in the semi-finals, substantially all of these fans in all 24 time zones, from Albania to Zimbabwe, knew what a red card was and understood the circumstances under which it would be issued to an offending player. When the referee issued the red card to Blanc eliminating him from the championship game, the action was accepted as correct and in accordance with the rules of the game. These viewers likewise accepted the ejection of Marcel Desailly when he was sent off with his second "yellow card" with 22 minutes left in the game.[1]

1. WHAT IS ETHICS?

a. Political Philosophy and Ethics

Like sports, ethics is a system of rules. Rather than creating or governing a game, ethics creates rules for life. These rules are created so that we can live together in groups as human beings, without doing violence to each other, by requiring the group and each individual to treat every other person in the group with justice.

When we develop these rules for the group we are discussing political philosophy. Political philosophy is that social science which sets forth the rules and principles for a community that promotes peace and justice among its people. It identifies the communitarian values of the society that are eventually incorporated into the laws of that society. Politics is the science of the ideal social organization and it studies monarchy, aristocracy, democracy, etc. as models of social organization.

When we apply the rules of social organization to the individual members of a society, we are discussing ethics. Ethics personalizes those values for the good of the commonweal. Ethics is the study of ideal individual conduct. It is the need of the community for peace and justice, however, that determines and justifies the duties imposed upon the individual.

Ethics in this book is a continuing search for pragmatic principles of social interaction that work to produce a peaceful and just society. Do not think of ethics as the study of religious values or as theological mandates. Rather, think of ethics as a part of the science of sociology, a study of the rules necessary for us to live together, in harmony, in social groups. Our study is not concerned with acts or habits that are primarily private. Many religions hold that thinking thoughts or holding beliefs that they consider heresy or blasphemy is immoral and subjects the unbeliever to punishment. Some religions hold that lusting after another "in your heart" is a sin; we leave such strictly personal conduct to your religious or philosophical moral teachings. Our inquiry is concerned with conduct that affects others; this book focuses on that public morality that binds all the members of society.

While the rules of soccer are arbitrary and can be changed at will by the participants, the basic rules of ethics are the same everywhere and throughout human history since the fundamental rules that govern our social relationships flow from our nature as human beings. However, our discovery or understanding of these principles will change from time to time.

[1] *New York Times*, 13 July 1998, p. A1, C1, C4-5.

I find the dictionary definition of ethics inadequate. What is "good" or "bad" is the consequence of right or wrong behavior. Psychologists tell us that one is psychologically incapable of doing an act that is perceived as bad. Every person acts according to what he or she perceives to be good. Even when one commits a crime or a blatantly unethical act, such as murder, at the time the act is perceived as good. For example, it would be the good of the moment if I was paid to commit a murder; it might be expedient to eliminate an unwanted spouse; and one might claim that I was entitled to my personal revenge for some injury done to me. What is good or bad needs to be defined in terms of what is right or wrong. Our conduct needs to be measured by an objective and predetermined standard of what is right and wrong. It is never right to murder. It is always wrong. So when we talk of the common good we mean what is right for the commonweal. In this discussion on ethics, I will assume that good means right and that evil and bad mean wrong.

It is the job of ethics, as a code of personal morality, to identify and establish objective principles as standards to guide our choice in what is right. Conscience is our understanding of this objective right that prompts us to choose the good that is right and to avoid the perceived or immediate or the expedient good that is wrong. Morality is to follow the dictates of conscience.

There are two kinds of ethical conduct, obligations and virtues. Ethical obligations are those rules of conduct that respect individual human rights that we have a duty to obey. Virtues are those acts that benefit others and that go beyond our obligations, that we voluntarily assume. It is ethical to obey the law; it is virtuous to do more than the law requires.

This book explores the question: what constitutes ethical conduct or right and wrong behavior? That is determined by the good or the bad effects which our conduct has upon others and upon our society. So I would offer a more precise and descriptive definition of ethics. *Ethics is the system of human rights and duties that governs the relationships among members of a society and those of the society toward its members, a system which seeks to promote peace with justice, as well as the development and promotion of altruistic values that enhance the commonweal.*

The perspective of this book is, first, to examine American ethics from the point of view of political philosophy, the study of the ideal society. Our study will examine those communitarian rules and principles that constitute the values that underlie our Constitution, laws, and the court decisions that make our society civil. Second, it will incorporate these rules and principles into a code of ethics, a system of ideal personal conduct, as our personal code of morality that supports and defends civil society. When viewed from this perspective, ethics is a value system that considers conduct right or wrong depending on whether the conduct promotes the communitarian values that society needs to be peaceful and just. Only those duties that society needs will be imposed upon the individual as the rules of ethics. Altruistic or virtuous conduct that enhances the commonweal is encouraged.

b. The Purpose of Ethics

The ultimate purpose of political philosophy is to define those principles and rules that will, if adhered to by all, create a peaceful and just society. The purpose of ethics, according to Aristotle, is individual happiness that he describes as "...an activity of soul in accordance with perfect virtue..."[2] However, I see our community's values and our individual ethical conduct as so intertwined as to be the same thing viewed from different perspectives. So I would say that the object of our ethics is the same as the community's need: the establishment and continuance of a peaceful and just society. Happiness is the consequence or the fruit of ethical conduct by all in the society.

At the beginning of this study, the question arises whether the object of ethics is merely a device by some to control others within the society. The Greek Sophists proclaimed that might is right, and justice is the interest of the stronger: "...the sophist Callicles denounces morality as an invention of the weak to neutralize the strength of the strong..."[3] I would answer "Yes" to this complaint; in our time we call this imposition upon the strong and the powerful for the benefit of all in the society, "The Rule of Law."

We need to be cautious, however, that our ethical system is not perverted and used as a mechanism to control the masses, to maintain law and order without any real justice, for the benefit of a privileged few.

c. Our Sense of Justice

The demand for justice among the members of a society gives rise to ethical rules. Justice has been defined as giving to each his or her due. Ethics sets forth the rules by which each person receives his or her due. It is clear that our sense of justice will define the quality of our ethical system. *How justly do we assign basic rights and duties and distribute the political, social and economic benefits of our social cooperation among all the members of the society?* Without justice, ethics will favor the privileged. If our understanding of justice is that it divides the society into classes and operates according to different standards within each class, then the ethical system will give preference to the privileged class in that society, as in the case of monarchy, aristocracy, or oligarchy, where privilege is based upon the accident of birth or extreme wealth. It is, indeed, possible to construct an ethical system that reinforces unequal classes within a society and uses ethical rules, not to achieve what a reasonable person would consider right and good for the commonweal, but as a means of imposing upon the unprivileged acceptance of a lower social and economic status and a meager share of that society's blessings. In short, that society uses unjust ethical rules to enforce peace and order.

---

[2] Aristotle, *Ethics*, Everyman's Library (Dutton, New York 1975), p. 25; See Book I.

[3] Durant, *Op. Cit.,* p. 17.

If, on the other hand, a society is *truly democratic,* then its sense of justice will recognize the equality of all and the ethical system it constructs will seek to distribute the benefits of social cooperation on an equal basis to all. It is clear that the higher the sense of justice—that is, the more equally all members of the society are treated—the greater the probability that the society will be peaceful and orderly. "No Justice! No Peace!" is the real cry of those who are treated unjustly. Domestic unrest by the victims against their oppressors is the natural consequence of perceived injustice.

Our sense of justice defines the quality of our ethical system; our ethical principles are the rolling out of our standard of justice. Our sense of justice ultimately turns upon how equally we treat all the members of our society—that is, how equally we impose duties, assign rights, and distribute the political, social, and economic benefits of social cooperation.

Since ethics imposes rules mandating future conduct, it implies that there be a high degree of trust that rules will be enforced or obeyed by all. The corruption of public officials responsible for the adoption or the enforcement of just laws by a wealthy and powerful oligarchy undermines the public's trust that all will be treated equally and fairly by society. The existence of organized crime in our society seriously violates the people's trust that law breakers will be apprehended and punished. When natural disaster creates scarcity of food, water, or sexual partners, the rule of law breaks down. It is not because the rules of ethics no longer apply. Rather, it is because the strong take advantage of the opportunity to attack the weak out of avarice or because the necessary trust that all others will continue to honor the rules, in the face of calamity, collapses. When the sense of order disappears, the sense that the rules do not apply appears. There is an immediate and proximate relationship between the fair and equal treatment of all citizens, corruption of public officials, the economic well-being of a community and the commitment of its citizens to ethical conduct.

2. WHAT IS THE NATURE OF HUMAN BEINGS?

a. Reason and Memory

All of us need to embrace the counsel of Socrates. "Know thyself." There is no real philosophy until the mind turns round and examines itself. What does it mean to be a "human being"? The classic definition is that "Man (meaning men and women) is a rational animal." Scientists define our species as *Homo sapiens sapiens.* We should look at ourselves as very intelligent animals who can think and understand complex ideas (or have the potential to think, in the case of children, or are imputed to have the capacity to think, in the case of the mentally disabled). We are only one of the five great apes but only we can reason at an abstract level and understand concepts like being, justice, good, evil, right, wrong, beauty, and truth. We can speak in complex languages, make sophisticated tools and organize ourselves into groups. We have long and short term memory so we can plan and we have learned how to cooperate with each other in order to survive.

b. Knowledge

Ethics is a set of rules and principles that guide our future conduct to do what is right and avoid what is wrong or do the greater good. Like law, ethics deals with future conduct and gives us guidelines to make an ethical choice. For an act to be ethical or moral or virtuous, one must be presented with two or more choices of conduct, have time to reflect, and make a conscious choice of a course of action. This implies that an individual has sufficient knowledge to make an informed decision. Acting ethically cannot be separated from the duty to learn and acquire knowledge about the rules and choices.

c. Free Choice and Determinism

The ability to freely choose is essential to the ethical act. Unlike any other species, humans have the ability to make free choices about what we understand to be right and wrong. Humans are not driven solely by instinct, nor are choices necessarily determined by genes and experience or by mere chance. The assumption is that human beings have free will—that is, the psychological capacity to make a free and voluntary choice between two (or more) courses of conduct. From this assumption arises the responsibility to choose the right, the objective good, pre-established by the rules and principles of ethics. Moreover, this choice must be a voluntary act, not one forced or coerced by another nor compelled by instinctive behavior. Instinctive behavior cannot, strictly speaking, be considered ethical conduct since it does not involve choice. While it is good for a parent to love and care for his or her child, it does not become an ethical act unless and until the parent has the choice not to care for the child and makes the conscious and voluntary decision to do so. An act is ethical when one chooses to act in compliance with one's obligations in accordance with the rights of another or knowingly and voluntarily performs an altruistic act. An act that is compelled or instinctual, however good, is not ethical unless there is an informed choice.

Furthermore, what has been said applies not just to performance of one's obligations or acts of virtue but to immoral, unethical and criminal acts as well. Generally, one cannot commit an unethical act or a crime that is wrong in itself, without knowledge of the wrong to be done, and a premeditated choice to do the evil forbidden.

Sigmund Freud and some of his followers have questioned the assumption that humans have choice. They have concluded that the human being does not have free will but that a person's choice between two or more courses of conduct is determined by one's genes and experience from the instant of conception down to the very moment that the decision is made. The theory is that every act is caused and that, therefore, the "choice" is merely the effect of a very complex series of prior causes and effects that now result in the particular course of conduct over which the individual has no real control. In effect, criminal acts as well as ethical acts are compelled. Words like choice, responsibility, moral culpability, right and wrong, have no relevance since they suggest the power and the obligation to control choices. The determinists, as these individuals are known, describe criminal or unethical conduct as anti-social behavior and reform in terms of conditioning.

Later psychologists have returned to the free choice theory. After the Second World War, Viktor E. Frankl was a professor of neurology and psychiatry at the University of Vienna Medical School and a distinguished professor of logotherapy at the U.S. International University. He was the founder of the School of Logotherapy, what has come to be called the Third Viennese School of Psychotherapy (after Freud's psychoanalysis, that looks to one's past, and Adler's individual psychology). He describes logotherapy, in comparison with psychoanalysis, as less retrospective and less introspective. "...logotherapy focuses rather on the future, that is to say, on the meanings to be fulfilled by the patient in his future. Logotherapy, indeed, is a meaning-centered psychotherapy...."[4] He relates his experiences during the war, as a prisoner in the Nazi death camps at Dachau and Auschwitz, and analyses the psychological response of the prisoners to the inhuman conditions they suffered. He explores whether they retain any free choice in the way they respond to their mistreatment.

> In attempting this psychological presentation and a psychopathological explanation of the typical characteristics of a concentration camp inmate, I may give the impression that the human being is completely and unavoidably influenced by his surroundings. (In this case the surroundings being the unique structure of camp life, which forced the prisoner to conform his conduct to a certain set pattern.) But what about human liberty? Is there no spiritual freedom in regard to behavior and reaction to any given surroundings? Is that theory true which would have us believe that man is no more than a product of many conditional and environmental factors—be they of a biological, psychological or sociological nature? Is man but an accidental product of these? Most important, do the prisoners' reactions to the singular world of the concentration camp prove that man cannot escape the influences of his surroundings? Does man have no choice of action in the face of such circumstances?

> We can answer these questions from experience as well as on principle. The experiences of camp life show that man does have a choice of action. There were enough examples, often of a heroic nature, which proved that apathy could

---

[4] Viktor E. Frankl, *Man's Search for Meaning* (Washington Square Press, Simon and Schuster, New York, 1946), p. 120.

be overcome, irritability suppressed. Man *can* preserve a vestige of spiritual freedom, of independence of mind, even in such terrible conditions of psychic and physical stress.

We who lived in concentration camps can remember the men who walked through the huts comforting others, giving away their last piece of bread. They may have been few in number, but they offer sufficient proof that everything can be taken from a man but one thing: the last of the human freedoms—to choose one's attitude in any given set of circumstances, to choose one's own way.

And there were always choices to make. Every day, every hour, offered the opportunity to make a decision, a decision which determined whether you would or would not submit to those powers which threatened to rob you of your very self, your inner freedom; which determined whether or not you would become the plaything of circumstance, renouncing freedom and dignity to become molded into the form of the typical inmate.

Seen from this point of view, the mental reactions of the inmates of a concentration camp must seem more to us than the mere expression of certain physical and sociological conditions. Even though conditions such as lack of sleep, insufficient food and various mental stresses may suggest that the inmates were bound to react in certain ways, in the final analysis it becomes clear that the sort of person the prisoner became was the result of an inner decision, and not the result of camp influences alone. Fundamentally, therefore, any man can, even under such circumstances, decide what shall become of him—mentally and spiritually. He may retain his human dignity even in a concentration camp....[5]

Although the debate still rages, for the purposes of this discussion, the question is moot since the claim that one acts under compulsion—that is, without free and voluntary intent in performing an illegal act—has been rejected by American courts. An exception to the rule exists, however, for infants under the age of seven who are considered incapable of committing a crime (or, for that matter, an ethical act). The same is true for mentally incompetent persons, who do not understand the nature and wrongfulness of the act contemplated.

In this book, I begin with the assumption that a human being has the capacity to make a free and voluntary choice—whether it be right or wrong—that he or she can control the decision, a decision that it is neither determined nor compelled nor the result of merely random selection.

d. The Right Choice

The whole purpose in developing an ethical system is to provide us with guidelines to help us make the right choice when faced with an ethical or moral problem. It is the capacity to choose rightly, even under difficult circumstances, that makes us ethical. It is the ability to see the right and to choose the right course of action, even when many others around you urge the expedient

---

[5] *Ibid.,* pp. 85-86.

course, that turns ordinary leaders into great leaders.

Harry Truman is an example of how an ordinary leader became a great leader by making the right ethical choices. Truman became president upon the death of Franklin Roosevelt, in April, 1945. He was an ordinary man by all accounts, who had two great qualities: he was honest and he had a clear understanding of right and wrong. By 1947, Western Europe was in shambles following the devastation of the Second World War. He was running for election for his second term and was facing a Republican congress which was hostile on virtually every spending measure he presented. General George C. Marshall, the chief of staff during the war, was his secretary of state. In April, 1947, Marshall was returning from Moscow where he was unable to reach an agreement with Stalin regarding the future of Germany.

Before leaving Washington, he received an urgent memo from Under Secretary for Economic Affairs Will Clayton warning that conditions in Western Europe were more serious than generally understood. During stops in Paris and Berlin, while going to and from Moscow, Marshall was stunned by what he saw and heard. On the plane back to Washington, he talked of little else but what could be done to save Western Europe.

Time was of the essence, Marshall stressed to Truman. "The patient is sinking while the doctors deliberate," he told the nation in a radio broadcast, April 28....

The idea of economic aid to Europe had been on Truman's mind for some while. Two years past, in one of their earliest conversations in the Oval Office, Henry Stimson had pointedly told him that an economically strong, productive Germany was essential to the future stability of Europe, a concept Truman readily accepted. In his State of the Union message in January, Truman had struck the theme of sharing American bounty with war-stricken peoples, as a means of spreading "the faith" of freedom and democracy, and on March 6, even before the announcement of the Truman Doctrine, he had said in a speech at Baylor University, "We are the giant of the economic world. Whether we like it or not, the future pattern of economic relations depends upon us...."

The situation was worse than anyone supposed. Millions of people were slowly starving.

A collapse in Europe would mean revolution and a tailspin for the American economy....

[Marshall declared in a speech at Harvard] "Our policy is directed not against any country or doctrine, but against hunger, poverty, desperation and chaos. Its purpose should be the revival of a working economy in the world so as to permit the emergence of political and social conditions in which free institutions can exist...."

The Republicans were determined to cut taxes and expenditures, and already since the war, three billion dollars had been spent in foreign relief. In a single grant in 1946 the United States had loaned Britain 3.25 billion dollars and now, it seemed, to little purpose. By Bill Clayton's calculations, the Europeans would need six or seven billion dollars in the coming two or three years. When Arthur Vandenberg read this in

The New York Times, in an article by James Reston, he telephoned Reston to say that surely he was misinformed. Congress, Vandenberg said, would never approve such sums, not to save anybody.[6]

In fact, the Marshall Plan, as it came to be called, eventually spent over $17 billion. It is no exaggeration that Truman's decision, in the face of tremendous opposition and at the risk of his second term, saved Western Europe from going communist. Today, Truman is considered one of our great presidents, in part because he made ethically sound choices in the face of great opposition.

e. *Evolutionary Psychology*

As animals, humans need air to breathe, space to live in, food to eat and drink, as well as shelter and clothing to shield us from the elements. Humans are, therefore, predators who have learned to cooperate with each other to hunt and gather, to occupy territory and plant food. We are sexual creatures who need mates for companionship, pleasure and procreation. The new science of evolutionary psychology is shedding new light on the early moral development of the human species.

> ...But today's Darwinian anthropologists, in scanning the world's peoples, focus less on surface differences among cultures than on deep unities. Beneath the global crazy quilt of rituals and customs, they see recurring patterns in the structure of family, friendship, politics, courtship, morality. They believe the evolutionary design of human beings explains these patterns: why people in all cultures worry about social status (often more than they realize); why people in all cultures not only gossip, but gossip about the same kinds of things: why in all cultures men and women seem different in a few basic ways; why people everywhere feel guilt, and feel it in broadly predictable circumstances; why people everywhere have a deep sense of justice, so that the axioms "One good turn deserves another" and "an eye for an eye, a tooth for a tooth" shape human life everywhere on this planet.

> In a way, it's not surprising that the rediscovery of human nature has taken so long. Being everywhere we look, it tends to elude us. We take for granted such bedrock elements of life as gratitude, shame, remorse, pride, honor, retribution, empathy, love, and so on—just as we take for granted the air we breathe, the tendency of dropped objects to fall, and other standard features of living on this planet. But things didn't have to be this way. We could live on a planet where social life featured none of the above. We could live on a planet where some ethnic groups felt some of the above and others felt others. But we don't. The more closely Darwinian anthropologists look at the world's peoples, the more they are struck by the dense and intricate web of human nature by which all are bound. And the more they see how the web was woven.

> Even when the new Darwinians do focus on differences—whether among groups of people or among people within groups—they are not generally inclined to

---

[6] David McCullough, *Truman* (Simon and Schuster, New York, 1992), pp. 561-4.

explain them in terms of genetic differences. Darwinian anthropologists see the world's undeniably diverse cultures as products of a single human nature responding to widely varying circumstances....[7]

I do not begin with the value judgement that human nature is either good or bad. Rather, *I begin with the proposition that the basic motivation for a system of rules to govern our unruly conduct is the basic instinct of human beings to survive.* We have learned that our chances of survival are better when we cooperate with others in the hunt and in protecting mates and territory. The Darwinians would claim that, through the process of natural selection, it is only those who have learned to cooperate who have survived. Such cooperation necessitates rules for the group at least to the extent that we don't hunt each other. As children of these ancient cooperators, our basic ethical values to promote the group may be hard-wired; that would account for the universality of basic ethical values. Ethics can be viewed as the rules necessary to resolve the tension between our nature as predators and our need to cooperate with each other in order to, first, survive in a hostile jungle, and second, build a peaceful and just society.

3. WHAT IS AMERICAN ETHICS?

a. *American Ethics and Our Standard of Justice*

All ethical values are based in human nature and to that extent are universal both among all people living today and over the course of the history of human beings on this planet. Specific ethical systems arise as part of the culture and the sense or standard of justice of the diverse peoples of the world. American ethical values, although essentially founded in human nature, are the outgrowth of our historical experiences, our cultural, political and philosophical values, and in particular our unique sense of justice. American ethics builds upon, but is different from, the Judeo-Christian tradition and from our heritage under the British Common Law. American ethics is the *public morality* of the American people.

As we shall see, the American standard of justice is very high although not completely fulfilled. American ethics requires that all people be treated equally regarding human, political and civil rights and that all be treated fairly regarding economic rights.

b. *Public Wrongs versus Private Wrongs*

In analyzing our laws we need to understand that the violation of a criminal law is considered a wrong done to the people as a whole. The crime of murder, for example, although it involves the killing of a particular human

---

[7] Robert Wright, *The Moral Animal* (Vintage Books, A Division of Random House, New York, 1995), pp. 7-8.

being, is an injury done to the whole society and is punished by fine and/or imprisonment. On the other hand, civil wrongs or torts are wrongs against an individual for which he or she can receive monetary damages to compensate him or her for the injury. When we look at our laws to discover the underlying moral or ethical principles, we will generally be examining the crimes that are considered "malum in se"—evil in itself. These crimes always violate some moral or ethical value.

c. Principles of American Ethics

The expression of fundamental ethical principles is unique in American ethics. I have identified five principles that characterize American ethics:

1. American ethics assumes that all people are created equal and free; that is, that they are equal in the eyes of the law with respect to human, political, and civil rights and that all are to be treated fairly with respect to economic rights;[8]

2. American ethics bases ethical obligations upon consent, upon the social contract, rather than some authority;

3. American ethics recognizes human rights as the quid pro quo for our ethical obligations under the social contract;

4. American ethics declares that its values are secular; that is, our ethical system is expressed in terms of secular goals and objectives; and,

5. The scope of American ethics—the public morality that binds us all— is limited by the Right of Privacy.

This study shall examine each of these principles in the next five chapters.

SUMMARY

Ethics identifies basic obligations and rights that govern the relation-ships among the members of a society and those between the society and its members, and promotes virtuous conduct. Personal ethical obligations arise from and are justified by the need and desire to create and maintain a peaceful and just society. These rules and principles guide our future conduct to choose what is right and avoid what is wrong and in promoting altruistic or virtuous conduct. Conduct is right or wrong depending on whether it supports and de-fends the peace and justice of society. The virtuous citizen will follow his or her conscience, will choose the right course of action and will avoid wrongful conduct by acting in his or her enlightened self-interest for the common good. The virtuous citizen will seek to do more than fulfil obligations and will per-form virtuous or altruistic acts that enhance the commonweal.

The quality of our ethical system depends upon our sense of justice—

---

[8] Economic rights will be treated in another work.

that is, how equally we treat all the members of the society in imposing basic duties; acknowledging human, political, and civil rights; and distributing the political, social, and economic benefits of social cooperation. Willful abuse of the rights of the minority, official corruption, permissiveness toward organized crime, or serious economic hardship in a society will undermine the commitment to ethical principles and the rule of law and will result in domestic unrest.

Every ethical act (and every unethical or criminal act) requires knowledge regarding the nature and the consequences of the act sufficient to make an informed choice and time to reflect and make a voluntary choice. Our obligations and rights are founded upon our nature as human beings and are therefore universal in scope although every society will express these universal values according to each society's history, culture, philosophy and sense of justice. American ethical values are built upon, but are different from, the Judeo-Christian tradition, our heritage under the British Common Law, and our high standard of justice. American ethics is based upon the principles that:

1. All people are created free and are equal regarding human, political and civil rights and all are to be treated fairly regarding economic rights;

2. Ethical obligations are assumed by mutual consent in the social contract;

3. Human rights are the benefits received from the social contract;

4. Our ethical values have secular purposes and objectives; and

5. Our public morality is limited by the Right of Privacy.

MY PERSONAL OBLIGATION:
Deal in Good Faith

"Good faith" is a term taken from equity jurisprudence. Good faith is a state of mind that has an honest intention in dealings with others and abstains from any unconscientious advantage over another under the guise of the letter of the law. Good faith is dealing with an honest purpose and without collusion. Good faith is dealing without knowledge of fraud and without bad faith, i.e. without intent to assist in a fraudulent or otherwise unlawful scheme. "In the traditional sense good faith connotes a moral quality; it is equated with honesty of purpose, freedom from fraudulent intent and faithfulness to duty or obligation."[9] To bargain in good faith means that there is a willingness to reach an agreement and to make reasonable compromises to do so, and to enter into an agreement intending that both parties receive the benefits of their bargain. However, it does not always require sound judgement and business sagacity.

Our business dealings impose an obligation of good faith; "Every con-

---

[9] *Raab v. Casper*, 124 Cal Rptr 590 at 593.

tract or duty within [the Uniform Commercial Code] imposes an obligation of good faith in its performance or enforcement"[10] and "good faith means honesty in fact in the conduct or transaction concerned."[11] In fact, "...in every contract there exists an implied covenant of good faith and fair dealing...."[12]

For our study of ethics, good faith requires intellectual honesty—to approach new ideas with an open mind and not to lock out reasonable argument based on credible evidence. In this regard I ask all to withhold judgement on this work until you have read it and have had an opportunity to reflect upon its merits.[13]

MY PERSONAL VIRTUE:
Patience

Patience is what brings civility to our society. Patience is our practiced habit of dealing with others in a rational manner rather than in emotional outbursts. In our most basic society—the family—patience is the most necessary virtue for a good spouse and parent. Impatience within the family leads to domestic violence between parents and the use of excessive corporal punishment of children. In teaching children, parents must avoid the desire to be controlling of their children's conduct, especially when controlling discipline is motivated by the ego needs of the parent for the child to be perfect rather than the needs or safety of the child.

Too often, we instruct children on their conduct of the moment. "Eat your vegetables." "Don't watch the TV." "Do your homework." "Don't be late." What we should do instead is instruct our children in basic values and close family relationships. In our home the first rule was "brothers and sisters help each other; they do not hurt each other." Our basic value was to care for each other. When they were old enough, each child was encouraged to take charge of his or her own time and TV watching, consistent with his or her other responsibilities.

Years ago, when my children were youngsters, we were getting ready to go to church and had to leave in a few minutes to be on time for the service. One had been dilly-dallying for over an hour and was not yet dressed. This lack-a-daisical, slow-poke attitude was typical and frustrating when we were pressed for time. I became impatient and angry and spanked the offender. Rather than respond with patience and rational counsel that his delay was going to make the family late, in an emotional outburst, I reacted to his indifference

---

[10] *New York's Uniform Commercial Code,* Sec. 1-203.

[11] *UCC* , Sec. 1-201.

[12] *Kirke La Shelle Co. v. Paul Armstrong Co.* , 263 N.Y. 79, 87, 188 N.E. 163, 167 (1933). sec. 1-201.

[13] See: 28 Corpus Juris 715.

with the stick to enforce my demand for obedience.

As I look back on that and several other similar instances involving others, I must conclude that, at the time I thought that I had acted properly for the benefit of the family. However, from the perspective of years gone by, I regret ever having struck any of my children, regardless of however justified it was at the time. Physical discipline can destroy good relationships that take years to build and children never remember the cause or the justification for their discipline, only the physical hurt caused by a much more powerful parent. Better that we had all missed church services that day long ago than for him to remember me as an angry father. "Spare the rod and spoil the child" is a pernicious and harmful teaching. And yelling and screaming is just as bad; it does almost as much emotional harm to children as physical violence. When you yell and scream, you prove to those around you that you have lost control over yourself and that "they" are in control of you.

I believe that I am and have been a good father. I care for my children; I'm interested in what's happening in their lives; I help them when they are in need, and my great joy is to share their joy. I am not perfect. I still lack strong patience—but I am still working on it. I hope that you can learn from my mistakes.

ADDITIONAL READINGS

John Rawls was a Professor of Philosophy at Harvard in the 1960s. In his work A Theory of Justice, *he re-examines our concepts of the Social Contract that we will explore further in Chapter 3. In this segment he shows that our sense of Justice is the foundation of all our social relationships.*

Chapter 1: Justice as Fairness

1. The Role of Justice

Justice is the first virtue of social institutions, as truth is of systems of thought. A theory however elegant and economical must be rejected or revised if it is untrue; likewise laws and institutions no matter how efficient and well-arranged must be reformed or abolished if they are unjust. Each person possesses an inviolability founded on justice that even the welfare of society as a whole cannot override. For this reason justice denies that the loss of freedom for some is made right by a greater good shared by others. It does not allow that the sacrifices imposed on a few are outweighed by the larger sum of advantages enjoyed by many. Therefore in a just society the liberties of equal citizenship are taken as settled; the rights secured by justice are not subject to political bargaining or to the calculus of social interests. The only thing that permits us to acquiesce in an erroneous theory is the lack of a better one; analogously, an injustice is tolerable only when it is necessary to avoid an even greater injustice. Being first virtues of human activities, truth and justice are uncompromising.

These propositions seem to express our intuitive conviction of the primacy of justice. No doubt they are expressed too strongly. In any event I wish to inquire whether these contentions or others similar to them are sound, and if so how they can be accounted for. To this end it is necessary to work out a theory of justice in the light of which these assertions can be interpreted and assessed. I shall begin by considering the role of the principles of justice. Let us assume, to fix ideas, that a society is a more or less self-sufficient association of persons who in their relations to one another recognize certain rules of conduct as binding and who for the most part act in accordance with them. Suppose further that these rules specify a system of cooperation designed to advance the good of those taking part in it. Then, although a society is a cooperative venture for mutual advantage, it is typically marked by a conflict as well as by an identity of interests. There is an identity of interests since social cooperation makes possible a better life for all than any would have if each were to live solely by his own efforts. There is a conflict of interests since persons are not indifferent as to how the greater benefits produced by their collaboration are distributed, for in order to pursue their ends they each prefer a larger to a lesser share. A set of principles is required for choosing among the various social arrangements which determine this division of advantages and for underwriting an agreement on the proper distributive shares. These principles are the principles of social justice: they provide a way of assigning rights and duties in the basic institutions of society and they define the appropriate distribution of the benefits and burdens of social cooperation....[14]

---

[14] John Rawls, *A Theory of Justice* (Harvard University Press, Cambridge, MA 1971), pp. 3-4. Sec. 1-201.

CHAPTER II

Equality

...We hold these truths to be self-evident, that all men are created equal, that they are endowed by their Creator with certain unalienable Rights, that among these are Life, Liberty and the pursuit of Happiness. That to secure these rights, Governments are instituted among Men, deriving their just powers from the consent of the governed...

—*Thomas Jefferson*
& The Second Continental Congress
Declaration of Independence, *July 4,1776*

Four score and seven years ago, our fathers brought forth on this continent a new nation, conceived in liberty, dedicated to the proposition that all men are created equal....

—*Abraham Lincoln*
Gettysburg Address *(1863)*

When I was about 12 years old my mother asked me to help her with the wash. By that time, I had developed a very strong sense of justice, especially when it applied to me. Now I did not object to doing "my fair share" of the household work but I objected to doing more than my younger brothers simply because I was the oldest of a large family. When I considered myself to be treated unequally, as compared to others within the family, I raised the eternal cry of the adolescent: "It's not fair!"

Later, when I had children of my own, many things were not fair: "He has a larger piece of cake." "She has a piece of cake with roses on top." "Why can she stay up later than me?" "Why does he have a later curfew?" "His allowance is more than mine." And so on. Children are accountants; they measure and compare everything for indications of unequal treatment although neither I nor they ever complained about injustice when we received the larger piece of cake.

4. FROM INEQUALITY TO EQUALITY

a. Equality as the First Principle

It seems to be a universal truth that when human beings come together in groups, we demand equal treatment within the group as a condition of our peaceful cooperation. This may be a hard-wired demand that is the consequence of our most basic instinct to survive, since inequality leads to violence to establish dominance over the group. It may be the result of the learning process of our early ancestors that survival is easier when we learn to cooperate and it may be the result of the process of natural selection that those who have learned to cooperate are those whose children have survived to the present day. Our demand for equal treatment within the group, and the agreement by others to equality for all, forms the basis for peaceful social cooperation. Equal treatment for all is the first principle for every human society that wants to be peaceful and that considers itself just. Equal treatment for all is the foundation of a society that replaces rule by the strong with the rule of law. As we discussed earlier, the quality of our justice and, therefore, the quality of our ethical system, is directly proportional to how equally all in the society are treated.

The proposition that "all men are created equal" is one of the defining principles of American ethics. Equality is the bedrock foundation of the American sense of justice and it is this ethical ideal that underlies all of our laws and governmental actions. The equal treatment of all should be at the heart of our own personal code of morality. In this chapter we will discuss the conviction that all persons have the same human, political, and civil rights, and that all are entitled to have these rights protected equally by the government and respected by each other.

We cannot talk of equality without declaring our freedom in the same breath. Ours is not the equality of the slaves but the equality of free men and women. In colonial times, freedom was claimed as one of the rights of Englishmen everywhere. And, indeed, the English enjoyed a modicum of freedom, exercised within an unequal, rigid caste system that continues to this day in Great Britain. By the time that the Revolution had arrived, the Americans demanded more than the freedom of Englishmen; they demanded equal freedom—independence from the Crown and the aristocracy; they demanded a republic. They would no longer be content with replacing a tyrannical king with another ruler as the British had done, after beheading Charles I, following the Protectorate of Cromwell. The presumption that "the king that can do no wrong," continued with the ascension of Charles II and is still good law in Britain today. In fact, the common law fiction asserted that the king is not only incapable of *doing* wrong but even of *thinking* wrong.[1] If wrong was done it

---

[1] William Blackstone, *Commentaries on the Laws of England,* (University of Chicago Press, Chicago, IL, 1979), p. 246.

could not be imputed to the king but must be laid to the charge of the ministers who advised him.[2] When I speak of equality in this book, I mean full equality that includes freedom.

b. Equality under the King

This march toward fuller equality and freedom proceeded slowly and in halting stages. Early enlightenment thinkers were content with claiming their equality under a king. They were content with the equality of children—the equality that children seek from their father and mother. Later American thinkers would demand the full equality of free and independent adults that necessarily leads to self government.

The writer of the Enlightenment who had the greatest influence on our founding fathers was John Locke (1632–1704). The idea of equal treatment for all arose from his notion that human beings existed as free individuals in a state of nature before they came together in society under a social contract and before governments were instituted, i.e. before individuals incurred or assumed obligations to the community. To understand how this concept of full equality developed, we need to place this idea in an historical context.

In 1519 the political unity of the Holy Roman Catholic Church was torn asunder by Martin Luther with the nailing of his 95 theses to the door of the Wittenburg Cathedral. In 1534, Henry VIII further split the central authority of the church by demanding that the church leaders in England give allegiance to him as the head of the church in England and renounce the authority of the pope. Most of the bishops acquiesced and the Anglican Church was established as the official tax-supported Church of England. Bitter religious wars and persecutions broke out in Germany, France, Italy, Spain, England, Scotland, and other countries in Europe. The daughter of Henry VIII succeeded him as Queen Elizabeth. She executed Mary Queen of Scots, a Catholic. Mary's son, James VI of Scotland, was raised as a Protestant and in 1604 succeeded Elizabeth as James I of England, uniting England and Scotland under one Protestant monarch. This was the period of the rise of the national state and James was foremost in asserting the divine right of kings in both political and spiritual matters. This was a time in the western world when most people were not equal. At the time, Europe was ruled by kings and queens, czars and czarinas, emperors and empresses, princes and princesses, dukes and duchesses, barons and baronesses, sultans, popes, and cardinals, many of whom were absolute monarchs. The nobility acquired great wealth at the expense of the peasants they ruled and were able to pass on their thrones and their wealth to their children. Society was divided into royalty and their privileged, aristocratic entourage on the one hand and the unprivileged peasants—those who did the work—on the other hand.

---

[2] *Langford v. United States*, 225 L. Ed. 1010 at 1011.

King James asserted that monarchy is a divinely ordained institution, that he was God's representative on earth, and that he was not responsible to the people for his actions but to God alone. Kings derive their power through heredity succession, the idea that hereditary right cannot be abolished and that even if the kingdom was originally subdued by conquest that too was God's will. The king, James asserted, is above the law of the land (rejecting the medieval notion that the king was subject to natural law and the moral law or traditional customs of the land) and his subjects are charged by God not to resist their monarch but passively to obey him, even if, in their view, he is wicked.

His views were staunchly defended by the bishops of the Church of England. Sir Robert Filmer, a later writer, defended the divine right of kings theory in his work *Patriarcha or a Defence of the Natural Power of Kings Against the Unnatural Liberty of the People* (1680). He taught that political obligation was based upon scriptural patriarchy and that God had never intended people to elect their own rulers or limit the power of their rulers. Similar views were held by Louis XIV of Catholic France, who declared that "I am the State!" His views were similarly defended by the pope (who had long before asserted similar claims to absolute authority for himself since he was God's representative on earth) and the French bishops. In both cases these broad claims led to the execution of their successors, Charles I in England and Louis XVI in France.

Persecution of Catholics was widespread in England since they opposed the rejection of papal supremacy in spiritual matters and the confiscation of church lands. Later, as new Protestant denominations sprang up, they too were persecuted for opposing the Church of England. The most important of these was the Calvinist sect of Puritans, those within the Church of England who wanted to purify the church by ridding it of the rituals and trappings of the old church. They represented the growing merchant class that developed as feudalism and the power of the manor waned and people moved to the cities. This rich and powerful gentry supported a strong and independent parliament, The House of Commons, at the expense of the king and the House of Lords.

In the midst of this religious turmoil, James' son, Charles I, came to the throne in 1624. He continued to assert the divine right theory and clashed directly with Parliament, now controlled by the Puritans. Civil war broke out between the Cavaliers, the supporters of the king, and the Roundheads (so called for their closely shaved heads), made up of the Puritans and their allies supported by the emerging merchant class; Charles was defeated. To be sure, the civil war was no struggle for religious freedom but a struggle for political (and economic) power between would-be persecutors.

At his trial for treason before the Court convened by Parliament, Charles challenged its jurisdiction; he asked pointedly, by what authority do you presume to try your king anointed by God?

In 1649, the House of Commons alone—without the Lords and King—

established a special "High Court of Justice" to try King Charles I for attempting "to subvert the ancient and fundamental laws and liberties of this nation" and establish in their place "an arbitrary and tyrannical government." The court brought detailed charges against him, but Charles denied its jurisdiction. The Commons could not make laws or create such a court without the consent of the Lords and King, he said, nor could it claim the right to try a king "without the consent of every man in England of whatsoever quality or condition." He was nonetheless tried, convicted, and executed. The Commons went on to abolish monarchy and the House of Lords and to establish a short-lived "Commonwealth" in which power was exercised by "the representatives of the people in Parliament, and by such as they shall appoint."[3]

John Locke was a young Puritan student at the Westminster Abbey School when Charles I was found guilty of treason and beheaded in 1649 without getting an answer to his question. During his lifetime, another king, a Catholic, James II, was opposed by Parliament, precipitating yet another religious civil war that culminated in the defeat of James at the Battle of the Boyne in Ireland in 1688. Thereafter, Parliament invited James' sister Mary and her husband, the Dutch stadtholder, William of Orange, to assume the throne as joint monarchs.

In 1689, the victorious Constitution Parliament, as it was now known, enacted the Declaration of Rights or Bill of Rights, whereby the new monarchs gave up the prerogatives of suspending laws, erecting special courts, keeping a standing army, or levying taxes except with Parliamentary consent. Furthermore, it provided for frequent sessions of Parliament, freedom of speech for its deliberations, freedom of petition, and restrictions against excessive bail and cruel and unusual punishment.

By far the best-known and most influential English declaration among Americans was the Declaration of Rights of 1689, which formally ended the reign of James II and inaugurated that of William and Mary. It became for the colonists a sacred text, a document which, although not celebrated with religious imagery, provided a statement of established, fundamental political and legal truths. Like all such documents in English and American history, the Declaration of Rights was itself built on a substantial body of precedents. On five occasions between 1327 and 1485, then twice again in the seventeenth century, Englishmen brought the reign of a living king to an end. English kings were never disposed of lightly or silently; official statements of one sort or another always explained and justified the change of regime. Those justifications served over time to limit the legitimate deposition of a monarch to cases in which he was blatantly incompetent (rex inutilis) or bad in the sense of having violated established laws, customs, and moral standards, whether on his own initiative or by stubbornly following (as was said of Edward IV in 1484) "the counsel of persons insolent, vicious, and of inordinate avarice, despising the counsel of good, virtuous, and prudent persons." But who could judge a king? God, of course, and the language of the fourteenth

---

[3] Pauline Maier, *American Scripture* (Alfred A. Knopf, New York, 1997), p.52.

and fifteenth centuries suggested that the community of the governed could also decide whether a reigning king was incompetent or evil and who would replace him on the throne, although in practice a small number of high-placed men made the critical decisions. Gradually, however, the right to speak for "the whole community of the kingdom" became invested in Parliament, which included the King, Lords, and Commons, and so in theory represented all the "estates" or social classes within the realm.[4]

The Glorious Revolution had significant long-term effects on colonial thinking. The overthrow of James II set an example and a precedent for revolution against the monarch.

It is in this historical context that John Locke, whose ideas had now fully matured, published his *Two Treatises On Government* in 1690. His writings became the philosophical justification for the overthrow of James II. His political theory affected England most deeply and had enormous impact on political thought in the colonies. It penetrated into the North American colonies, and passed through Samuel Adams and Thomas Jefferson into the Declaration of Independence and, through Rousseau, into the French Revolution.

In his *First Treatise*, he attacked and refuted the theory of the divine right of kings and in particular the *Patriarcha* of Sir Robert Filmer. The more important *Second Treatise* set forth Locke's contract theory of government. People were endowed with certain natural rights, including the rights to life, liberty and property. Without government, in a state of nature, these fundamental rights were unprotected. To provide adequate safeguards for the exercise of these rights, people came together and, by mutual agreement, established governments among themselves. Monarchs were parties to these agreements and were entrusted by them to protect these basic rights. When the king violated this trust and abrogated the rights of the people, the people had the right—in the extreme case—to overthrow the king and replace the government.

His statement of the equality of all people was enunciated at the beginning of his *Second Treatise*. He taught that:

4. To understand political power right, and derive it from its original, we must consider, what state all men are naturally in, and that is, a state of perfect freedom to order their actions, and dispose of their possessions and persons, as they think fit, within the bounds of the law of nature, without asking leave, or depending upon the will of any other man.

A state also of equality, wherein all the power and jurisdiction is reciprocal, no one having more than another; ...[5]

What is interesting is that he spoke not merely of equality in the legal sense but equality of power. I suspect that he made this assertion because a

---

[4] *Ibid.*, pp. 51-2.
[5] John Locke, *The Second Treatise on Government*, in *Social Contract, Essays by Locke, Hume and Rousseau* with an Introduction by Sir Ernest Barker (Oxford University Press, New York, 1969), p. 4.

relative equality of power to bargain is essential to achieving a mutually advantageous agreement to come together. Otherwise, no community would be formed based upon mutual agreement. Of course, the concept that governments are the result of agreements reached at the dawn of human society is purely hypothetical and was not intended to relate some historical fact of pre-history. It is an intellectual device to analyze a complex idea. Locke was attempting to provide a rational explanation for the origin of government and a justification for revolution.

Fifty-eight years later, David Hume (1711-1776), the great leader of the Scottish Enlightenment, published his work, *Of the Original Contract*, in 1748. Although he takes issue with the notion that modern governments are the result of some original contract, he does support the principle of equality in the state of nature before the formation of government.

> When we consider how nearly equal all men are in their bodily force, and even in their mental powers and faculties, till cultivated by education, we must necessarily allow, that nothing but their own consent could, at first, associate them together, and subject them to any authority. The people, if we trace government to its first origin in the woods and deserts, are the source of all power and jurisdiction, and voluntarily, for the sake of peace and order, abandoned their native liberty and received laws from their equal and companion. The conditions upon which they were willing to submit, were either expressed, or were so clear and obvious, that it might well be esteemed superfluous to express. If this, then, is meant by the *original contract*, it cannot be denied, that all government is, at first, founded on a contract, and that the most ancient rude combinations of mankind were formed chiefly by that principle. In vain are we asked in what records this charter of our liberties is registered. It was not written on parchment, nor yet on leaves or barks of trees. It preceded the use of writing, and all the other civilized arts of life. But we trace it plainly in the nature of man, and in the equality, or something approaching equality, which we find in all the individuals of that species. The force, which now prevails, and which is founded on fleets and armies, is plainly political, and derived from authority, the effect of established government. A man's natural force consists only in the vigour of his limbs, and the firmness of his courage; which could never subject multitudes to the command of one. Nothing but their own consent, and their sense of the advantages resulting from peace and order, could have had that influence.[6]

His understanding of equality is more literal than the legal abstraction later developed by the American colonists.

Jean-Jacques Rousseau (1712-1778) was not as influential as Locke and Hume, in America. He too was influenced by Locke, however, and supported the assumption of equality in the state of nature. He began his essay, *The Social Contract*, published in 1762, with the fiery words "Man is born free, and everywhere he is in chains." In his second chapter he stated:

---

[6] David Hume, *Of the Original Contract*, in *Ibid.*, pp. 148-9.

The oldest form of society—and the only natural one—is the family. Children remain bound to their father for only just so long as they feel the need of him for their self-preservation. Once that need ceases the natural bond is dissolved. From then on, the children, freed from the obedience which they formerly owed, and the father, cleared of his debt of responsibility to them, return to a condition of equal independence. If the bond remains operative it is no longer something imposed by nature, but has become a matter of deliberate choice. The family is a family still, but by reason of convention only.

This shared liberty is a consequence of man's nature. Its first law is that of self-preservation: its first concern is for what it owes itself. As soon as a man attains the age of reason he becomes his own master, because he alone can judge of what will best assure his continued existence.[7]

With the Declaration of Rights, the English abolished absolute monarchy, strengthened Parliament, and provided for an immature equality—that is, an equality under a constitutional monarchy—for most Englishmen.

c. Full Equality and Self Government

The move toward political and social equality—toward independence from the Crown and toward a Republic—came slowly and reluctantly in the American colonies. Armed hostilities had broken out on April 19, 1775, at Lexington and Concord, but still there was no general call for independence, so deeply ingrained was the aversion to treason. Even as the Americans, now under Washington's command, surrounded British troops occupying Boston, fought the battles of Breed's Hill and Bunker Hill, the Second Continental Congress attempted a reconciliation with the King. The *Olive Branch Petition*, written by John D. Dickenson and adopted by Congress on July 5, 1775, professed the attachment of the American people to George III, appealed to him for the restoration of harmony, and begged that he prevent further hostilities until a reconciliation could be negotiated. The following day, a *Declaration of the Causes and Necessities of Taking Up Arms*, jointly written by Jefferson and Dickenson, was adopted by the Congress. It rejected any call for independence but declared that Americans were ready to die rather than be enslaved. The king refused to receive the petition; instead, after the evacuation of Boston on March 17, 1776, he raised an Army of 40,000 British regulars and German mercenaries, the largest army ever dispatched to the North American continent, to subdue the rebellion.[8]

The first clarion call for independence came on January 9, 1776, only six months before the eventual separation, with the publication of *Common Sense* by Thomas Paine. In plain but fiery words, he attacked George III as the "Royal Brute" and declared him chiefly responsible for the obnoxious measures

---

[7] Jean-Jacques Rousseau, *The Social Contract*, in *Ibid.*, p. 170.

[8] George Brown Tindall, *America, A Narrative History*, Vol. 1 (W. W. Norton & Company, New York, 2nd Ed. 1984), pp. 212-13.

taken against the colonies. He roundly denounced the monarchical form of government and won many to the cause of independence. He wrote:

MANKIND being originally equals in the order of creation, the equality could only be destroyed by some subsequent circumstance; ...

But there is another and greater distinction for which no truly natural or religious reason can be, and that is, the distinction of men into KINGS and SUBJECTS...[9]

England, since the conquest, hath known some few good monarchs, but groaned beneath a much larger number of bad ones, yet no man in his senses can say that their claim under William the Conqueror is a very honorable one. A French bastard landing with an armed banditti, and establishing himself king of England against the consent of the natives, is in plain terms a very paltry rascally original. It certainly hath no divinity in it...[10]

...Everything that is right or natural pleads for separation. The blood of the slain, the weeping voice of nature cries, 'TIS TIME TO PART...[11]

O ye that love mankind! Ye that dare oppose, not only the tyranny, but the tyrant, stand forth! every spot of the old world is over-run with oppression. Freedom hath been hunted round the globe. Asia, and Africa, have long expelled her. Europe regards her like a stranger, and England hath given her warning to depart. O! receive the fugitive, and prepare in time an asylum for mankind.[12]

Within three months 100,000 copies had been sold in a total population of about 4,000,000. By the spring of 1776, the sentiment for a break with the crown was clear. The very independent farmers, planters, and merchants who constituted a substantial percentage of the colonial population, would no longer tolerate a hereditary nobility in the New World.

American freedom would never be secure under British rule, Paine argued, because "the so much boasted Constitution of England" was deeply flawed. The problem lay in two major *"constitutional errors"*—monarchy and hereditary rule. To prove the point he cited, with more passion than order, one kind of evidence after another. The Bible, he insisted, condemned monarchy as "one of the sins of the Jews." Nature also disapproved of monarchy, which was why it so often presented capable kings with inept sons, or gave mankind *"an ass for a lion."* Monarchy and hereditary rule made bad rulers even of capable individuals by breeding arrogance, and by separating them from the rest of mankind whose interests they needed to know well. Moreover, the ambitions of kings and those who would be kings caused civil and foreign wars that had laid both Britain and "the world in ashes." The problem, then, was not just that evil persons were exercising power. It was systemic, in the very design of British government, which, like all governments, was incapable of constraining the power of hereditary rulers. The only way to solve that problem was to redesign the machine of government, eliminating monarchy and hereditary rule and expanding the "republican" element of British government which derived power not from birth

---

[9] Thomas Paine, *Common Sense* (Penguin Books, New York, 1976), pp. 71-2.
[10] *Ibid.*, pp. 76-8.   [11] *Ibid.*, p. 78.   [12] *Ibid.*, p. 100.

but from the ballot. The solution, in short, was revolution...[13]

Today we forget the difficulties that the proponents had in overcoming the fear of independence. Many of the state delegates to the Second Continental Congress were under instructions from their colonial legislatures to seek reconciliation with the crown and to take no actions toward independence, and some were slow to change even after Lexington and Concord. Supporters of independence knew that Congress would move only with popular support so that between April and July 1776 an intense appeal for independence was made at the provincial level. At least ninety local "declarations of independence" were adopted by colonies, states, and localities before Congress considered its declaration. Nothing provides a better explanation of why the American people finally chose to leave the British Empire and to take up the reins of government themselves.

> In truth, those state and local "declarations of independence," only a select few were called "declarations" at the time, are a somewhat miscellaneous set of documents written for a variety of related purposes. Some officially ended the old regime within a state. Virginia and New Jersey formally concluded British rule with provisions that opened their first state constitutions, which were adopted before Congress declared Independence. Rhode Island passed a separate law that served the same purpose, and Maryland—as if to fulfill John Adams's prediction that Maryland would "go beyond every body else, when they begin to go"— adopted its own, separate "Declaration" on July 6, 1776. The list of "declarations of independence" also includes instructions that authorized states' Congressional delegates to approve Independence. Those carefully drafted, formal statements proclaimed a state's commitment to separate nationhood and almost always summarized the events that had provoked and justified that position. Moreover, in Massachusetts, Virginia, and Maryland, substantial numbers of towns or counties instructed their state representatives to work for Independence, and, again, often explained why. Elsewhere other groups, such as New York's mechanics, militia units in Pennsylvania, or grand jurymen in South Carolina, announced their support for Independence and reflected on its causes or, sometimes, its benefits.[14]

But these declarations were to a purpose; the colonists did not wish merely to abolish the monarchy and the aristocracy but to establish a government that would respect and protect their basic rights and recognize that they were both free and equal. That spring, George Mason offered the Virginia legislature the first bill of rights in the colonies. He declared "...That all men are born equally free and independent...." His language was copied by many other state constitutions and bills of rights. When Thomas Jefferson wrote the Declaration of Independence for the Second Continental Congress, he turned to the English Declaration of Rights and to Mason's Declaration of Rights and drew heavily on the language as well as the principles of both. However, he

---

[13] Maier, *Op. Cit.*, pp. 31-2.
[14] *Ibid.*, pp. 48-9.

modified Mason's words to read "...that all men are created equal...."

By declaring separation from the English Crown, Jefferson advanced the cause of individual liberty by declaring the freedom of all to be *equal*. The Revolution was not only fought to overthrow the British monarchy but, in many ways, it was also a civil war that pitted Republicans against the Tories.

> The many Americans who debated Independence did not need Thomas Jefferson to remind them that the "whole point" of the controversy that had absorbed their lives lay not in the ending of an old regime but in the founding of a better one, or that their future would be bound up with that powerful but ambiguous word, equality. Their resolutions and instructions on Independence provided together an eloquent expression of the American mind, which the Congressional Declaration of Independence was also meant to do, and they gradually captured "the proper tone and spirit called for by the occasion."[15]

This aversion to a political and social privileged class was later and most clearly stated in our first Constitution, that "firm league of friendship," The Articles of Confederation:

> VI. ...nor shall any person holding any office of profit or trust under the United States, or any of them, accept of any present, emolument, office or title of any kind whatever from any king, prince or foreign state; nor shall the United States in Congress assembled, or any of them, grant any title of nobility....

Our present Constitution (1787) continued the prohibition in Article I, Section 9 (last paragraph):

> No Title of Nobility shall be granted by the United States: And no Person holding any Office of Profit or Trust under them, shall, without the Consent of the Congress, accept of any present, Emolument, Office, or Title, of any kind whatever, from any King, Prince, or foreign State.

And Article I, Section 10 provides that:

> No State shall...grant any Title of Nobility.

Article IV, Section 4, requires that:

> The United States shall guarantee to every State in this Union a Republican Form of Government...

After the Constitutional Convention of 1787, there was a great national debate regarding its adoption. The Massachusetts Convention (Feb. 7, 1788), called to ratify the Constitution, recommended an amendment (that was never adopted) that:

> Ninethly, Congress shall at no time consent that any person holding an office of trust or profit under the United States shall accept of a title of Nobility or any other title or office from any King, prince or Foreign State.[16]

---

[15] *Ibid.*, p. 95.

[16] Ralph Ketcham, ed., *The Anti-Federalist Papers and the Constitutional Convention Debates* (Penguin Books USA Inc., New York, NY, 1986), p. 219.

Madison, referring to the guarantee of Republican government in *The Federalist Papers #43* observes that:

> 6...In a confederacy founded on republican principles, and composed of republican members, the superintending government ought clearly to possess authority to defend the system against aristocratic or monarchical innovations....[17]

He continues his defence of Republicanism in *The Federalist Papers #57*.

> The *third* charge against the House of Representatives is that it will be taken from that class of citizens which will have least sympathy with the mass of the people, and be most likely to aim at an ambitious sacrifice of the many to the aggrandizement of the few.

> Of all the objections which have been framed against the federal Constitution, this is perhaps the most extraordinary. Whilst the objection itself is leveled against a pretended oligarchy, the principle of it strikes at the very root of republican government...

> Who are to be the electors of the federal representatives? Not the rich, more than the poor; not the learned, more than the ignorant; not the haughty heirs of distinguished names, more than the humble sons of obscure and unpropitious fortune. The electors are to be the great body of the people of the United States...

> Who are to be the objects of popular choice? Every citizen whose merit may recommend him to the esteem and confidence of his country. No qualification of wealth, of birth, of religious faith, or of civil profession is permitted to fetter the judgment or disappoint the inclination of the people...[18]

With the Declaration of Independence, the successful conclusion of the Revolutionary War, and the adoption of our second Constitution, Americans abolished the monarchy and the aristocracy, declared their aberrance to oligarchy in this country, established the rule of law through self government, and declared the principle of full equality with freedom for all. However, at the time, Jefferson's statement of rights and the origins of government in the Declaration were considered secondary to the operative language declaring independence. After all, the whole purpose of the Declaration was to be a statement of separation from Great Britain, not a recitation of human rights. As we shall see in the next section, the ideal of freedom and equality for all does not mature until Abraham Lincoln redefines the Declaration of Independence in the struggle over slavery. Lincoln viewed the rebellion as a base effort to overthrow the principle that "all men are created equal."[19]

---

[17] James Madison, *The Federalist Papers #43*, in *The Federalist Papers: Hamilton, Madison, Jay,* ed. Clinton Rossiter (NAL Penguin, Inc., New York 1961), p. 274.

[18] *Ibid.,* pp. 350-1.

[19] Maier, *Op. Cit.,* p. 207.

SUMMARY

The proposition of equal treatment and freedom for all is a defining principle of American ethics. Equality of human, political and civil rights for all is our standard of justice and is the bedrock foundation of our legal system. The fundamental purpose of government is to protect those rights equally for every person in our society.

The struggle for full freedom and equality came slowly. In 16th Century England, the Puritans, representing the emerging mercantile class, pitted Parliament against Charles I, who was tried and executed for subverting "... the ancient and fundamental laws and liberties of this nation...." The monarchy was abolished and a Commonwealth established that only survived 12 years. In 1660 his son, Charles II, assumed the throne.

In 1688 Parliament again removed a monarch when they replaced James II with William and Mary as wars over religion culminated in the Glorious Revolution. The Declaration of Rights of 1689 invested in Parliament i.e. all estates or social classes the right to remove a king and fix the conditions of his reign.

The move toward a republic took hold in the American colonies only after armed hostilities had occurred at Lexington and Concord in April, 1775. The call for independence did not come until January of 1776 with the publication of *Common Sense* by Thomas Paine. He challenged "...the distinction of men into KINGS and SUBJECTS..." and he asserted that "...no man in his senses can say that their [the English Kings'] claim under William the Conqueror is a very honorable one..." He cried out "...'TIS TIME TO PART..."

At least 90 local declarations of independence were adopted by colonies, mechanics, militia groups and grand jurymen before the Second Continental Congress took up its Declaration in July, 1776. The most notable was the Declaration of Rights written by George Mason and adopted by the Virginia legislature, that declared "...That all men are born equally free and independent..."

Jefferson's Declaration of Independence, drawing on the English Declaration of Rights and Mason's ideas and language in the Virginia Declaration, set forth the basic underlying principle of equality that is the foundation of our federal and state governments and declared the independence of the American colonies from the English crown. At the time, only the operative statement declaring independence was considered important. It was only later, when Abraham Lincoln gave full meaning to equality that these self-evident truths became important and equal rights for all emerged, imperfectly at first, as the standard of Justice for our society.

ADDITIONAL READINGS

The Second Treatise on Government (1690)
by John Locke[20]

5. This equality of men by nature, the judicious Hooker looks upon as so evident in itself, and beyond all question, that he makes it the foundation of that obligation to mutual love amongst men, on which he builds the duties they owe one another, and from whence he derives the great maxims of justice and charity.....

6. ...The state of nature has a law of nature to govern it, which obliges every one, and reason, which is that law, teaches all, who will but consult it, that being all equal and independent, no one ought to harm another in his life, health, liberty, or possessions:....

22. The natural liberty of man is to be free from any superior power on earth, and not to be under the will or legislative authority of man, but to have only the law of Nature for his rule. The liberty of man in society is to be under no other legislative power but that established by consent in the common-wealth, nor under the dominion of any will, or restraint of any law, but what the legislative shall enact according to the trust put in it. Freedom, then, is not what Sir Robert Filmer tells us, O. A. 55. "A liberty for every one to do what he lists, to live as he pleases, and not to be tied by any laws;" but freedom of men under government is to have a standing rule to live by, common to every one of that society, and made by the legislative power erected in it. A liberty to follow my own will in all things where the rule prescribes not, not to be subject to the inconstant, uncertain, unknown, arbitrary will of another man, as freedom of nature is to be under no other restraint but the law of nature.

23. This freedom from absolute, arbitrary power is so necessary to, and closely joined with, a man's preservation, that he cannot part with it but by what forfeits his preservation and life together.

54. Though I have said above (Chap. 2) "That all men by nature are equal," I cannot be supposed to understand all sorts of "equality": Age or virtue may give men a just precedency. Excellency of parts and merit may place others above the common level. Birth may subject some, and alliance or benefits others, to pay an observance to those to whom Nature, gratitude, or other re-spects, may have made it due; and yet all this consists with the equality which all men are in respect of jurisdiction or dominion one over another, which was the equality I there spoke of as proper to the business in hand, being that equal right that every man hath to his natural freedom, without being subjected to the will or authority of any other man....

---

[20] Locke, *Op. Cit.*

61. Thus we are born free as we are born rational; not that we have actually the exercise of either: age that brings one, brings with it the other too...

Common Sense
by Thomas Paine[21]

Government by kings was first introduced into the world by the Heathens, from whom the children of Israel copied the custom. It was the most prosperous invention the Devil ever set on foot for the promotion of idolatry. The Heathens paid divine honors to their deceased kings, and the Christian world hath improved on the plan by doing the same to their living ones....(p. 72.)

...To the evil of monarchy we have added that of hereditary succession; and as the first is a degradation and lessening of ourselves, so the second, claimed as a matter of right, is an insult and an imposition on posterity. For all men being originally equals, *no one by birth* could have a right to set up his own family in perpetual preference to all others forever, and though himself might deserve *some* decent degree of honors of his contemporaries, yet his descendants might be far too unworthy to inherit them. One of the strongest *natural* proofs of the folly of hereditary rights in kings, is, that nature disapproves it, otherwise she would not so frequently turn it into ridicule by giving mankind an *ass for a lion.*

Secondly, as no man at first could possess any other public honors than were bestowed upon him, so the givers of those honors could have no power to give away the right of posterity, and though they might say 'We choose you for *our* head,' they could not, without manifest injustice to their children, say 'that your children and your children's children shall reign over *ours* for ever.' Because such an unwise, unjust, unnatural compact might (perhaps) in the next succession put them under the government of a rogue or a fool. Most wise men, in their private sentiments, have ever treated hereditary right with contempt; yet it is one of those evils, which when once established is not easily removed; many submit from fear, others from superstition, and the more powerful part shares with the king the plunder of the rest....

...In England a k—— hath little more to do than to make war and give away places; which in plain terms, is to impoverish the nation and set it together by the ears. A pretty business indeed for a man to be allowed eight hundred thousand sterling a year for, and worshipped into the bargain! Of more worth is one honest man to society, and in the sight of God, than all the crowned ruffians that ever lived....(p. 81.)

---

[21] Paine, *Op. Cit.*

Federalist Papers, No. 39.

The charge was raised that the proposed constitution would undermine the republican spirit. James Madison, under the nom de plume "Publicus" responds in The Federalist Papers, No. 39.[22]

...The question that offers itself is whether the general form and aspect of the government be strictly republican. It is evident that no other form would be reconcilable with the genius of the people of America; with the fundamental principles of the Revolution; or with that honorable determination which animates every votary of freedom to rest all our political experiments on the capacity of mankind for self government. If the plan of the convention, therefore, be found to depart from the republican character, its advocates must abandon it as no longer defensible.

What, then, are the distinctive characters of the republican form?...

If we resort for a criterion to the different principles on which different forms of government are established, we may define a republic to be, or at least may bestow that name on, a government which derives all its powers directly or indirectly from the great body of the people, and is administered by persons holding their offices during pleasure for a limited period, or during good behavior. It is *essential* to such a government that it be derived from the great body of the society, not from an inconsiderable proportion or a favored class of it; otherwise a handful of tyrannical nobles, exercising their oppression by a delegation of their powers, might aspire to the rank of republicans and claim for their government the honorable title of republic. It is *sufficient* for such a government that the persons administering it be appointed, either directly or indirectly, by the people; and that they hold their appointments by either of the tenures just specified; otherwise every government in the United States, as well as every other popular government that has been or can be well organized or well executed, would be degraded from the republican character....

Could any further proof be required of the republican complexion of this system, the most decisive one might be found in its absolute prohibition of titles of nobility, both under the federal and the State governments; and in its express guaranty of the republican form to each of the latter?

---

[22] Rossiter, *Op. Cit.*, p. 240.

American Scripture
by Pauline Maier[23]
Equality and Rights

But the right of revolution was not, it seems, the only "principle of liberty" in the Declaration of Independence, or even the most important for the guidance of posterity. "The same venerated instrument that declared our separation from Great Britain," said John Sergeant in Philadelphia, "contained also the memorable assertion, that 'all men are created equal, that they are endowed by their Creator with certain unalienable rights, and that to secure these rights, governments are instituted among men, deriving their just powers from the consent of the governed.'" And that, he said, "was the text of the revolution— the ruling vital principle—the hope that animated the patriot's heart and nerved the patriot's arm, when he looked forward through succeeding generations, and saw stamped upon all their institutions, the great principles set forth in the Declaration of Independence." For Sprague, too, the Declaration of Independence was a "Declaration, by a whole people, of what before existed, and will always exist, the native equality of the human race, as the true foundation of all political, of all human institutions."

By including human equality among the "great principles" that the Declaration stated and describing it as "the foundation of all political, of all human institutions," Sergeant and Sprague contributed to a modern reading of the document that had begun to develop among Jeffersonian Republicans in the 1790s but became increasingly common after the 1820s, and gradually eclipsed altogether the document's assertion of the right of revolution. It is important to understand, however, that the issue of equality had a place in American life and politics long before it was associated with the Declaration of Independence. In the eighteenth century, the republican form of government was commonly considered best suited to egalitarian societies, and Americans, conscious that they lacked the extremes of wealth characteristic of older European countries, generally accepted equality as a characteristic of their society and of the governments they were founding. The state and local declarations of independence made that abundantly clear. Remember that on May 15, 1776, the Virginia convention authorized the drafting of a new state constitution that would "secure substantial and equal liberty to the people." Two months earlier Judge William Henry Drayton praised South Carolina's new constitution for allowing voters to raise even the poorest Carolinian to the highest office in the state, while the Grand Jury at Charlestown took pleasure in the founding of a government whose benefits extended "generally, equally, and indiscriminately to all," and another grand jury in the Cheraws District took delight in the new constitution because

---

[23] Maier, *Op. Cit.*, pp. 191-7.

under it "the rights and happiness of the whole, the poor and the rich, are equally secured." Meanwhile, Massachusetts coastal towns argued that the people's right to equal liberty and equal representation mandated a reallocation of legislative seats so they would be more closely keyed to population (which would, of course, shift power toward them). None of those references to equality had anything to do with the Declaration of Independence since they predated it. And together they suggested enough different meanings of the word "equality"—equal rights, equal access to office, equal voting power—to keep Americans busy sorting them out and fighting over practices that seemed inegalitarian far into the future. The equality mentioned, moreover, was generally between rich and poor white men, or those who lived in different geographical sections; its application to women or people of other races or persons with conflicting religious convictions would open whole new fields for conflict....

LANDMARK CASE #1

William Jefferson Clinton, Petitioner
v.
Paula Corbin Jones, Respondent
65 Law Week 1372 (1997)

Landmark cases have been selected for your review in this work to demonstrate a particular principle of American Ethics. This case is the first to apply the principle of the equality of all to a president. Although we give immunity to public officials for official acts, the common law assertion that "the king can do no wrong," was rejected at the birth of the Republic. "...[T]he Constitution admits that he [the President] may do wrong, and has provided a means for his trial for wrong-doing, and his removal from office if found guilty by the proceedings of impeachment...."[24] The founding fathers insured that the American president would be no king. This case confirms that not even the president is above the law and may be sued in a civil matter not involving official duties.

Justice Stevens delivered the opinion of the Court.

This case raises a constitutional and a prudential question concerning the Office of the President of the United States. Respondent, a private citizen, seeks to recover damages from the current occupant of that office based on actions allegedly taken before his term began. The President submits that in all but the most exceptional cases the Constitution requires federal courts to defer such litigation until his term ends and that, in any event, respect for

---
[24] *Langford v. United States, Ibid.*

the office warrants such a stay. Despite the force of the arguments supporting the President's submissions, we conclude that they must be rejected....

Those allegations principally describe events that are said to have occurred
on the afternoon of May 8, 1991, during an official conference held at the
Excelsior Hotel in Little Rock, Arkansas. The Governor [Clinton] delivered
a speech at the conference; respondent [Jones]—working as a state employee—staffed the registration desk. She alleges that Ferguson [a former
Arkansas State Police officer] persuaded her to leave her desk and to visit
the Governor in a business suite at the hotel, where he made "abhorrent"
sexual advances that she vehemently rejected....(p. 4373)

...it is perfectly clear that the alleged misconduct of petitioner was unrelated
to any of his official duties as President of the United States and, indeed,
occurred before he was elected to that office....(p. 4374)

The principal rationale for affording certain public servants immunity from
suits for money damages arising out of their official acts is inapplicable to
unofficial conduct. In cases involving prosecutors, legislators, and judges
we have repeatedly explained that the immunity serves the public interest in
enabling such officials to perform their designated functions effectively
without fear that a particular decision may give rise to personal liability.
We explained in *Ferri v. Ackerman,*:

> "As public servants, the prosecutor and the judge represent the interest of
> society as a whole. The conduct of their official duties may adversely affect a
> wide variety of different individuals, each of whom may be a potential source
> of future controversy. The societal interest in providing such public officials
> with the maximum ability to deal fearlessly and impartially with the public at
> large has long been recognized as an acceptable justification for official
> immunity. The point of immunity for such officials is to forestall an atmos-
> phere of intimidation that would conflict with their resolve to perform their
> designated functions in a principled fashion."

That rationale provided the principal basis for our holding that a former
President of the United States was "entitled to absolute immunity from damages liability predicated on his official acts." Our central concern was to
avoid rendering the President "unduly cautious in the discharge of his official duties."

This reasoning provides no support for an immunity for *unofficial* conduct.
As we explained in Fitzgerald "the sphere of protected action must be related closely to the immunity's justifying purposes." Because of the President's broad responsibilities, we recognized in that case an immunity from
damages claims arising out of official acts extending to the "outer perimeter
of his authority." But we have never suggested that the President, or any
other official, has an immunity that extends beyond the scope of any action
taken in an official capacity.... "...a President, like Members of Congress,

judges, prosecutors, or congressional aides—all having absolute immunity—are not immune for acts outside official duties...."

Moreover, when defining the scope of an immunity for acts clearly taken within an official capacity, we have applied a functional approach. "Frequently our decisions have held that an official's absolute immunity should extend only to acts in performance of particular functions of his office." Hence, for example, a judge's absolute immunity does not extend to actions performed in a purely administrative capacity. As our opinions have made clear, immunities are grounded in "the nature of the function performed, not the identity of the actor who performed it."

Petitioner's effort to construct an immunity from suit for unofficial act grounded purely in the identity of his office is unsupported by precedent....(p. 4376)

5. SLAVERY

Slavery was the blind spot in the American sense of justice. Many saw the inconsistency of those who recognized the inequality of oppressed subjects under a tyrannical monarch, but would not see the cruel inequality of slaves suffering under masters who had absolute authority over them. They could be bought and sold, families could be separated and they could be punished, raped, and even put to death with no accountability. Nothing fired passions on both sides of the debate as much as the publication, in 1852, of the compelling novel, *Uncle Tom's Cabin,* by Harriet Beecher Stowe. It was a dramatization of the horrors of slavery that gives us a shocking insight into the brutality of human bondage in mid-nineteenth century America. When she visited the White House in 1863, during the Civil War, Lincoln greeted her as "the little woman who wrote the book that made this great war." Here is a short excerpt from the powerful story by this Unitarian preacher's daughter. She describes the slave sale of a mother and daughter, sold to pay the debts of their master.

Uncle Tom's Cabin
by Harriet Beecher Stowe[25]
The Slave Warehouse

The day after the letter arrived in New Orleans, Susan and Emmeline were attached, and sent to the depot to await a general auction on the following morning; and as they glimmer faintly upon us in the moonlight which steals through the grated window, we may listen to their conversation. Both are weeping, but each quietly, that the other may not hear.

"Mother, just lay your head on my lap, and see if you can't sleep a little," says the girl, trying to appear calm.

---

[25] Harriet Beecher Stowe, *Uncle Tom's Cabin* (Bantam Books, New York, 1981).

"I haven't any heart to sleep, Em; I can't, it's the last night we may be together!"

"O, mother, don't say so! perhaps we shall get sold together,—who knows?"

"If 'twas anybody's else case, I should say so, too, Em," said the woman; "but I'm so feard of losin' you that I don't see anything but the danger."

"Why, mother, the man said we were both likely, and would sell well."

Susan remembered the man's looks and words. With a deadly sickness at her heart, she remembered how he had looked at Emmeline's hands, and lifted up her curly hair, and pronounced her a first-rate article. Susan had been trained as a Christian, brought up in the daily reading of the Bible, and had the same horror of her child's being sold to a life of shame that any other Christian mother might have; but she had no hope, no protection....(pp. 328-9)

....but still the bidding went on, rattling, clattering, now French, now English. Down goes the hammer again,—Susan is sold! She goes down from the block, stops, looks wistfully back, her daughter stretches her hands towards her. She looks with agony in the face of the man who has bought her,—a respectable middle-aged man, of benevolent countenance.

"O Mas'r, please do buy my daughter!"

"I'd like to, but I'm afraid I can't afford it!" said the gentleman, looking, with painful interest, as the young girl mounted the block, and looked around her with a frightened and timid glance.

The blood flushes painfully in her otherwise colorless cheek, her eye has a feverish fire, and her mother groans to see that she looks more beautiful than she ever saw her before. The auctioneer sees his advantage, and expatiates volubly in mingled French and English, and bids rise in rapid succession.

"I'll do anything in reason," said the benevolent-looking gentleman, pressing in and joining with the bids. In a few moments they have run beyond his purse. He is silent; the auctioneer grows warmer; but bids gradually drop off. It lies now between an aristocratic old citizen and our bullet-headed acquaintance. The citizen bids for a few turns, contemptuously measuring his opponent; but the bullet-head has the advantage over him, both in obstinacy and concealed length of purse, and the controversy lasts but a moment; the hammer falls, he has got the girl, body and soul, unless God help her!

Her master is Mr. Legree, who owns a cotton plantation on the Red River. She is pushed along into the same lot with Tom and two other men, and goes off, weeping as she goes.

The benevolent gentleman is sorry; but, then, the thing happens every day! One sees girls and mothers crying, at these sales, *always*! It can't be helped, etc.; and he walks off, with his acquisition, in another direction.

Two days after, the lawyer of the Christian firm of B. & Co., New York, sent on their money to them....(pp. 333-4)

....Scenes of blood and cruelty are shocking to our ear and heart. What man has nerve to do man has not nerve to hear. What brother-man and brother-Christian must suffer, cannot be told us, even in our secret chamber, it so harrows up the soul! And yet, oh my country! these things are done under the shadow of thy laws! O Christ! Thy church sees them, almost in silence!...(p. 411)

a. Colonial History

Slavery had been a dying institution in Europe but flourished in Spanish and Portuguese America, including Florida, for a century before the establishment of the first English colony. Black slavery was introduced to the English colonies in 1619 when a Dutch vessel dropped off twenty Negroes in Jamestown. At first, they were treated as indentured servants but gradually because of racial differences and the fact that they were "heathens" perpetual slavery became the law of the land.

...Evidence that in 1664 some blacks were being held in hereditary life service appears in Virginia court records. In 1660 and 1661, and 1663 in Maryland, the colonial Assembly recognized slavery by laws that later expanded into elaborate and restrictive slave codes. In South Carolina, by contrast, Barbadians after 1670 simply transplanted the institution of slavery full-blown from the Caribbean before they discovered its value in the rice paddies, where indentured servants could hardly be enticed to work in the mud and heat.

...Though British North America took less than 5 percent of the total slave imports to the Western Hemisphere during the more than three centuries of that squalid traffic—400,000 out of some 9,500,000—it offered better chances for survival if few for human fulfillment. The natural increase of black immigrants in America approximated that of whites by the end of the colonial period.

Negro slavery was recognized in the laws of all the colonies, but flourished in the Tidewater South—one colony, South Carolina, had a black majority through most of the eighteenth century.[26]

America had white slavery as well, in all the colonies. These indentured servants—British subjects who sold themselves or were impressed into servitude for a term of years, to buy their passage to the New World—came to our shores in large numbers, until the Revolution. By one estimate voluntary indentured servitude accounted for probably half the arrivals of white settlers in all the colonies outside New England. (In a recent visit, I was surprised to find that the Ellis Island museum stated that 75% of all white colonial immigrants were indentured servants.)

The name derived from the indenture, or contract, by which a person could bind himself to labor in return for transportation to the New World. Usually one made the contract with a shipmaster who would then sell it to a new master upon arrival. Not all went voluntarily. The London underworld developed a flourishing trade in "kids" and "spirits," who were kidnapped or spirited into servitude. On occasion orphans were bound off to the New World; from time to time the mother country sent convicts into colonial servitude, the first as early as 1617. After 1717, by act of Parliament, convicts guilty of certain crimes could escape the hangman by "transportation." Most of these, like Moll Flanders, the lusty heroine of Daniel Defoe's novel, seem to have gone to the Chesapeake. And after 1648 political and military offenders met a like fate, beginning with some

---

[26] Tindall, *Op. Cit.*, pp. 102-3.

captives of the Parliamentary armies.

In due course, however, the servant reached the end of his term, usually after four to seven years, claimed the freedom dues set by custom and law—some money, tools, clothing, food—and took up land of his own....[27]

It is fair to say that, at the time of the Revolution, there was a slave mentality in all of the thirteen colonies in America that accepted the servitude of blacks and whites. The holding of white slaves continued until well after the establishment of the new nation.

b. The Declaration of Independence

It appears that, at the time the Declaration of Independence was professing the equality of all, the majority of the inhabitants of the colonies were slaves or indentured servants or former indentured servants. Jefferson's first draft accused the king of tyranny in that:

> [20] he has waged cruel war against human nature itself, violating its most sacred rights of life & liberty in the persons of a distant people who never offended him, captivating & carrying them into slavery in another hemisphere, or to incur miserable death in their transportation thither. This piratical warfare, the opprobrium of *infidel* powers is the warfare of the *Christian* king of Great Britain. Determined to keep open a market where MEN should be bought & sold, he has prostituted his negative for suppressing every legislative attempt to prohibit or to restrain this execrable commerce and that he is now exciting those very people to rise in arms among us, and to purchase that liberty of which he obtruded them; thus paying off former crimes committed against the *liberties* of one people, with crimes which he urges them to commit against the *lives* of another....[28]

The delegates to the Second Continental Congress would have none of it, in deference to South Carolina and Georgia and to those northerners who had been engaged in the slave trade. Those who recognized the inconsistency between equality in theory and slavery in practice also realized that the abolition of slavery and the slave trade could not be accomplished at that time. They inserted instead an accusation that the king had "excited domestic insurrections among us," covering both slaves and Loyalists, and in the process eliminated any reference to slavery. Their purpose was to declare independence and the document did that. It was not their purpose to write a neat and completely consistent Bill of Rights and the document did not do that.

c. The Articles of Confederation

When the several new states, acting through their representatives in the Second Continental Congress, entered into that "firm league of friendship" under the Articles of Confederation, they provided that:

---

[27] *Ibid.*, pp. 101-2.
[28] Maier, *Op. Cit.*, p.120.

IV. The better to secure and perpetuate mutual friendship and intercourse among the people of the different states in this union, the free inhabitants of each of these states, paupers, vagabonds, and fugitives from justice excepted, shall be entitled to all privileges and immunities of free citizens in the several states;...

IX. ...The United States in Congress assembled shall have authority...to agree upon the number of land forces, and to make requisitions from each state for its quota, in proportion to the number of white inhabitants in such state...[29]

d. The Constitutional Convention

The debate over slavery continued in the Constitutional Convention during the summer of 1787. The discussion intertwined with disagreements over the method of taxation and the question of apportionment in the House of Representatives. The Articles of Confederation had apportioned its appropriations on the basis of the value of the real estate in each state. The New Jersey Plan now proposed that:

3. Resolved that whenever requisitions shall be necessary, instead of the rule for making requisitions mentioned in the articles of Confederation, the United States in Congress be authorized to make such requisitions in proportion to the whole number of white and other free citizens and inhabitants of every age sex and condition including those bound to servitude for a term of years and three fifths of all other persons not comprehended in the foregoing description, except Indians not paying taxes;...[30]

After heated and extensive debate on apportionment that summer, it was decided that the House of Representatives should be popularly elected. Then they decided that there should be one Representative for every 40,000 (later 30,000) in population. The formula in the New Jersey Plan for direct taxation was adopted and became the formula for apportionment as part of the Great Compromise, the agreement to have the Senate represent the States and the House of Representatives the people. The final language reads:

Section 2. [Third paragraph]...Representatives and direct taxes shall be apportioned among the several states which may be included within this union, according to their respective numbers, which shall be determined by adding to the whole number of free persons, including those bound to service for a term of years, and excluding Indians not taxed, three-fifths of all other persons....

———United States Constitution.

The first federal census was held in 1790. It determined that the white population of the United States was 3,172,444, freed Negroes added 59,557 and there were 697,624 slaves, in all 13 states, for a total population of 3,929,625.[31]

---

[29] Ketcham, *Op. Cit.*, p. 357, 362.

[30] *Ibid.*, p. 63, quoting Madison's notes on the convention.

[31] Richard B. Morris and Henry Steele Comminger, eds., *Encyclopedia of American History*, Bicentennial Edition (Harper & Row, New York, 1976), p.754.

The debate over the decisive issue regarding the continuation and the regulation of the slave trade was the last remaining obstacle to be overcome before the delegates could reach final agreement on the proposed Constitution, and the debate on August 21 and 22 was passionate. The draft constitution— the Virginia Plan—forbade either a prohibition or tax on "the migration or importation of such persons as the several states shall think proper to admit." This provision was staunchly supported by the Southern States, especially South Carolina and Georgia; they suggested that these states would not ratify the Constitution without this protection of the slave trade. Luther Martin, the lawyer and politician from Maryland, said that the slave trade "was inconsistent with the principles of the revolution and dishonorable to the American character to have such a feature in the Constitution."[32] This was part of a larger debate that proposed a two-thirds vote in Congress to pass laws regulating foreign commerce. This provision was opposed by the New England states who wanted stronger federal regulation of foreign commerce. In the end, New England would not vote to prohibit the slave trade if Georgia and South Carolina would not insist on the two-thirds vote regulating foreign commerce. The final compromise read:

> Section 9. The migration or importation of such persons as any of the states now existing shall think proper to admit, shall not be prohibited by the Congress prior to the year 1808, but a tax or duty may be imposed on such importation, not exceeding 10 dollars for each person.

The Southerners took the precaution to require that this provision could not be deleted from the document:

> Article V. [Amendments]...provided, that no amendment which may be made prior to the year 1808, shall in any manner affect [the slave trade]...

Finally, runaway slaves were required to be returned to their masters:

> Article IV. Section 2. [Par. 3] No person held to service or labour in one state, under the laws thereof, escaping into another, shall, in consequence of any law or regulation therein, be discharged from such service or labour, but shall be delivered up on claim of the party to whom such service or labour may be due.
>
> —United States Constitution.

Later, on June 20, 1788, in a speech before the New York Constitutional Convention, opposing the Constitution, Melancton Smith stated that "He could not see any rule by which slaves are to be included in the ratio of representation: The principle of a representation, being that every free agent should be concerned in governing himself, it was absurd to give that power to a man who could not exercise it—slaves have no will of their own: The very operation of it was to give certain privileges to those people who were so wicked as to keep slaves...."[33]

---

[32] Ketchem, *Op. Cit.*, See pp. 160-5.
[33] Ketchem, *Op. Cit.*, p. 340.

e. Slavery in the New Nation

Slavery was *the* moral issue of the first part of the nineteenth century in this country. The slaveholders asserted that all men are free and equal who come into society, but that the Negro is not a part of our society. The fight over slavery dogged the young Republic as Congress allowed slavery to move west as new states were admitted into the union. Abolitionist groups formed to abolish slavery and to help the slaves escape to the North or to Canada.

In 1834, Dred Scott was a Negro slave owned by Doctor Emerson, an Army surgeon, who brought him first to Rock Island in the free state of Illinois and then to Fort Snelling in Upper Louisiana, free territory under the Missouri Compromise. After four years, they returned to Missouri, a slave state, where Dred Scott, his wife, and their two daughters born in free territory were sold to John F. A. Sandford of New York City, who took them by force at St. Louis. Dred Scott claimed that he and his family were free since he had been taken to a free state or territory and his children were born there. He sued Sandford, his purported owner, for his release. When he lost in the State, he appealed to the United States Supreme Court. Chief Justice Roger Taney spoke for the majority of the Court.

...In the opinion of the court, the legislation and histories of the times, and the language in the Declaration of Independence, show, that neither the class of persons who had been imported as slaves, nor their descendants, whether they had become free or not, were then acknowledged as part of the people, nor intended to be included in the general words used in that memorable instrument.

...They had for more than a century before been regarded as beings of an inferior order; and altogether unfit to associate with the white race, either in social or political relations; and so far inferior, that they had no rights which the white man was bound to respect; and that the Negro might justly and lawfully be reduced to slavery for his benefit. He was bought and sold, and treated as an ordinary article of merchandise and traffic, whenever a profit could be made by it. This opinion was at that time fixed and universal in the civilized portion of the white race. It was regarded as an axiom in morals as well as in politics, which no one thought of disputing, or supposed to be open to dispute; and men in every grade and position in society daily and habitually acted upon it in their private pursuits, as well as in matters of public concern, without doubting for a moment the correctness of this opinion.

And in no nation was this opinion more fixed or more uniformly acted upon than by the English government and English people. They not only seized them on the coast of Africa, and sold them or held them in slavery for their own use; but they took them as ordinary articles of merchandise to every country where they could make a profit on them, and were far more extensively engaged in this commerce than any other nation in the world.

The opinion thus entertained and acted upon in England was naturally impressed upon the colonies they founded on this side of the Atlantic. And, accordingly, a Negro of the African race was regarded by them as an article of property, and held, and bought and sold as such, in every one of the thirteen Colonies which united in the Declaration of Independence, and afterwards formed the Constitution of the United States. The slaves were more or less numerous in the different Colonies, as slave labor was found more or less profitable. But no one seems to have doubted the correctness of the prevailing opinion of the time...

...The general words above quoted [the Preamble to the Declaration of Independence] would seem to embrace the whole human family, and if they were used in a similar instrument at this day, would be so. But it is too clear for dispute, that the enslaved African race were not intended to be, and formed no part of the people who framed and adopted this Declaration;...

...They perfectly understood the meaning of the language they used, and how it would be understood by others; and they knew that it would not, in any part of the civilized world, be supposed to embrace the Negro race, which, by common consent, had been excluded from civilized governments and the family of nations, and doomed to slavery. They spoke and acted according to the then established doctrines and principles, and in the ordinary language of the day, and no one misunderstood them.   The unhappy black race were separated from the white by indelible marks, and laws long before established, and were never thought of or spoken of except as property, and when the claims of the owner or the profit of the trader were supposed to need protection.[34]

Dred Scott and his family were returned to their slave master. This decision constitutes the low water mark in American jurisprudence. I was very upset when I first read this case. It's one thing to hear uneducated and ignorant people speak of other human beings in such degrading and disparaging terms, but it is quite another thing to read about the acceptance of such mistreatment in the language of the law. To read the words of the Chief Justice of the United States, that the civilized world considered the Negros "...so far inferior, that they had no rights which the white man was bound to respect; and that the Negro might justly and lawfully be reduced to slavery for his benefit," is shocking and outrageous. It flies in the face of everything that I believed good about our country and the reasons why we were right to rebel against a tyrannical king. It brings home the terrible damage caused by the indelible mark that early Americans branded upon the black race, a brand that we have not yet fully erased. Needless to say, those opposed to slavery at the time were outraged. This decision probably did more than any other single incident to polarize sentiment and create the climate for the Civil War. There are more excerpts from this case at the end of this section.

The defence of the Declaration of Independence fell to Abraham Lincoln, who gave new life to that document by focusing upon its statement of equality and rights now that its revolutionary purpose was over.

...Before the 1850s, however, Lincoln seems to have had relatively little interest in the Declaration of Independence. Then, suddenly, that document, and, above

---

[34] 19 How. 393-633; 15 L Ed 691. (1857)

all, its assertion that all men were created equal, became his "ancient faith," "the father of all moral principles," an "axiom" of free society. He was provoked, it seems, by the attacks on the Declaration of Calhoun, Pettit, and Rufus Choate of Massachusetts, who called its affirmations of natural rights "glittering and sounding generalities." Lincoln recalled each of those denunciations of the Declaration, always with regret. And he made the arguments of those who defended the Declaration his own, much as Jefferson had done with the texts upon which he drew in drafting that document, reworking the ideas from speech to speech, pushing their logic, and eventually arriving at a simple statement of profound eloquence. Later Lincoln would say that he "never had a feeling politically that did not spring from the sentiments embodied in the Declaration of Independence." His understanding of the document became in time that of the nation.

Lincoln's position emerged most fully and powerfully during his debates with Illinois' Senator Stephen Douglas, a Democrat who had proposed the Kansas-Nebraska Act. Lincoln ran for the Senate against Douglas in 1858 as a member of the new Republican Party—whose first national convention, which convened at Philadelphia on June 17, 1856, the anniversary of the Battle of Bunker Hill, adopted a platform that described maintaining "the principles promulgated in the Declaration of Independence" and embodied in the Constitution as "essential to the preservation of our republican institutions...."

...Douglas defended the Kansas-Nebraska Act, which allowed the people of those states to decide whether to allow slavery within their borders, as perfectly consistent with the principles and practices of the Revolution. While instructing their Congressional delegates to vote for Independence in 1776, Douglas recalled correctly, one state after another had explicitly retained the exclusive right of defining its domestic institutions. The Kansas-Nebraska Act only confirmed that right, he said. Moreover, the Declaration of Independence carried no implications whatsoever with regard to slavery since the signers referred to white men only, to "men of European birth and European descent, when they declared the equality of all men." In fact, Douglas asserted, the equality they asserted was between American colonists and British subjects in Great Britain, both of whom had equal rights and neither of whom could be justly held subject to the other. The signers were not thinking of "the negro or... savage Indians, or the Feejee, or the Malay, or any other inferior or degraded race." Had they meant to include blacks, the signers would have been honor-bound to go home and immediately free their slaves, which not even Thomas Jefferson did. To say that "every man who signed the Declaration of Independence declared the negro his equal" was therefore to call the signers hypocrites. The Declaration had one purpose and one purpose only: to explain and justify American Independence from the British Crown.

To Lincoln, Douglas's argument left a "mere wreck," a "mangled ruin," of the Declaration of Independence, whose "plain, unmistakable language" said "*all* men" were created equal, which meant "there can be no moral right in connection with one man's making a slave of another." In affirming that government derived its "just powers from the consent of the governed," the Declaration said that no man could govern another without his consent, which was "the leading principle—the sheet anchor—of American republicanism." If, then, "the negro is a man," was it not a "total destruction of self-government, to say that he too shall not govern *himself*"? To govern another man without his consent was "despotism." Like Benjamin Wade and others before him, Lincoln understood that it was impossible to separate the Declaration's condemnation of monarchy from a condemnation of slavery. To deny that kings can justly rule by right of birth was to deny that anyone could rule another, of any race or creed or national origin, without his or her consent. Moreover, to confine the Declaration's significance to the British peoples of 1776 meant that the document lost significance not only for Douglas's "inferior races," but for the French, Irish, German, Scandinavian, and other immigrants who came to America after the Revolution (and who were well represented among Illinois voters). For them the promise of equality for all men was a moral sentiment that linked newly arrived Americans with the rounding generation, an "electric cord" that bound them into the nation "as though they were blood of the blood, and flesh of the flesh of the men who wrote that Declaration," and so made one people out of many.[35]

It took a Civil War to end slavery in this country and 630,000 American lives—North and South.

f. Constitutional Amendments

Following the Civil War, the Thirteenth Amendment was added to the Constitution to end slavery in America forever:

Neither slavery nor involuntary servitude, except as a punishment for crime whereof the party shall have been duly convicted, shall exist within the United States, or any place subject to their jurisdiction.

The Fourteenth Amendment made the former slaves citizens, bringing them into full participation in the political life of our society and guaranteeing all persons due process—fair procedures in enforcing the law and equal protection of the law:

Section 1. All persons born or naturalized in the United States, and subject to the jurisdiction thereof, are citizens of the United States and of the State wherein they reside....

...No State shall make or enforce any law which shall abridge the privileges or immunities of citizens of the United States; nor shall any State deprive any person of life, liberty or property, without due process of law; nor deny to any person within its jurisdiction the equal protection of the laws.

The Fifteenth Amendment gave the former slaves the right to vote:

The right of citizens of the United States to vote shall not be denied or abridged by the United States or by any State on account of race, color, or previous condition of servitude.

But still, the great ideal of equality for all remained unfinished business.

---

[35] Maier, *Op. Cit.*, pp. 197 et sec.

g. *Continuing the Indelible Mark of Inferiority*

After the Civil War the armies of the North imposed an onerous occupation upon the South—the Era of Reconstruction—inciting guerrilla warfare and the rise of the Ku Klux Klan. The misery of the South was turned with a vengeance upon the defenseless former slaves and "Jim Crow" laws—intended to deprive these new citizens of their newfound human, political and civil rights—were enacted everywhere in the South.

In the early 1890s, Homer Adolph Plessy, an African American, was a first class passenger on a train for travel within the State of Louisiana. He was removed when he refused to move to a "colored only" area and was charged with a crime and found guilty. He appealed to the United States Supreme Court on the ground that the law was unconstitutional since it denied him "equal protection of the law." The United States Supreme Court held that:

> ...The object of the [Fourteenth] amendment was undoubtedly to enforce the absolute equality of the two races before the law, but in the nature of things it could not have been intended to abolish distinctions based upon color, or to enforce social, as distinguished from political equality, or a commingling of the two races upon terms unsatisfactory to either. Laws permitting, and even requiring, their separation in places where they are liable to be brought into contact do not necessarily imply the inferiority of either race to the other, and have been generally, if not universally, recognized as within the competency of the state legislatures in the exercise of their police power. The most common instance of this is connected with the establishment of separate schools for white and colored children, which have been held to be valid exercise of the legislative power even by courts of states where the political rights of the colored race have been longest and most earnestly enforced....

Mr. Justice Harlan voiced strong opposition to the majority opinion, expressing the fear that such stigmatizing laws could spread to many other areas of political and social interaction:

> ...If a state can prescribe as a rule of civil conduct, that whites and blacks shall not travel as passengers in the same railroad coach, why may it not so regulate the use of the streets of its cities and towns as to compel white citizens to keep on one side of the street and black citizens to keep on the other? Why may it not, upon like grounds, punish whites and blacks who ride together in street cars or in open vehicles on a public road or street? Why may it not require sheriffs to assign whites to one side of a court-room and blacks to the other? And why may it not also prohibit the commingling of the two races in the galleries of legislative halls or in public assemblages, convened for the political questions of the day? Further, if this statute of Louisiana is consistent with the personal liberty of citizens, why may not the state require the separation in railroad coaches of native and naturalized citizens of the United States, or of Protestants and Roman Catholics?...p. 263.[36]

---

[36] *Plessy v. Ferguson*, 41 L Ed 256 (1896)

Of course, following this decision, that is exactly what happened. Jim Crow laws of every imaginable kind were enacted all through the Southern States to separate, humiliate and dehumanize 12% of our population because of skin pigmentation. It would take another 58 years for the Supreme Court to undo the damage it caused to African Americans in this case. Not until the civil rights movement of the 1960s did real political integration begin and only then were the basic human rights of African Americans effectively enforced.

Although I have focused on the evil of slavery to emphasize the horror of racism and the inequality that it causes, I have not intended to ignore the crimes committed against Native Americans throughout our history, the bigotry against the Chinese, Irish, Italians, Jews and others when they arrived as immigrants beginning in the 1850s, and the discrimination against many Hispanic groups in our day. All of these mistreated groups represent additional examples of our need to work harder in our present world for equality with justice for all.

SUMMARY

Slavery was *the* moral issue at the time our country was founded and into the middle of the 19th century. It took a terrible Civil War and 630,000 lives, on both sides of the issue, to abolish slavery and bring the former slaves into civil society. The indelible mark of inferiority that earlier Americans branded upon the black race has not yet been fully erased. The task of making the ideal of "equality for all" the reality of "equal treatment for all," blacks, whites, Native Americans, Asians, and Hispanics remains *the* moral issue of the 21st century for this generation of Americans.

ADDITIONAL READING

American Scripture
by Pauline Maier[37]
Equality and Rights

Lincoln saw the Declaration of Independence's statements on equality and rights as setting a standard for the future, one that demanded the gradual extinction of conflicting practices as that became possible, which was the way Cooke had interpreted the opening section of Virginia's Declaration of Rights. The authors of the Declaration of Independence, Lincoln said, meant simply to declare the right so that the *enforcement* of it might follow as fast as the circumstances should permit. They meant to set up a standard maxim for free men which should be familiar to all, and revered by all; constantly looked to,

---

[37] Maier, *Op. Cit.*, pp. 197-207.

and constantly labored for, and even though never perfectly attained, constantly approximated and thereby constantly spreading and deepening its influence, and augmenting the happiness and value of life to all people of all colors everywhere.

He was therefore able to agree with Calhoun that the assertions of human equality and inalienable rights were unnecessary in the Declaration of Independence: the Americans could have declared their independence without them. But that made their inclusion even more wonderful. "All honor to Jefferson," Lincoln wrote in a letter of 1859—to the man who, in the concrete pressure of a struggle for national independence by a single people, had the coolness, forecast, and capacity to introduce into a merely revolutionary document, an abstract truth, applicable to all men and all times, and so to embalm it there, that to-day, and in all coming days, it shall be a rebuke and a stumbling-block to the very harbingers of reappearing tyranny and oppression."

JEFFERSON AND THE MEMBERS of the Second Continental Congress had not understood what they were doing in quite that way on July 4, 1776. For them, it was enough for the Declaration to be "merely revolutionary." Their text would not risk becoming wadding left to rot on the battlefield until the war with Britain was over, a memorial to the dead past until time had silenced the contests of their day. They sought to extend support for their cause and enhance the chances of victory; more they did not ask. In many ways, Douglas's history was more faithful to the past and to the views of Thomas Jefferson, who to the end of his life saw the Declaration of Independence as a revolutionary manifesto, and who understood that slavery violated the values of the Revolution but saw federal coercion of Western slaveholders in exactly the same way. Lincoln's view of the past, like Jefferson's in the 1770s, was a product of political controversy, not research, and his version of what the founders meant was full of wishful suppositions. But Lincoln was the greater statesman. By the mid-nineteenth century, when the standard of revolution had passed to radical Abolitionists and Southern secessionists who wanted to dismember the Union, the Declaration of Independence was in need of another reading. In Lincoln's hands, the Declaration of Independence became first and foremost a living document for an established society, a set of goals to be realized over time, and so an explanation less of the colonists' decision to separate from Britain than of their victory in the War for Independence. Men would not fight and endure "as our fathers did," Lincoln wrote in a fragment probably composed early in 1861, "without the promise of something better, than a mere change of masters." He understood the Northern cause in the Civil War in much the same way: the North fought not only to save the Union, but to save a form of government, as Lincoln told Congress on July 4, 1861, "whose leading object is to elevate the condition of men; to lift artificial weights from all shoulders—to clear the paths of laudable pursuit for all—to afford all, an unfettered start and a fair chance in the race of life." The rebellion it opposed was at base an effort "to overthrow the principle that all men were created equal."

LANDMARK CASE # 2

Dred Scott v. John F. A. Sandford
19 How. 393-633; 15 L. Ed. 691. (1857)

Mr. Justice Taney:

...The words "people of the United States" and "citizens" are synonymous terms, and mean the same thing. They both describe the political body, who, according to our republican institutions, form the sovereignty, and who hold the power and conduct the government through their representatives. They are what we familiarly call the "sovereign people," and every citi- zen is one of this people, and a constituent member of this sovereignty. The question before us is, whether...[Negroes]...compose a portion of this people, and are constituent members of this sovereignty. We think they are not, and that they are not included, and were not intended to be included, under the word "citizens" in the Constitution, and can, therefore, claim none of the rights and privileges which that instrument provides for and secures to citizens of the United States. On the contrary, they were at that time consid- ered as a subordinate and inferior class of beings, who had been subjugated by the dominant race, and whether emancipated or not, yet remained subject to their authority, and had no rights or privileges but such as those who held the power and the government might choose to grant them....(p. 700)

...We give both of these laws [slave laws] in the words used by the respec- tive legislative bodies, because the language in which they are framed, as well as the provisions contained in them, show, too plainly to be misunder- stood, the degraded condition of this unhappy race. They were still in force when the Revolution began, and are a faithful index to the state of feeling towards the class of persons of whom they speak, and of the position they occupied throughout the thirteen colonies, in the eyes and thoughts of the men who framed the Declaration of Independence and established the State constitutions and governments. They show that a perpetual and impassable barrier was intended to be erected between the white race and the one which they had reduced to slavery, and governed as subjects with absolute and despotic power, and which they then looked upon as so far below them in the scale of created beings, that intermarriages between white persons and Negroes or mulattoes were regarded as unnatural and immoral, and punished as crimes, not only in the parties, but in the person who joined them in mar- riage. And no distinction in this respect was made between the free Negro or mulatto and the slave, but this stigma, of the deepest degradation, was fixed upon the whole race.

...This state of public opinion had undergone no change when the Constitution was adopted, as is equally evident from its provisions and language.

...But there are two clauses in the Constitution which point directly and specifically to the Negro race as a separate class of persons, and show clearly that they were not regarded as a portion of the people or citizens of the government then formed.

One of these clauses reserves to each of the thirteen States the right to import slaves until the year 1808, if it thinks proper. And the importation which it thus sanctions was unquestionably of persons of the race of which we are speaking, as the traffic in slaves in the United States had always been confined to them. And by the other provision the States pledge themselves to each other to maintain the right of property of the master, by delivering up to him any slave who may have escaped from his service, and be found within their respective territories. By the first above-mentioned clause, therefore, the right to purchase and hold this property is directly sanctioned and authorized for twenty years by the people who framed the Constitution. And by the second, they pledge themselves to maintain and uphold the right of the master in the manner specified, as long as the government they then formed should endure. And these two provisions show, conclusively, that neither the description of persons therein referred to, nor their descendants, were embraced in any of the other provisions of the Constitution; for certainly these two clauses were not intended to confer on them or their posterity the blessings of liberty, or any of the personal rights so carefully provided for the citizen....(pp. 702-3)

The legislation of the States therefore shows, in a manner not to be mistaken, the inferior and subject condition of that race at the time the Constitution was adopted, and long afterwards, throughout the thirteen States by which that instrument was framed; and it is hardly consistent with the respect due to these States, to suppose that they regarded at that time, as fellow citizens and members of the sovereignty, a class of beings whom they had thus stigmatized; whom as we are bound, out of respect to the State sovereignties, to assume they had deemed it just and necessary thus to stigmatize, and upon whom they had impressed such deep and enduring marks of inferiority and degradation; or that when they met in convention to form the Constitution, they looked upon them as a portion of their Constituents, or designed to include them in the provisions so carefully inserted for the security and protection of the liberties and rights of their citizens. It cannot be supposed that they intended to secure to them rights, and privileges, and rank, in the new political body throughout the Union, which every one of them denied within the limits of its own dominion. More especially, it cannot be believed that the large slaveholding States regarded them as included in the word "citizens," or would have consented to a constitution which might compel them to receive them in that character from another State. For if they were so received, and entitled to the privileges and immunities of citizens, it would exempt them from the operation of the special laws and from the police regulations which they considered to be necessary for their own safety. It would give to persons of the Negro race, who were recognized as citizens in any one State of the Union, the right to enter every other State whenever they pleased, singly or in companies, without pass or passport, and without obstruction, to sojourn there as long as they pleased, to go where they pleased at every hour of the day or night without molestation, unless they committed some violation of law for which a white man would be punished; and it would give them the full liberty of speech in public and in private upon all subjects upon which its own citizens might speak; to hold public meetings upon political affairs, and to keep and carry arms wherever they went. And all of this would be done in the face of the subject race of the same color, both free and slaves, inevitably producing discontent and insubordination among them, and endangering the peace and safety of the State....(p. 705)

Mr. Justice Curtis, dissenting:

I shall not enter into an examination of the existing opinions of that period respecting the African race, nor into any discussion concerning the meaning of those who asserted, in the Declaration of Independence, that all men are created equal; that they are endowed by their Creator with certain inalienable rights; that among these are life, liberty, and the pursuit of happiness. My own opinion is, that a calm comparison of these assertions of universal abstract truths, and of their own individual opinions and acts, would not leave these men under any reproach of inconsistency; that the great truths they asserted on that solemn occasion, they were ready and anxious to make effectual, wherever a necessary regard to circumstances, which no statesman can disregard without producing more evil than good, would allow; and that it would not be just to them, nor true in itself, to allege that they intended to say that the Creator of all men had endowed the white race, exclusively, with the great natural rights which the Declaration of Independence asserts....(p. 771)

Did the Constitution of the United States deprive them or their descendants of citizenship? That Constitution was ordained and established by the people of the United States through the action, in each State, of those persons who were qualified by its laws to act thereon, in behalf of themselves and all other citizens of that State. In some of the States, as we have seen, colored persons were among those qualified by law to act on this subject. These colored persons were not only included in the body of "the people of the United States by whom the Constitution was ordained and established," but in at least five of the States they had the power to act, and doubtless did act, by their suffrages, upon the question of its adoption. It would be strange, if we were to find in that instrument anything which deprived of their citizenship any part of the people of the United States who were among those by whom it was established....(p. 771)

LANDMARK CASE #3

Plessy v. Ferguson
41 Law Ed 256 (1896)

A Louisiana statute stated that all railway companies (other than street railway companies) carrying passengers in that state were required to have separate but equal accommodations for white and colored persons, "by providing two or more passenger coaches for each passenger train, or by dividing the passenger coaches by partition as to secure separate accommodations." Homer Plessy challenged that law as unconstitutional since it denied him equal protection of the law in violation of the 14th Amendment.

Mr. Justice Brown:

...it was said that the act of a mere individual, the owner of an inn, a public conveyance, or place of amusement, refusing accommodations to colored people, cannot be justly regarded as imposing any badge of slavery or servitude upon the applicant, but only as involving an ordinary civil injury, properly cognizable by the laws of the state, and presumably subject to redress by those laws until the contrary appears, "It would be running the slavery argument into the ground," said Mr. Justice Bradley, "to make it apply to every act of discrimination which a person may see fit to make as to the guests he will entertain, or as to the people he will take into his coach or cab or car, or admit to his concert or theater, or deal with in other matters of intercourse or business."

A statute which implies merely a legal distinction between the white and colored races—a distinction which is founded in the color of the two races, and which must always exist so long as white men are distinguished from the other race by color—has no tendency to destroy the legal equality of the two races, or re-establish a state of involuntary servitude....

...So far, then, as a conflict with the 14th amendment is concerned, the case reduces itself to the question whether the statute of Louisiana is a reasonable regulation, and with respect to this there must necessarily be a large discretion on the part of the legislature. In determining the question of reasonableness it is at liberty to act with reference to the established usages, customs, and traditions of the people, and with a view to the promotion of their comfort, and the preservation of the public peace and good order. Gauged by this, we cannot say that a law which authorizes or even requires the separation of the two races in public conveyances is unreasonable or more obnoxious to the 14th Amendment than the acts of Congress requiring separate schools for colored children in the District of Columbia, the constitutionality of which does not seem to have been questioned, or the corresponding acts of state legislatures.

We consider the underlying fallacy of the plaintiff's argument to consist in the assumption that the enforced separation of the two races stamps the colored race with a badge of inferiority. If this be so, it is not by reason of anything found in the act, but solely because the colored race chooses to put that construction upon it. The argument necessarily assumes that if, as has been more than once the case, and is not unlikely to be so again, the colored race should become the dominant power in the state legislature, and should enact a law in precisely similar terms, it would thereby relegate the white race to an inferior position. We imagine that the white race, at least, would not acquiesce in this assumption. The argument also assumes that social prejudices may be overcome by legislation, and that equal rights cannot be secured to the Negro except by an enforced commingling of the two races. We cannot accept this proposition. If the two races are to meet on terms of social equality, it must be the result of natural affinities, a mutual appreciation of each other's merits and a voluntary consent of individuals....(pp. 260-1)

Legislation is powerless to eradicate racial instincts or to abolish distinctions based upon physical differences, and the attempt to do so can only result in accentuating the difficulties of the present situation. If the civil and political rights of both races be equal, one cannot be inferior to the other civilly or politically. If one race be inferior to the other socially, the Constitution of the United States cannot put them upon the same plane. (p. 261)

Mr. Justice Harlan, dissenting:

...The white race deems itself to be the dominant race in this country. And so it is, in prestige, in achievements, in education, in prestige, and in power. So, I doubt not that it will continue to be for all time, if it remains true to its great heritage and holds fast to the principles of constitutional liberty. But in view of the Constitution, in the eye of the law, there is in this country no superior dominant, ruling class of citizens. There is no caste here. Our Constitution is color-blind, and neither knows nor tolerates classes among citizens. In respect of civil rights, all citizens are equal before the law. The humblest is the peer of the most powerful. The law regards man as man, and takes no account of his surroundings or of his color when his civil rights as guaranteed by the supreme law of the land are involved....In my opinion, the judgment this day rendered will, in time, prove to be quite as pernicious as the decision made by this tribunal in the *Dred Scott* case. It was adjudged in that case that the descendants of Africans who were imported into this country and sold as slaves were not included nor intended to be included under the word "citizens" in the Constitution, and could not claim any of the rights and privileges which that instrument provided for and secured to citizens of the United States; that at the time of the adoption of the Constitution they were "considered as a subordinate and inferior class of beings, who had been subjugated by the dominant race, whether emancipated or not, yet remained subject to their authority, and had no rights or privileges but such as those who held the power and the government might choose to grant them." 60 U.S. 19 How. 393,[1: 691, 700]. The recent amendments of the Constitution, it was supposed, had eradicated these principles from our institutions. But it seems that we have yet, in some of the states, a dominant race, a superior class of citizens, which assumes to regulate the enjoyment of civil rights, common to all citizens, upon the basis of race....What can more certainly arouse race hate, what more certainly create and perpetuate a feeling of distrust between these races, than state enactments which in fact proceed on the ground that colored citizens are so inferior and degraded that they cannot be allowed to sit in public coaches occupied by white citizens? That, as all will admit, is the real meaning of such legislation as was enacted in Louisiana.

The sure guaranty of the peace and security of each race is the clear, distinct, unconditional recognition by our governments, national and state, of every right that inheres in civil freedom, and of the equality before the law of all citizens of the United States without regard to race....This question is not met by the suggestion that social equality cannot exist between the white and black races in this country. That argument, if it can be properly regarded as one, is scarcely worthy of consideration, for social equality no more exists between two races when traveling in a passenger coach or a public highway than when members of the same races sit by each other in a street car or in the jury box, or stand or sit with each other in a political assembly, or when they use in common the streets of a city or town, or when they are in the same room for the purpose of having their names placed on the registry of voters, or when they approach the ballot-box in order to exercise the high privilege of voting....

...The arbitrary separation of citizens, on the basis of race, while they are on a public highway, is a badge of servitude wholly inconsistent with the civil freedom and the equality before the law established by the Constitution. It cannot be justified upon any legal grounds.

If evils will result from the commingling of the two races upon public highways established for the benefit of all, they will be infinitely less than those that will surely come from state legislation regulating the enjoyment of civil rights upon the basis of race. We boast of the freedom enjoyed by our people above all other peoples. But it is difficult to reconcile that boast with a state of the law which, practically, puts the brand of servitude and degradation upon a large class of our fellow citizens, our equals before the law. The thin disguise of "equal" accommodations for passengers in railroad coaches will not mislead anyone, or atone for the wrong this day done.... (pp. 263-5)

6. EQUAL IN THE EYES OF THE LAW

But what do we mean by equality? Certainly it is clear to any casual observer that people in our society are very unequal. Inequalities have always existed among us in physical stature and health, intellectual ability, material wealth and our racial, ethnic or social status. So in what sense are all people equal?

a. Equal by Definition

Human beings are equal in the sense that we are all members of the same species—*Homo sapiens sapiens*. We are the same in that we are all rational animals. We should look at ourselves as very intelligent animals who can think and understand complex ideas and we have the ability to make free choices about what we understand to be right and wrong. We are not driven solely by instinct nor are our choices necessarily determined by our genes and experience. We are predators who have learned to cooperate with each other to hunt, plant and occupy territory. We are sexual creatures who need companionship with the opposite sex for pleasure and procreation. And we will all die. All human beings are equal in these characteristics and needs. But the enlightenment thinkers meant much more than a mere equality by definition. Our founding fathers considered all people to be equal in the sense that all are equal in the eyes of the law. But what does it mean to be "equal in the eyes of the law"?

b. Equal in Participation: The Franchise

To be equal in the eyes of the law means that all members of our society have an equal right to participate in that society. In this respect, America has not been perfect. Full participation remained a goal that has only recently become a reality. At the time of the Revolution only those men who owned $200 worth of property could vote. Neither slaves nor Native Americans had any recognized human or civil rights. Neither women nor young adults could vote.

Property requirements to exercise the franchise were generally eliminated by the mid 20th century although the requirement that office holders own property persisted until the 1960s. It was not until 1924 that Native Americans were made citizens by an act of Congress. It was not until 1920 that women in this country were granted the right to vote by the passage of the Nineteenth Amendment:

The right of citizens of the United States to vote shall not be denied or abridged by the United States or by any State on account of sex.

In an effort to give greater meaning to our equality of participation and recognizing that since the Civil War some States were frustrating by various means the right of black people to vote, we adopted the Twenty-Fourth Amendment in 1964 at the height of the Civil Rights movement in this country:

> The right of citizens of the United States to vote in any primary or other election for President or Vice President, for electors for President or Vice President, or for Senator or Representative in Congress, shall not be denied or abridged by the United States or any State by reason of failure to pay any poll tax or other tax.

Finally, in 1971, with the passage of the Twenty-Sixth Amendment, young adults obtained the right to the franchise:

> The right of citizens of the United States, who are eighteen years of age or older, to vote shall not be denied or abridged by the United States or by any State on account of age.

c. Equal in Rights

Section One of the Fourteenth Amendment requires that state governments recognize human, political, and civil rights to the same extent enjoyed by citizens of the United States. It is one of the strongest bonds that makes us one nation and one people:

> ...No State shall make or enforce any law which shall abridge the privileges or immunities of citizens of the United States; nor shall any State deprive any person of life, liberty or property, without due process of law...

Professor Dworkin reminds us that the Bill of Rights is a restriction upon the power of government for the equal benefit of all:

> I believe that the principles set out in the Bill of Rights, taken together, commit the United States to the following political and legal ideas: government must treat all those subject to its dominion as having equal moral and political status; it must attempt, in good faith, to treat them all with concern; and it must respect whatever individual freedoms are indispensable to those ends, including but not limited to the freedoms more specifically designated in the document, such as the freedoms of speech and religion.[38]

d. Equal in Protection

"Equal in the eyes of the law" means that every member of our society is entitled to the "equal protection of the laws." Section One of the Fourteenth Amendment continues:

> nor deny to any person within its jurisdiction the equal protection of the laws.

Again, Professor Dworkin observes the history and the great sweep of the Fourteenth Amendment:

---

[38] Dworkin, *Op. Cit.*, p. 47.

...Most of [the Framers] no doubt had fairly clear expectations about what legal consequences the Fourteenth Amendment would have. They expected it to end certain of the most egregious Jim Crow practices of the Reconstruction period. They plainly did not expect it to outlaw official racial segregation in school—on the contrary, the Congress that adopted the equal protection clause itself maintained segregation in the District of Columbia school system. But they did not say anything about Jim Crow laws or school segregation or homosexuality or gender equality, one way or the other. They said that "equal protection of the laws" is required, which plainly describes a very general principle, not any concrete application of it...

...they declared a principle of quite breathtaking scope and power: the principle that government must treat everyone as of equal status and with equal concern.[39]

Although this Amendment was adopted in the aftermath of slavery, it is intended to apply to everyone in our country. At about the same time, Congress passed civil rights laws to implement these protections. Federal law[40] provides:

Sec. 1981. Equal rights under the law

All persons within the jurisdiction of the United States shall have the same right in every State and Territory to make and enforce contracts, to sue, be parties, give evidence, and to the full and equal benefit of all laws and proceedings for the security of persons and property as is enjoyed by white citizens, and shall be subject to like punishment, pains, penalties, taxes, licenses, and exactions of every kind, and to no other.

Sec. 1982. Property rights of citizens

All citizens of the United States shall have the same right, in every State and Territory, as is enjoyed by white citizens thereof to inherit, purchase, lease, sell, hold, and convey real and personal property.

Sec. 1983. Civil action for deprivation of rights

Every person who, under color of any statute, ordinance, regulation, custom, or usage, of any State or Territory or the District of Columbia, subjects, or causes to be subjected, any citizen of the United States or other person within the jurisdiction thereof to the deprivation of any rights, privileges, or immunities secured by the Constitution and laws, shall be liable to the party injured in an action at law, suit in equity, or other proper proceeding for redress.

It has been our sad history that these laws, intended to promote equality among the races, have been honored more in the breach than the observance since their adoption during the Reconstruction Era, until the advent of the Civil Rights Movement in the 1960s.

e. Equal in Opportunity

In recent times, equality has been broadened to include social and eco-

---

[39] *Ibid.*, p. 48.
[40] 42 USCA 1981, 1982 & 1983.

nomic rights. Under its power to regulate commerce, Congress passed laws prohibiting racial discrimination in transportation and public accommodations. In 1965 Congress passed the Civil Rights Act that imposed duties on employers not to discriminate on the basis of race (as well as religion and national origin) in the workplace and promoted economic fairness not by requiring equal jobs or wealth or education but requiring equal opportunity for all people to obtain these benefits. These laws were later broadened to forbid discrimination against women, older people, and the disabled in their employment. In recent years laws have been adopted to promote equal opportunity for admission to tax supported schools, for women and other minorities. And there are state and local laws that forbid discrimination in housing and that expand the protections afforded to other minority groups, such as gay and lesbian persons.

f. Affirmative Action

In an effort to promote greater equality, in 1965 President Lyndon Johnson signed an Executive Order requiring that the Federal government, state universities, other state programs that accepted federal money, and those that do business with the federal government, give preferences in hiring, promoting and laying off black employees over white employees in order to overcome the heritage of slavery and make up for the perceived social and economic disadvantages of the descendants of the slaves. After all, slavery is still very close to us; there are people alive today in 1999, who, as children, remember speaking to their grandparents or great-grandparents about their lives as slaves. And so too, the damage of slavery—the indelible mark of inferiority tolerated and imposed by law and reaffirmed by the United States Supreme Court, in the memory of living people—the degradation and humiliation of being treated as less than human that causes the destruction of a person's self-image, the breakup of the family that destroys cultural and social values—is also very close to us. Affirmative action programs in government were viewed as a means of leveling the playing field by promoting greater job opportunities for this disadvantaged minority. Later, President Richard Nixon added many more minority groups also perceived to be disadvantaged, including Native Americans, Hispanics and women, that diluted the original purpose of remedying the effects of slavery.

Those who oppose affirmative action programs, do so on the grounds that they offend our basic concepts of equality, that no person should be given a preference on the basis of race or sex in employment practices, that all should be treated equally. After all, we are all members of some minority and (except for that smallest of minorities—the very rich) many of the members of these groups can point to their own hardships and disadvantage. The jury in America is still out on this issue.

Perhaps Mr. Justice Blackmun sums up our hopes best in his concurring opinion in the Baake case:

...I yield to no one in my earnest hope that the time will come when an "affirmative action" program is unnecessary and is, in truth, only a relic of the past. I would hope that we could reach this stage within a decade at the most. But the story of *Brown v Board of Education*, (1954), decided almost a quarter of a century ago, suggests that that hope is a slim one. At some time, however, beyond any period of what some would claim is only transitional inequality, the United States must and will reach a stage of maturity where action along this line is no longer necessary. Then persons will be regarded as persons, and discrimination of the type we address today will be an ugly feature of history that is instructive but that is behind us....[41]

SUMMARY

This is not intended to be a comprehensive listing of all the human, political, or civil rights statutes that exist at the Federal and State level. Rather, these examples are intended to show the great commitment that we have to true equality—equality in the eyes of the law—and the extent that this fundamental concept affects every principle and rule of American ethics. We were the first to put this equality into practice; today, much of the world has followed us.

MY PERSONAL OBLIGATION:
Respect for Others as Human Beings

The proposition that "...all men are created equal..." is the most powerful force ever created by Western civilization. That concept was directly responsible for the American Revolution and the establishment of the American Republic. It was directly responsible for the French Revolution and was one of the causes of the American Civil War. In the 20th Century, the idea of equality was a contributing factor to the Russian Revolution and the overthrow of European monarchies after the First World War. And it was one of the causes for the establishment of democracy in India after the Second World War. Right until the present day, the power of the idea of the equality of all has caused dictatorships to fall and democratic states to rise up through most of South America and the Caribbean and is continuing to spread throughout Africa.

We must take this duty to treat all people as equals in the eyes of the law, which we impose upon our government and upon ourselves as a society, and make it our personal obligation. The virtuous citizen will treat neighbors as equals in their essential humanity, where they live, learn, work, and play. The virtuous citizen as lawyer, doctor, and banker will treat clients as equal human beings. The virtuous citizen as owner and manager will treat employees and customers as equal human beings. The rich will treat the poor as equal human beings. Each race and nationality will treat each other as equal human beings. Equality for all in our public and business relationships is our ethical

---

[41] *University of California Regents v. Baake*, 438 US 265, 98 S Ct 2733, 57 L Ed 2d 750, 842.

obligation and is, ultimately, in our own enlightened self-interest.

MY PERSONAL VIRTUE:
Kinship

The Plessy case observed that "If the two races are to meet on terms of social equality, it must be the result of natural affinities, a mutual appreciation of each other's merits and a voluntary consent of individuals."

While respect for others is our duty, that duty extends only to human rights and political and civil rights. These involve only some social interchange such as integrated schools and housing and equal opportunities in the workplace. When we acknowledge that we are all brothers and sisters as part of the human family, we do more than the law requires. It is a virtue that the virtuous citizen gladly accepts, to welcome all our brothers and sisters into our private clubs, our churches and our private schools. The virtuous citizen will welcome all members of the human family into his or her home and share food and drink at the family table. We cannot know or care for each and every one of the six billion people who now inhabit our planet. But the virtuous citizen will develop an attitude of caring for others, especially those in need in one's own small world.

Nor can we have more than a few close friends. But the virtuous citizen will make friends based not on the color of another's skin or the acceptability of another's religious or philosophical convictions but upon the quality and strength of one's character. The virtuous citizen will not see any "indelible mark of inferiority" that ignorant and fearful people have imprinted upon some of our brothers and sisters. The virtuous citizen will ignore the accidental characteristics of the individual and develop a circle of friends based upon the essential humanity of each person. Friends will be made depending upon whether that individual is a good person with whom you share things in common.

Above all, brothers and sisters help each other; they do not hurt each other.

LANDMARK CASE # 4

Baake v. The Board of Regents
438 US 265; 57 L Ed 2nd 750 (1978)

The University of California at Davis Medical School had a special admissions program, reserving 16 seats out of 100 for black and other disadvantaged minority applicants. Allan Baake, a white applicant, was denied admission although others less qualified than he were accepted through the special admissions program. He sued for admission to medical school, claiming reverse discrimination and the denial of equal protection of the law. Mr. Justice Pow-

ell delivers the majority opinion, concluding that the school's program violated Baake's rights to equal protection since, in giving preference to disadvantaged minorities, it excluded him from competing for the remaining 16 seats. However, the majority also held that race may be a factor in the admission decision in order to achieve diversity within the student body.

Mr. Justice Powell:

Over the past 30 years, this Court has embarked upon the crucial mission of interpreting the Equal Protection Clause with the view of ensuring to all persons "the protection of equal laws," in a Nation confronting a legacy of slavery and racial discrimination. Because the landmark decisions in this area arose in response to the continued exclusion of Negroes from the mainstream of American society, they could be characterized as involving discrimination by the "majority" white race against the Negro minority. But they need not be read as depending upon that characterization for their results. It suffices to say that "[o]ver the years, this Court has consistently repudiated [d]istinctions between citizens solely because of their ancestry 'as being odious to a free people whose institutions are founded upon the doctrine of equality.'"

[The University of California] urges us to adopt for the first time a more restrictive view of the Equal Protection Clause and holds that discrimination against members of the white "majority" cannot be suspect if its purpose can be characterized as "benign." The clock of our liberties, however, cannot be turned back to 1868. It is far too late to argue that the guarantee of equal protection to all persons permits the recognition of special wards entitled to a degree of protection greater than that accorded others. "The Fourteenth Amendment is not directed solely against discrimination due to a 'two-class theory'—that is, based upon differences between 'white' and Negro."

...The concepts of "majority" and "minority" necessarily reflect temporary arrangements and political judgments. As observed above, the white "majority" itself is composed of various minority groups, most of which can lay claim to a history of prior discrimination at the hands of the State and private individuals. Not all of these groups can receive preferential treatment and corresponding judicial tolerance of distinctions drawn in terms of race and nationality, for then the only "majority" left would be a new minority of white Anglo-Saxon Protestants. There is no principled basis for deciding which groups would merit "heightened judicial solicitude" and which would not. Courts would be asked to evaluate the extent of the prejudice and consequent harm suffered by various minority groups. Those whose societal injury is thought to exceed some arbitrary level of tolerability then would be entitled to preferential classifications at the expense of individuals belonging to other groups. Those classifications would be free from exacting judicial scrutiny. As these preferences began to have their desired effect, and the consequences of past discrimination were undone, new judicial rankings would be necessary. The kind of variable sociological and political analysis necessary to produce such rankings simply does not lie within the judicial competence—even if they otherwise were politically feasible and socially desirable.

Moreover, there are serious problems of justice connected with the idea of preference itself. First, it may not always be clear that a so-called preference is in fact benign. Courts may be asked to validate burdens imposed upon individual members of a particular group in order to advance the group's general interest. Nothing in the Constitution supports the notion that individuals may be asked to suffer otherwise impermissible burdens in order to enhance the societal standing of their ethnic groups. Second, preferential programs may only reinforce common stereotypes holding that certain groups are unable to achieve success without special protection based on a factor having no relationship to individual worth. Third, there is a measure of inequity in forcing innocent persons in [a] respondent's position to bear the burdens of redressing grievances not of their making. (pp. 773-5)

...If [The University of California's] purpose is to assure within its student body some specified percentage of a particular group merely because of its race or ethnic origin, such a preferential purpose must be rejected...as facially invalid. Preferring members of any one group for no reason other than race or ethnic origin is discrimination for its own sake. This the Constitution forbids. (p. 782)

...The fourth goal asserted by [The University of California] is the attainment of a diverse student body. This clearly is a constitutionally permissible goal for an institution of higher education. Academic freedom, though not a specifically enumerated constitutional right, long has been viewed as a special concern of the First Amendment. The freedom of a university to make its own judgments as to education includes the selection of its student body. (p. 785)

...the "nation's future depends upon leaders trained through wide exposure" to the ideas and mores of students as diverse as this Nation of many peoples....(p. 785)

Thus in arguing that its universities must be accorded the right to select those students who will contribute the most to the "robust exchange of ideas," [The University of California] invokes a countervailing constitutional interest, that of the First Amendment. In this light, [The University of California] must be viewed as seeking to achieve a goal that is of paramount importance in the fulfillment of its....(p. 786)

...Ethnic diversity, however, is only one element in a range of factors a university properly may consider in attaining the goal of a heterogeneous student body. Although a university must have wide discretion in making the sensitive judgments as to who should be admitted, constitutional limitations protecting individual rights may not be disregarded.

....In summary, it is evident that the Davis special admissions program involves the use of an explicit racial classification never before countenanced by this Court. It tells applicants who are not Negro, Asian, or Chicano that they are totally excluded from a specific percentage of the seats in an entering class. No matter how strong their qualifications, quantitative and extracurricular, including their own potential for contribution to educational diversity, they are never afforded the chance to compete with applicants from the preferred groups for the special admissions seats. At the same time, the preferred applicants have the opportunity to compete for every seat in the class....(pp. 789-90)

....[In the meantime] the courts below failed to recognize that the State has a substantial interest that legitimately may be served by a properly devised admissions program involving the competitive consideration of race and ethnic origin....(p.790)

Mr. Justice Marshall summarized the feelings of many African Americans in his concurring opinion.

...I agree with the judgment of the Court only insofar as it permits a university to consider the race of an applicant in making admissions decisions. I do not agree that petitioner's admissions program violates the Constitution. For it must be remembered that, during most of the past 200 years, the Constitution as interpreted by this Court did not prohibit the most ingenious and pervasive forms of discrimination against the Negro. Now, when a State acts to remedy the effects of that legacy of discrimination, I cannot believe that this same Constitution stands as a barrier.

Three hundred and fifty years ago, the Negro was dragged to this country in chains to be sold into slavery. Uprooted from his homeland and thrust into bondage for forced labor, the slave was deprived of all legal rights. It was unlawful to teach him to read; he could be sold away from his family and friends at the whim of his master; and killing or maiming him was not a crime. The system of slavery brutalized and dehumanized both master and slave....(p. 832)

...In the wake of *Plessy*, many States expanded their Jim Crow laws, which had up until that time been limited primarily to passenger trains and schools. The segregation of the races was extended to residential areas, parks, hospitals, theaters, waiting rooms, and bathrooms. There were even statutes and ordinances which authorized separate phone booths for Negroes and whites, which required that textbooks used by children of one race be kept separate from those used by the other, and which required that Negro and white prostitutes be kept in separate districts. In 1898, after Plessy, the *Charlestown News and Courier* printed a parody of Jim Crow laws:

"'If there must be Jim Crow cars on the railroads, there should be Jim Crow cars on the street railways. Also on all passenger boats....If there are to be Jim Crow cars, moreover, there should be Jim Crow waiting saloons at all stations, and Jim Crow eating houses....There should be Jim Crow sections of the jury box, and a separate Jim Crow dock and witness stand in every court—and a Jim Crow Bible for colored witnesses to kiss.'" Woodward 68.

The irony is that before many years had passed, with the exception of the Jim Crow witness stand, "all the improbable applications of the principle suggested by the editor in derision had been put into practice—down to and including the Jim Crow Bible."

Nor were the laws restricting the rights of Negroes limited solely to the Southern States. In many of the Northern States, the Negro was denied the right to vote, prevented from serving on juries, and excluded from theaters, restaurants, hotels, and inns. Under President Wilson, the Federal Government began to require segregation in Government buildings; desks of Negro employees were curtained off; separate bathrooms and separate tables in the cafeterias were provided; and even the galleries of the Congress were segregated. When his segregationist policies were attacked, President Wilson responded that segregation was "not humiliating but a benefit" and that he was "rendering [the Negroes] more safe in their possession of office and less likely to be discriminated against."

The enforced segregation of the races continued into the middle of the 20th century. In both World Wars, Negroes were for the most part confined to separate military units; it was not until 1948 that an end to segregation in the military was ordered by President Truman. And the history of the exclusion of Negro children from white public schools is too well known and recent to require repeating here. That Negroes were deliberately excluded from public graduate and professional schools—and thereby denied the opportunity to become doctors, lawyers, engineers, and the like—is also well established. It is of course true that some of the Jim Crow laws (which the decisions of this Court had helped to foster) were struck down by this Court in a series of decisions leading up to *Brown v. Board of Education.* Those decisions, however, did not automatically end segregation, nor did they move Negroes from a position of legal inferiority to one of equality. The legacy of years of slavery and of years of second-class citizenship in the wake of emancipation could not be so easily eliminated.

The position of the Negro today in America is the tragic but inevitable consequence of centuries of unequal treatment. Measured by any benchmark of comfort or achievement, meaningful equality remains a distant dream for the Negro.

A Negro child today has a life expectancy which is shorter by more than five years than that of a white child. The Negro child's mother is over three times more likely to die of complications in childbirth, and the infant mortality rate for Negroes is nearly twice that for whites. The median income of the Negro family is only 60% that of the median of a white family, and the percentage of Negroes who live in families with incomes below the poverty line is nearly four times greater than that of whites.

When the Negro child reaches working age, he finds that America offers him significantly less than it offers his white counterpart. For Negro adults, the unemployment rate is twice that of whites, and the unemployment rate for Negro teenagers is nearly three times that of white teenagers. A Negro male who completes four years of college can expect a median annual income of merely $110 more than a white male who has only a high school diploma. Although Negroes represent 11.5% of the population, they are only 1.2% of the lawyers and judges, 2% of the physicians, 2.3% of the dentists, 1.1% of the engineers and 2.6% of the college and university professors.

The relationship between those figures and the history of unequal treatment afforded to the Negro cannot be denied. At every point from birth to death the impact of the past is reflected in the still disfavored position of the Negro.

In light of the sorry history of discrimination and its devastating impact on the lives of Negroes, bringing the Negro into the mainstream of American life should be a state interest of the highest order. To fail to do so is to ensure that America will forever remain a divided society. (pp. 832-7)

While I applaud the judgment of the Court that a university may consider race in its admissions process, it is more than a little ironic that, after several hundred years of class-based discrimination against Negroes, the Court is unwilling to hold that a class-based remedy for that discrimination is permissible. In declining to so hold, today's judgment ignores the fact that for several hundred years Negroes have been discriminated against, not as individuals, but rather solely because of the color of their skins. It is unnecessary in 20th century America to have individual Negroes demonstrate that they have been victims of racial discrimination; the racism of our society has been so pervasive that none, regardless of wealth or position, has managed to escape its impact. The experience of Negroes in America has been different in kind, not just in degree, from that of other ethnic groups. It is not merely the history of slavery alone but also that a whole people were marked as inferior by the law. And that mark has endured. The dream of America as the great melting pot has not been realized for the Negro; because of his skin color he never even made it into the pot.

These differences in the experience of the Negro make it difficult for me to accept that Negroes cannot be afforded greater protection under the Fourteenth Amendment where it is necessary to remedy the effects of past discrimination. In the Civil Rights Cases, the Court wrote that the Negro emerging from slavery must cease "to be the special favorite of the laws." We cannot in light of the history of the last century yield to that view. Had the Court in that decision and others been willing to "do for human liberty and the fundamental rights of American citizenship, what it did for the protection of slavery and the rights of the masters of fugitive slaves," we would not need now to permit the recognition of any "special wards."

Most importantly, had the Court been willing in 1896, in *Plessy v. Ferguson*, to hold that the Equal Protection Clause forbids differences in treatment based on race, we would not be faced with this dilemma in 1978. We must remember, however, that the principle that the "Constitution is colorblind" appeared only in the opinion of the lone dissenter. The majority of the Court rejected the principle of color blindness, and for the next 60 years, from *Plessy* to *Brown v. Board of Education*, ours was a Nation where, by law, an individual could be given "special" treatment based on the color of his skin.

It is because of a legacy of unequal treatment that we now must permit the institutions of this society to give consideration to race in making decisions about who will hold the positions of influence, affluence, and prestige in America. For far too long, the doors to those positions have been shut to Negroes. If we are ever to become a fully integrated society, one in which the color of a person's skin will not determine the opportunities available to him or her, we must be willing to take steps to open those doors. I do not believe that anyone can truly look into America's past and still find that a remedy for the effects of that past is impermissible....(pp. 840-1)

CHAPTER III

The Social Contract

Life cannot subsist in society but by reciprocal concessions.
Samuel Johnson
Letter to Boswell *1766*

Once upon a time, ten reasonable people out hunting, five men and five women, converged upon each other in a jungle with swords in hand. Some were white, others were black, yellow, brown, and red. One was badly disabled and only one had many possessions. Everyone was startled upon confronting their competitors for food and all began to snarl and growl to defend themselves and to scare the others away from the hunting grounds.

After a while, a wise person said, "Let us not kill each other; rather, let us cooperate in the hunt and share the kill."

A second person, a large one, said, "Why should I share? I am stronger than you and can catch the prey alone."

A third person said, "I am swifter than you and can catch my quarry without you and I, too, need not share."

A fourth person said "I am smarter than you and can snare my hunt by myself and I will not share either."

The wise one answered, "If we hunt alone only one will eat, and eat well, and the others will starve. But if we work together, we have a much better chance of trapping our quarry more quickly and all will eat (although not as well as one) and all will live."

They answered, "How will we get our fair share?"

The wise one said, "Just over there in the crevice between those two large stones is the entrance to the Land of Impartiality, where rules can be made for the benefit of all. Would you like to join me?"

The weaker persons were eager for a guaranteed smaller share in the kill and so joined the wise one. The rich and powerful persons knew that only one of them would survive if they failed to cooperate. They had also learned from the elders that loners do not survive to reproductive age as often as team players. So, being reasonable people, they too, decided to join the wise one.

As they passed through the curtain that covered the entrance, they became abstract human beings; they shed all those accidental characteristics that do not define them as human beings. They were no longer male and female, white, black, yellow, brown, or red. The disabled person was no longer so, the rich person was shorn of possessions and status in the community, the large person was no longer big, the swift person no longer swift, and the smart person was of ordinary intelligence. Even the wise one was no longer wise but like the rest.

But as abstract human beings, they retained those essential characteristics that make people rational. They could think and reason and remember that, as animals, they needed food and water and a mate and territory. And they could plan and each could choose what was in each other's best interest.

Moreover, when they entered this dominion, they passed through the Veil of Ignorance so that they now did not know who or what they would be when they returned to the jungle. They did not know what their sex or race or health or wealth or status in life would be and therefore, they did not know how the rules that they were about to make would affect them hereafter. They had all been forced to become impartial. The ten reasonable people were somewhat bewildered and were trying to absorb all that had happened.

At last a fifth human being spoke; "Let us agree that we shall all be equal." A sixth said, "It is clear that, as abstract human beings, we *are* all equal since it is those accidental characteristics, which we have just shed, that make us unequal in the jungle. However, I agree that we should *recognize* that, as abstract human beings, we are all equal in the Land of Impartiality." All acknowledged the obvious fact. They recognized that they all had equal bargaining power—only the power of rational argument—and that no one had any other bargaining leverage.

Then the seventh reasonable human being said, "It is also clear that each of us is being forced to make rules for the benefit of all of us since I do not know whether our rules will benefit me or hurt me when we return to real life."

"Then our first agreement must be not to kill each other," said an eighth human being. "We must all agree to lay our swords upon the table when we return to the jungle."

A ninth said, "I will not agree to give up my sword since I may be strong when we return to the jungle." Then all the others were disturbed and said that all must relinquish their arms or no one could give up any weapons since no one would remain defenseless against a recalcitrant aggressor.

A tenth reasonable human being said to the ninth, "But you may return to the jungle as a weak person and therefore you may subject yourself to being killed at the whim of one who is strong, unless we all agree now, when we are equal and impartial, to peace and to sheathe our weapons."

The ninth human being, being reasonable, saw the dilemma and the wisdom of the argument and agreed to disarm upon the condition that all others did likewise. Then they all mutually promised not to kill each other and all agreed to come to the defense of any other who was attacked in violation of the agreement, and to punish the offender.

They were so happy with their initial success that they returned to the jungle without making rules to divide the kill.

7. THE SOURCES OF OUR DUTY TO OBEY THE LAW

a. Society and Its Laws

All societies have rules or laws and require their members to obey these laws, for the peace and good order of the society. In fact John Rawls in his *A Theory of Justice* assumes that a society is defined by its rules. "...[A] society is a more or less self-sufficient association of persons who in their relations to one another recognize certain rules of conduct as binding and who for the most part act in accordance with them...."[1]

But why should any free and independent person choose to obey these laws or any king or chieftain? There are essentially two sources of our duty to obey the laws of a society. The first is authority; the second is mutual consent.

b. Authority

Parents exercise an authority over their children during their minority and the children learn early to respect and accept the commands of their mother and father. By extension, chieftains, kings, czars, emperors, and popes fill the same role as parents. It is respect for the justice of the laws promulgated that gives rise to the free-will choice to obey these laws.

In the ancient world, inevitably, the authority of the king or Caesar was reinforced with the power and authority of the gods or God to persuade (or terrorize) the population into submission. Ancient kings declared themselves to be gods and were to be obeyed as gods. The law of Moses was declared to be the law of God speaking through Moses. The Caesars were all considered gods. Later in the Christian era, the fear of hell and the loss of heaven was used to enforce obedience to the authority of the king and pope.

i. The Natural Law

The medieval scholar, Thomas Aquinas, expanding upon the work of ancient Greek and Roman philosophers, asserted the proposition that God established a natural law that imposed duties upon all humankind and that the natural law is unchangeable, although our knowledge and understanding of it may change. The highest expression of the natural law is the Ten Commandments given by God to Moses about 3,000 years ago. Positive law, the particu-

---

[1] Rawls, *Op. Cit.*, p.4.

lar rules of a society, must conform to the demands of the natural law since the natural law is the standard by which we measure the legitimacy or the morality of man-made laws. Neither the natural law nor the law of Moses were conceived of as establishing individual rights but rather as rules to benefit the society as a whole and, more importantly, to honor and obey God.

ii. The Divine Right of Kings

In modern times, this unilateral authority was expressed as the divine right of kings, a doctrine we explored in the previous chapter. A further explanation of this theory was recorded by the encyclopedist who noted that it is a

> ...doctrine in defense of monarchical absolutism, which asserted that kings derived their authority from God and could not therefore be held accountable for their actions by any earthly authority such as a parliament. In its origins in Europe the divine right theory may be traced to the medieval conception of God's award of temporal power to the political ruler, paralleling the award of spiritual power to the church. By the 16th and 17th centuries, however, the new national monarchs were asserting their authority in matters of both church and state. King James I of England (reigned 1603-25) was the most exponent of the doctrine of the divine right of kings, but the doctrine virtually disappeared from English politics after the Revolution of 1688.[2]

Jean-Jacques Rousseau in his great work, *The Social Contract*,[3] questioned whether imposed authority could be a source of one's duty to obey the laws of a society:

> ...however strong a man, he is never strong enough to remain master always, unless he transform his Might into Right, and Obedience into Duty. Hence we have come to speak of the Right of the Strongest, a right which, seemingly assumed in irony, has, in fact, become established in principle. But the meaning of the phrase has never been adequately explained. Strength is a physical attribute, and I fail to see how any moral sanction can attach to its effects. To yield to the strong is an act of necessity, not of will. At most it is the result of a dictate of prudence. How, then, can it become a duty?

The legitimacy of the monarch or the government is a different issue from the justice of the laws it promulgates. From the point of view of ethics and the creation of a duty to obey the laws, it makes no difference whether the monarch was installed by tribal election, custom, lineage, conquest, or usurpation. The legitimacy of the duties imposed by the lawgiver depends not so much upon whether the law giver has de jure or merely de facto authority as whether the laws promulgated impose duties that are just—whether such laws are made for the common good. Obviously, duties imposed upon the society that promote the equality of its members will be perceived as for the common good and therefore just; such laws will be respected and will gain wider public support.

---

[2] *Encyclopedia Britannica*, Vol. 4, (1994), p. 132.
[3] Jean-Jacques Rousseau, "The Right of the Strongest," in Barker, *Op. Cit.*, p. 172.

However, when obedience is either enforced through conquest or slavery or simple blind and unthinking obedience to the law, then conduct is not an ethical act since no choice was involved. To yield to the strong is an act of prudence, not an act of respect for the law. But when submission to the authority of the society is learned and accepted as a conscious choice, then acceptance of these duties becomes an ethical act. Respect for the law is the basis for a free-will choice; without respect for the law there can be no freedom to choose the order of the law-giver, and there can be no ethical act. Obedience is an ethical act when it is an express act of consent.

c. Agreement

i. The Ancient Roots of the Contract Theory

The second source of duty to obey the laws of the society is negotiated consent to be obligated—a consent mutually given and accepted by all members in the society.

Plato (427 BC–347 BC) in his dialogue *Crito*, describes the obligation of the citizen to obey the law and is the first to offer the opinion that the obligation to obey the laws of a society is based upon an implied consent. In *Crito*, Socrates (who was Plato's teacher) had been condemned to die for corrupting the youth of Athens through his teachings. His friend Crito tries to persuade him to escape. Socrates answers:

SCENE: The Prison of Socrates

Socrates: ...What answer shall we make to his, Crito? Do the laws speak truly, or do they not?

Crito: I think that they do.

Socrates: The laws will say: "Consider, Socrates, if this is true, that in your present attempt you are going to do us wrong. For, after having brought you into the world, and nurtured and educated you, and given you and every other citizen a share in every good that we had to give, we further proclaim and give the right to every Athenian, that if he does not like us, when he has come of age and has seen the ways of the city, and made our acquaintance, he may go where he pleases and take his goods with him; and none of us laws will forbid him or interfere with him. Any of you who does not like us and the city, and who wants to go to a colony or to any other city, may go where he likes, and take his goods with him. But he who has experience of the manner in which we order justice and administer the state, and still remains, has entered into an implied contract that he will do as we command him. And he who disobeys us is, as we maintain, thrice wrong; first, because in disobeying us he is disobeying his parents; secondly, because we are the authors of his education; thirdly, because he has made an agreement with us that he will duly obey our commands; and he neither obeys them nor convinces us that our commands are wrong; and we do not rudely impose them, but give them the alternative of obeying or convincing us;—These are the sort of accusations to which, as we were saying, you, Socrates, will be exposed if you accomplish your intentions; you, above all other Athenians."

Suppose I ask, why is this? they will justly retort upon me that I above all other men have acknowledged the agreement....Then will they not say: "You, Socrates, are breaking the covenants and agreements which you made with us at your leisure, not in any haste or under any compulsion or deception, but having had seventy years to think of them, during which time you were at liberty to leave the city, if we were not to your mind, or if our covenants appeared to you to be unfair. You had your choice, and might have gone either to Lacedaemon or Crete, which you often praise for their good government, or to some other Hellenic or foreign state..."

Socrates, in fact, refused to disobey, did not escape, and was executed.[4]

ii. The British Heritage:

The denunciation of the divine right of kings that developed in the late 17th century at the dawn of the enlightenment was first enunciated by John Locke in his *First Treatise of Civil Government* (1689). In his *Second Treatise of Civil Government*, (1690), he developed his theory of self government. His work became the philosophical rationale that moved Western civilization from authority to agreement as the basis of our duty to obey society's rules and constituted one of the greatest paradigm shifts in history. He taught that:

95. Men being, as has been said, by nature all free, equal and independent, no one can be put out of his estate and subjected to the political power of another without his own consent, which is done by agreeing with other men, to join and unite into a community for their comfortable, safe, and peaceable living, one amongst another, in a secure enjoyment of their properties, and a greater security against any that are not of it. This any number of men may do, because it injures not the freedom of the rest; they are left, as they were, in the liberty of the state of nature. When any number of men have so consented to make one community or government, they are thereby presently incorporated, and make one body politic, wherein the majority have a right to act and conclude the rest.[5]

He attempted to show how mutual agreement to the Social Contract could be accepted as a general ground of political duty:

119. ...No body doubts but an express consent of any man, entering into any society, makes him a perfect member of that society, a subject of that government. The difficulty is, what ought to be looked upon as a tacit consent, and how far it binds, i.e. how far anyone shall be looked on to have consented, and thereby submitted to any government, where he has made no expressions of it at all. And to this I say, that every man that hath any possession or enjoyment of any part of the dominions of any government doth thereby give his tacit consent, and is as far forth obliged to obedience to the laws of that government, during such enjoyment, as any one under it, whether this his possession be of land to him and his heirs for ever, a lodging only for a week; or whether it be barely travelling freely on the highway; and, in effect, it reaches as far as the very being

---

[4] Plato, *Crito*, in *Social & Political Philosophy*, ed. John Arthur and William Shaw (Prentice Hall, Englewood Cliffs, NJ, 1992), pp. 6-7.

[5] Quoted in Barker, *Op. Cit.,* p. 56.

of anyone within the territories of that government.

He set forth his alternative to absolute power, the social contract, a theory used to justify the execution or dethronement of two kings in 40 years.

221. There is therefore Secondly another way whereby governments are dissolved, and that is, when the legislative, or the prince, either of them act contrary to their trust.

So, forty-one years later, John Locke gave Charles I the answer to the question he asked at his trial—by what authority he was being tried. Locke answered that the representatives of the people can try and execute a king for breach of trust to the people, pledged in the social contract. In so doing he gave the American revolutionaries the philosophical and legal argument to rid themselves of a later king. John Locke had a powerful influence upon our founding fathers, especially Thomas Jefferson, the author of the Declaration of Independence and the Virginia Statute of Religious Freedom, and James Madison, the Father of the Constitution and the prime mover of our Bill of Rights.

Locke's theories on the social contract were not without criticism right down to the present day. About a half a century later the great Scottish leader of the enlightenment, David Hume, published his criticism in 1748 entitled *Of the Original Contract*. He agreed that there may have been some form of very rudimentary "original contract" but disagreed that any existing state was formed or continues on the basis of agreement of the people. He observed that:

They [Locke and his followers] assert, not only that government in its earliest infancy arose from consent, or rather the voluntary acquiescence of the people; but also that, even at present, when it has attained its full maturity, it rests on no other foundation. They affirm, that all men are still born equal, and owe allegiance to no prince or government, unless bound by the obligation and sanction of a promise. And as no man, without some equivalent, would forego the advantages of his native liberty, and subject himself to the will of another, this promise is always understood to be conditional, and imposes on him no obligation, unless he meet with justice and protection from his sovereign. These advantages the sovereign promises him in return; and if he fail in the execution, he has broken, on his part, the articles of engagement, and has thereby freed his subject from all obligations to allegiance. Such, according to these philosophers, is the foundation of authority in every government, and such the right of resistance possessed by every subject.

But would the reasoners look abroad into the world, they would meet with nothing that, in the least, corresponds to their ideas, or can warrant so refined and philosophical a system. On the contrary, we find every where princes who claim their subjects as their property, and assert their independent right of sovereignty, from conquest or succession. We find also every where subjects who acknowledge this right in their prince, and suppose themselves born under obligations of obedience to a certain sovereign, as much as under the ties of reverence and duty to certain parents. These connexions are always conceived to be equally independent of our consent, in Persia and China; France and Spain; and even in Holland and England, wherever the doctrines above-mentioned have not been care-fully inculcated. Obedience or subjection become so familiar, that most men never make any inquiry about its origin or cause, more than about the principle of gravity, resistance, or the most universal laws of nature.

...Almost all the governments which exist at present, or of which there re-mains a record in story, have been founded originally, either on usurpation or conquest, or both, without any pretence of a fair consent or voluntary subjection of the people.

...The subsequent administration is also supported by power, and acquiesced in by the people, not as a matter of choice, but of obligation. They imagine not that their consent gives their prince a title: but they willingly consent, because they think, that, from long possession, he has acquired a title, independent of their choice or inclination.

Should it be said, that by living under the dominion of a prince which one might leave, every individual has given a *tacit* consent to his authority, and promised him obedience; it may be answered, that such an implied consent can only have place where a man imagines that the matter depends on his choice. But where he thinks (as all mankind do who are born under established governments) that, by his birth, he owes allegiance to a certain prince or certain form of government; it would be absurd to infer a consent or choice, which he expressly, in this case, renounces and disclaims.

Can we seriously say, that a poor peasant or artisan has a free choice to leave his country, when he knows no foreign language or manners, and lives, from day to day, by the small wages which he acquires? We may as well assert that a man, by remaining in a vessel, freely consents to the domination of the master; though he was carried on board while asleep, and must leap into the ocean and perish the moment he leaves her.[6]

Hume argued persuasively that implied or tacit consent can never be an adequate basis for binding all members of society to political duty. He con-ceded that the consent of the people is one just foundation of government and "It is surely the best and most sacred of any," but concluded "that it has very seldom had place in any degree, and never almost in its full extent; and that, therefore, some other foundation of government must also be admitted."

8. THE AMERICAN EXPERIENCE

a. The Mayflower Compact

Apparently, David Hume had never heard of the agreement reached by the first New England colonists approximately 128 years earlier. England was over 100 years behind Spain and Portugal in colonizing the New World. But by the turn of the 17th Century, the crown had granted charters to several mer-chant corporations to settle colonies and establish trade routes, and had in-vested them with governmental power—the power to enact laws in the name of

---

[6] *Ibid.*, p. 148-56.

the crown and to impose taxes. The Virginia Company was one of these new commercial/governmental corporations.

A small group of religious dissenters, who had fled to Holland to escape religious persecution, now returned to England, and on June 19, 1619, received a patent or grant from the Virginia Company, giving them the right to establish a colony somewhere in present day Virginia. On September 16, 1620, the Mayflower sailed from Plymouth bound for Virginia with the ship's crew and 101 persons including 14 indentured servants, several hired artisans, and one mercenary.

On November 9, 1620 they arrived in the New World off Cape Cod, about 600 miles north of their destination.[7] They were beyond the jurisdiction of their king and outside the franchise granted to them by their charter. As they prepared to disembark upon the wilderness of the North American continent and as Winter approached, they realized their need for political authority for their governance.

These dissenters had rejected the authority of the Church of Rome as the mediator between God and Man and as the final interpreter of sacred scriptures and asserted the general Protestant sentiment exalting the authority of the individual to deal directly with God and interpret the scriptures according to one's own conscience. They had separated from the established Church of England which had claimed the sole authority to ordain clergy and assumed the authority to found their own church and ordain their own ministers. So now, in the absence of the king or patent, it was a short step for them to assume the authority, by mutual agreement, to establish their own government. William Bradford, later a governor of Plymouth Colony, describes that moment on November 21, 1620:

The remainder of Ano: 1620

I shall a litle returne backe and begine with a combination made by them before they came ashore, being the first foundation of their govermente in this place; occasioned partly by the discontented and mutinous speeches that some of the strangers amongst them had let fall from them in the ship—That when they came a shore they would use their owne libertie: for none had power to command them, the patente they had being for Virginia, and not for New-england, which belonged to an other Government, with which the Virginia Company had nothing to doe. And partly that such an acte by them done (this their condition considered) might be as firme as any patent, and in some respects more sure.

The forme was as followeth.

In the Name of God, Amen. We whose names are under-writen, the loyall subjects of our dread soveraigne Lord, King James, by the grace of God, of Great Britaine, France, and Ireland king, defender of the faith,etc., haveing undertaken, for the glorie of God, and advancemente of the Christian faith, and honour of our

---
[7] Richard B. Morris and Henry Steele Comminger, eds., *Op. Cit.,* pp. 37-8.

king and countrie, a voyage to plant the first colinie in the Northerne parts of Virginia, doe by these presents solemnly and mutualy in the presence of God, and one of another, covenant and combine our selves togeather into a civill body politick, for our better ordering and preservation and furtherance of the ends aforesaid; and by vertue hearof to enacte, constitute, and frame such just and equall lawes, ordinances, acts, constitutions, and offices, from time to time, as shall be thought most meete and convenient for the generall good of the Colonie, unto which we promise all due submission and obedience. In witnes wherof we have hereunder subscribed our names at Cap-Codd the 11. of November, in the year of the raigne of our soveraigne lord, King James, of England, France, and Ireland the eighteenth, and of Scotland the fiftie fourth. Ano: Dom. 1620.

After this they chose, or rather confirmed, Mr. John Carver (a man godly and well approved amongst them) their Governour for that year. And after they had provided a place for their goods, or comone store, (which were long in unlading for want of boats, foulnes of winter weather, and sicknes of diverce,) and begune some small cottages for their habitation, as time would admitte, they mette and consulted of lawes and orders, both for their civill and military Govermente, as the necessitie of their condition did require, still adding therunto as urgent occasion in severall times, and as cases did require...[8]

b. The Connecticut River Towns

And so the first body politic established by agreement in modern history for which we have a written record was born. Seventy years later, John Locke in his *Second Treatise* would create the great myth of Western political philosophy—the social contract. Here at "Cap-Codd" was the reality of government by the consent of the governed. "A similar course was afterward followed by the river towns of Connecticut, at New Haven, by the settlers at Dover and Exeter on the Piscataqua, at Providence and elsewhere."[9]

c. The Federal Constitution

Later, as the colonies moved toward independence, government by the consent of the governed would become the justification for separation and the hallmark of all the constitutions of the new states and the federal government. The Preamble to our Federal Constitution declares that:

WE THE PEOPLE of the United States, in Order to form a more perfect Union, establish Justice, insure domestic Tranquility, provide for the common defence, promote the general Welfare, and secure the Blessing of Liberty to ourselves and our Posterity, do ordain and establish this CONSTITUTION for the United States of America.

Indeed, most of the governments that have been created in 19th and

---

[8] William Bradford, *Bradford's History of Plymouth Plantation*, 1606-46 (Charles Scribner's Sons, New York, 1908), pp. 106-7.

[9] *Ibid.*, p. 106.

[In the margin: 54]

...[sett]s by them done (this their condition considered) might be as firme as any patent; and in some respects more sure.
    The forme was as followeth.

In y[e] name of god Amen. We whose names are underwriten, the loyall subjects of our dread soueraigne Lord King James, by y[e] grace of god, of great Britaine, franc, & Ireland king, defender of y[e] faith, &c

Haueing undertaken, for y[e] glorie of god, and aduancemente of y[e] christian faith, and honour of our king & countrie, a voyage to plant y[e] first colonie in y[e] Northerne parts of Virginia, doe by these presents solemnly & mutualy in y[e] presence of god, and one of another, couenant, & combine our selues togeather into a civill body politick, for y[e] beter ordering, & preseruation & fur-therance of y[e] ends aforesaid; and by vertue hearof to enacte, constitute, and frame shuch just & equall lawes, ordinances, Acts, constitutions, & offices, from time to time, as shall be thought most meete & conuenient for y[e] generall good of y[e] colonie: unto which we promise all due submission and obedience. In witnes wherof we haue hereunder subscribed our names at Cap-Codd y[e] .11. of Nouember, in y[e] year of y[e] raigne of our soueraigne Lord king James of England, franc, & Ireland y[e] eighteenth and of Scotland y[e] fiftie fourth. An°: Dom .1620.]

After this they chose, or rather confirmed Mr John Carver (a man godly & well approued amongst them) their Gouernour for that year. And after they had prouided a place for their goods, or comone store (which were long in unlading, for want of boats, foulnes of y[e] winter weather, and sicknes of diuers) and begune some small cottages for their habitation; as time would admitte they mette and consulted of lawes, & orders, both for their civill & military gouernmente, as y[e] necessitie of their condi-tion did require, still adding therunto as urgent occasion in seuerall times, and cases did require.

In these hard & dificulte beginings they found some discontents & murmurings arise amongst some, and mutinous speeches & cariags in other; but they were soone quelled, & ouercome, by y[e] wisdome, patience, and just & equall carrage of things by y[e] Gou[er]: and better part wth clave faithfully togeather in y[e] maine. but that which was most sadd & lamentable, was, that in 2 or 3 moneths time halfe of their company dyed, espetialy in Jan: & february, being y[e] depth of winter, and wanting houses & other comforts; being infected with y[e] scurvie &

The Mayflower Compact
From the original Bradford manuscript

20th Centuries have been based upon the assumption of the social contract and the idea that their constitutions were established with the consent of their people.

9. MODERN THINKERS

a. *The Social Contract Revisited*

Modern authors, likewise, have questioned whether implied consent can be the basis for a general obligation to obey the law. John Simmons in his *Moral Principles and Political Obligations*, states:

> All of this has been leading, of course, to the conclusion that tacit consent must meet the same fate as express consent concerning its suitability as a general ground of political obligation. For it seems clear that very few of us have ever tacitly consented to the government's authority in the sense developed in this essay; the situations appropriate for such consent simply do not arise frequently. Without major alterations in modern political processes and conventions, consent theory's big gun turns out to be of woefully small caliber. While consent, be it tacit or express, may still be the firmest ground of political obligation (in that people who have consented probably have fewer doubts about their obligations than others), it must be admitted that in most modern states consent will only bind the smallest minority of citizens to obedience. Only attempts to expand the notion of tacit consent beyond proper limits will allow consent to appear to be a suitably general ground of political obligation.[10]

Others have suggested that fair play, gratitude or some other principle of repayment forms the basis of general obligation. John Rawls develops a novel approach.

3. THE MAIN IDEA OF THE THEORY OF JUSTICE

> My aim is to present a conception of justice which generalizes and carries to a higher level of abstraction the familiar theory of the social contract as found, say, in Locke, Rousseau, and Kant. In order to do this we are not to think of the original contract as one to enter a particular society or to set up a particular form of government. Rather, the guiding idea is that the principles of justice for the basic structure of society are the object of the original agreement. They are the principles that free and rational persons concerned to further their own interests would accept in an initial position of equality as defining the fundamental terms of their association. These principles are to regulate all further agreements; they specify the kinds of social cooperation that can be entered into and the forms of government that can be established. This way of regarding the principles of justice I shall call justice as fairness.

> Thus we are to imagine that those who engage in social cooperation choose together, in one joint act, the principles which are to assign basic rights and duties and to determine the division of social benefits. Men are to decide in advance how they are to regulate their claims against one another and what is to

---

[10] John Simmons, *Moral Principles and Political Obligations*, in Arthur Shaw, *Op. Cit.* (Princeton University Press, Princeton, New Jersey 1979), p. 17.

be the foundation charter of their society. Just as each person must decide by rational reflection what constitutes his good, that is, the system of ends which it is rational for him to pursue, so a group of persons must decide once and for all what is to count among them as just and unjust. The choice which rational men would make in this hypothetical situation of equal liberty, assuming for the present that this choice problem has a solution, determines the principles of justice.

In justice as fairness the original position of equality corresponds to the state of nature in the traditional theory of the social contract. This original position is not, of course, thought of as an actual historical state of affairs, much less as a primitive condition of culture. It is understood as a purely hypothetical situation characterized so as to lead to a certain conception of justice. Among the essential features of this situation is that no one knows his place in society, his class position or social status, nor does any one know his fortune in the distribution of natural assets and abilities, his intelligence, strength and the like. 1 shall even assume that the parties do not know their conceptions of the good or their special psychological propensities. The principles of justice are chosen behind a veil of ignorance. This ensures that no one is advantaged or disadvantaged in the choice of principles by the outcome of natural chance or the contingency of social circumstances. Since all are similarly situated and no one is able to design principles to favor his particular condition, the principles of justice are the result of a fair agreement or bargain. ....[11]

John Rawls transforms the classic conception of the social contract from the great myth of Western political philosophy into a parable, a story that is used to analyze an abstract concept or explain a moral or ethical process. (His analysis is pure game theory before game theory was popular, since he designs a scenario that must produce the desired result.) We imagine a gathering where all human beings are stripped of those accidental characteristics of their human nature, one's sex, age, race, nationality or tribe, social status, wealth or poverty, good health or disability. We are left with only the essential characteristics of our human nature as human beings. Each one of us is an animal that is a predator with needs and appetites for food, clothing and shelter. Each of us needs and wants a mate and territory and we have basic instincts to protect ourselves and our children. Each of us is rational, that is we can think at a very abstract and symbolic level; and we have memory that reminds us that our actions or inaction have consequences and we can plan. We can make free choices about what is in our own self interest and we understand that our enlightened self interest sometimes values long term interest over short term goals. And, above all, we are social animals that know how to cooperate with each other, to build a peaceful and just society.

What we have described is what the law refers to as "the reasonable man." Each of us becomes that hypothetical person who will act reasonably under any circumstance. When we add to this condition the fact that our rea-

---

[11] Rawls, *Op. Cit.*, pp. 11-2.

sonable people will now come together and make rules for the commonweal behind "the veil of ignorance," without knowledge of how it will affect each of them, then these reasonable people, completely equal in bargaining power and absolutely impartial, will make rules that are both reasonable and just, meaning that the rules will burden and benefit each equally. We need to understand that this is not the description of an historical event but rather an exercise in rational analysis.

Few people actually consider and explicitly agree to the duties of the social contract. Implied or tacit consent is an actual consent implied from our conduct. It is similar to our tacit agreement to play by the rules of soccer when we participate in the game or when we make a bet on the game. We implicitly consent that we will win or lose on the basis of these pre-established rules. As Hume and Simmons observed, the implied or tacit consent of most citizens or subjects would be difficult to establish. How then can people generally be obligated to obey the law? Our consent to the duties of the social contract is an *assumed consent* since it is assumed—that is, taken as granted or true—that every reasonable person in a state of perfect equality and absolute impartiality will give such consent. Where consent is actually withheld from time to time, in real life, it is assumed that the conditions of rationality, equality or impartiality are imperfect. Therefore every member of a given society is automatically bound by the social contract since every member's consent is *assumed and required*. It is this universally assumed consent to the social contract that constitutes the general basis for political duty.

Assumed consent is not an actual consent, however; it is consent that is imputed to you as a member of society. It is therefore not an ethical act. Only when we explicitly acknowledge and accept the duties imposed by the social contract, with knowledge and forethought, do we perform an ethical act. *The essence of our personal code of morality is our explicit consent to the duties of the social contract that creates our personal obligation to obey those laws.*

b. Developing the Substantive Provisions of the Social Contract

Basic duties are natural duties since they arise from our nature as human beings. However, these natural duties are not perfected until we form ourselves into social groups since duties are relationships. For example, the duty not to kill each other becomes a duty only with the formation of the social contract. Before that it is an inchoate idea.

Basic or natural duties are the substantive provisions of the social contract. But not all the duties in our society are basic. How then, do we discover which among our many duties are basic? We use the reasonable person test. *A duty is basic and a substantive provision of the social contract if reasonable people, with equal bargaining power and no knowledge of how the duty will affect them, will agree to it, unanimously, everywhere, and at all times.*

Let's take an example. Our process of rational analysis concludes that when reasonable people gather in a state of perfect equality and absolute impartiality to negotiate the basic rules for a peaceful and just society, the first subject must be war or peace. By definition, there must be a mutual agreement (or law) not to kill (or injure) each other. The agreement not to kill each other is the condition precedent to a peaceful society. Since we begin with the presumption that a reasonable person is motivated by rational self-interest and the basic instinct to survive and therefore desires a peaceful society, every reasonable person will mutually agree not to kill any other member of that society. Moreover, this agreement must be unanimous since this negotiation is in the nature of a disarmament negotiation. Consider the possibility that there is one holdout to the accord. No other party to the proposed compact would surrender his or her sword unless and until all others in the group have laid their weapons upon the table. So the consent must be unanimous and the duty imposed by the agreement universal. The same analysis, using the reasonable person test, can be made of every basic duty that we are obligated to respect. These will be very few.

c. The Definition of the Social Contract

So at last, we can define what we mean by the Social Contract. It is the compilation of all our basic or natural duties. *The social contract is that fundamental compact that consists of the rules imposing basic duties, assigning rights, and distributing the benefits of political, social, and economic cooperation, which is unanimously agreed to by reasonable people in a state of perfect equality and absolute impartiality.* Of course, we are not speaking of an historical event. The social contract is the result of rational and legal analysis and hypothesis. The reasonable person test asks: Would reasonable people agree to this or that duty? Would their agreement be unanimous—cross-cultural and cross-generational? The answers are usually given by lawyers, judges, politicians, philosophers, professors and sometimes by popular vote. While the assembly of reasonable people is hypothetical and their deliberations behind the veil of ignorance a parable, the social contract that results from this rational analysis is real. It is the fundamental compact that is assumed to exist in every society.

When governments are formed and laws are made, the social contract becomes positive law. It is similar to an oral contract becoming a written contract. However, positive law, the laws of a particular society, must conform to the agreements of the social contract. Basic natural duties necessarily imposed by the social contract, must continue under the laws of every society and government. Organic documents or constitutions must respect the basic duties of the social contract for, as we shall see in our next chapter, it is these basic natural duties that give rise to natural or human rights.

SUMMARY

Political duties are imposed by the authority of the lawgiver or by the mutual agreement of those in a society. In the 17th Century, at the dawn of the enlightenment, John Locke created the paradigm of mutual consent as the foundation of law. The enlightenment marks the coming of age of political societies in France, England and Scotland and later, in the thirteen British colonies in America. The Americans matured from the childhood acceptance of the authority of the king to where they demanded the right to govern themselves by mutual consent as independent and equal adults.

American ethics is based on the social contract, that fundamental agreement to which we are assumed to have consented, which imposes basic duties, assigns rights, and distributes the benefits and burdens of political, social, and economic cooperation. The basic or natural duties of the social contract are those that reasonable people acting with complete equality and absolute impartiality will agree to unanimously, everywhere, and at all times. There are only a few basic or natural duties. The constitutions and laws of every government must enforce these natural duties since they give rise to human rights.

MY PERSONAL OBLIGATION:

Keep Your Promises

A contract is a promise that each party gives to the other; each party becomes obligated to the other and each reciprocally acquires a right to what is promised by the other.

As you move from childhood to adulthood, as a virtuous citizen you will strive to become aware of the promises that you are assumed to have made for the benefit of society. The virtuous citizen will knowingly and with premeditation make these promises and obligate oneself to basic laws and all other laws that conform to basic laws. The natural duties of the social contract will become the virtuous citizen's code of personal morality.

The virtuous citizen honors business contracts and agreements and recognizes that in all dealings "My word is my bond." Commitment to your agreements is the essence of credibility, and an absolutely necessary quality of character in any successful person in business. *Be slow to promise, but when your word is out, you must keep your promises.*

MY PERSONAL VIRTUE:

Courtesy

Courtesy is the oil that lubricates social relationships. Courtesy makes civil society civil. It is the gentleness and kindness and consideration that makes interpersonal relations easier and more pleasant. Courtesy cannot be commanded but it is the hallmark of a civilized person. There is never an excuse for discourtesy. It takes only a moment; but it requires a good atti-tude—a willingness not to be macho or aggressive or personally abusive. Thank you!

ADDITIONAL READINGS

A Theory of Justice
by John Rawls[12]

24. The Veil of Ignorance

....The idea of the original position is to set up a fair procedure so that any principles agreed to will be just. The aim is to use the notion of pure procedural justice as a basis of theory. Somehow we must nullify the effects of specific contingencies which put men at odds and tempt them to exploit social and natural circumstances to their own advantage. Now in order to do this I assume that the parties are situated behind a veil of ignorance. They do not know how the various alternatives will affect their own particular case and they are obliged to evaluate principles solely on the basis of general considerations.

.....As far as possible, then, the only particular facts which the parties know is that their society is subject to the circumstances of justice and whatever this implies. It is taken for granted, however, that they know the general facts about human society. They understand political affairs and the principles of economic theory; they know the basis of social organization and the laws of human psychology. Indeed, the parties are presumed to know whatever general facts affect the choice of the principles of justice.

....These remarks show that the original position is not to be thought of as a general assembly which includes at one moment everyone who will live at some time; or, much less, as an assembly of everyone who could live at some time. It is not a gathering of all actual or possible persons. To conceive of the original position in either of these ways is to stretch fantasy too far; the conception would cease to be a natural guide to intuition. In any case, it is important that the original position be interpreted so that one can at any time adopt its perspective. It must make no difference when one takes up this viewpoint, or who does so: the restrictions must be such that the same principles are always chosen. The veil of ignorance is a key condition in meeting this requirement. It insures not only that the information available is relevant, but that it is at all times the same.

......Now the reasons for the veil of ignorance go beyond mere simplicity. We want to define the original position so that we get the desired solution. If a

[12] Rawls, *Op. Cit.*, pp. 136-42.

knowledge of particulars is allowed, then the outcome is biased by arbitrary contingencies. As already observed, to each according to his threat advantage is not a principle of justice. If the original position is to yield agreements that are just, the parties must be fairly situated and treated equally as moral persons. The arbitrariness of the word must be corrected for by adjusting the circumstances of the initial contractual situation. Moreover, if in choosing principles we required unanimity even when there is full information, only a few rather obvious cases could be decided. A conception of justice based on unanimity in these circumstances would indeed be weak and trivial. But once knowledge is excluded, the requirement of unanimity is not out of place and the fact that it can be satisfied is of great importance. It enables us to say of the preferred conception of justice that it represents a genuine reconciliation of interests....

25. The Rationality of the Parties

....I have assumed throughout that the persons in the original position are rational. In choosing between principles each tries as best he can to advance his interests. But I have also assumed that the parties do not know their conception of the good. This means that while they know that they have some rational plan of life, they do not know the details of this plan, the particular ends and interests which it is calculated to promote....

CHAPTER IV

Human Rights

The true civilization is where every man gives to every other every right he claims for himself.

—*Robert G. Ingersoll*
Interview, *November 14, 1880*

In 1732, King George II appointed William Cosby as governor of the colony of New York and New Jersey. Cosby arrived six months late. In the interim Rip Van Dam, a New York merchant of Dutch extraction, who was the senior member of the provincial council, assumed the executive powers. Upon taking office, the new governor demanded one half of Van Dam's salary for the six months preceding, as was the custom. However, Van Dam refused and Cosby sued him in the newly established Court of the Exchequer, a court established by the council, not the legislature, for the purpose of this suit. The Chief Justice, Lewis Morris, one of the wealthiest landowners in the colony, refused the claim on the grounds that the new court was not properly established and he had no jurisdiction. The new governor promptly removed Morris from the bench.

Morris, Van Dam and his attorneys, James Alexander and William Smith, formed an opposition party to Cosby. In 1733 Morris and his son ran for seats in the popularly elected Assembly, representing Eastchester in Westchester County. The sheriff, appointed by Cosby, required the Quakers, who were Morris supporters, to swear that they were landowners in order to be eligible to vote, knowing that they were forbidden to take an oath. They refused and were disqualified; nevertheless, both father and son were elected.

There was only one newspaper in New York, William Bradford's *New York Gazette*, and he received a salary from Cosby as the king's printer for the Province of New York. The Morris faction now determined to start a second newspaper in New York as their political voice to expose Governor Cosby as a tyrannical and greedy public official who sold appointed offices, fixed elections, and controlled judges to do his bidding. Morris, Alexander, Smith, and others, all experienced pamphleteers, founded the *New York Weekly Journal*, "containing the Freshest Advices, Foreign and Domestic." For their publisher, they found a young immigrant printer by the name of John Peter Zenger.[1]

Most of the writings attacking the governor were by innuendo and were done anonymously. On January 28, 1734, the Journal published a letter to the editor, under a pseudonym (it was probably written by John Alexander), claiming to speak for "the people of this city and province":

> ...They think, as matters now stand, that their LIBERTIES and PROPERTIES are precarious, and that SLAVERY is like to be entailed on them and their posterity, if some past things be not amended. And this they collect from many past proceedings.

> ...You gentlemen think that things past are right, and that things may go on in the same way without such consequence....[2]

On April 8, 1774, he published a similar letter:

> ...[The writer] should be glad to hear the Assembly would exert themselves as became them, by showing that they have the interest of their country more at heart than the gratification of any private view of any of their members, or being at all affected by the smiles or frowns of a governor; both which ought equally to be despised when the interest of their country is at stake. You...complain of the lawyers, but I think the law itself is at an end: We see men's deeds destroyed, judges arbitrarily displaced, new courts erected without consent of the legislature, by which it seems to me trials by juries are taken away when a governor pleases; men of known estates denied their votes contrary to the received practice, the best expositor of any law: Who is then in that province that call anything his own, or enjoy any liberty longer than those in the administration will condescend to let him do it?[3]

After two months of publication, the governor decided to close the paper and charge Zenger with seditious libel. Free speech and free press, at the time, meant that there could be no prior restraint on any statement or publication, but the publisher was subject to criminal prosecution and punishment after the publication of spoken or written words found to be libelous. Seditious libel was a common law crime—a crime established by judges in prior cases—not by the legislature by statute. Judges were appointed by the governor in the name of the king. They held that seditious libel included fair and truthful criticism. The charges against Zenger included:

> ....That by government we were protected in our lives, religion and properties; and that for these reasons great care had always been taken to prevent everything that might tend to scandalize magistrates and others concerned in the administration of the government, especially the supreme magistrate. And that there were many instances of very severe judgments, and of punishments inflicted upon

---

[1] James Alexander, *A Brief Narrative of the Case and Trial of John Peter Zenger, Printer of the New York Weekly Journal*, (1736), ed. Stanley Nider Katz (The Belknap Press of Harvard University Press, Cambridge, Massachusetts, 1972). pp. 2-35.

[2] *Ibid.*, p. 133.   [3] *Ibid.*, p. 136.

such, as had attempted to bring the government into contempt; by publishing false and scurrilous libels against it, or by speaking evil and scandalous words of men in authority; to the great disturbance of the public....[4]

However, two successive grand juries refused to indict, i.e. to accuse Zenger of a crime. Nor was Cosby able to persuade the Assembly to charge him according to the practice of the day. Likewise, the City Council of New York refused to burn the offending issues of the *Journal* as ordered by the governor. So, Cosby therefore directed the Attorney General, Richard Bradley, to accuse, arrest, and imprison Zenger, which he did in December, 1734. Zenger could not raise excessively high bail (and his wealthy friends saw the political advantage to his incarceration and did not post bail) and so he remained in jail for eight months until his trial. Such was the state of natural and political rights in colonial America before the Revolution.

10. THE DEFINITION OF HUMAN RIGHTS

a. Rights are Relationships

What is a "right"? A right is one side of a relationship; one's right is the duty of another.

What is a "human right"? A human right is a relationship arising from our nature as human beings that entitles one to certain conduct from all others. It is a contractual right flowing from the social contract that imposes upon all others the *necessary and universal duty* to act or refrain from acting in a certain way. American ethics is based on the contract paradigm that developed historically out of the enlightenment of France, England and Scotland in the 18th Century. It expresses ethical values not as laws or commandments but as negotiated duties and rights. So, for example, American ethics forbids murder because, in the fundamental agreement that creates our society, we accept (or are assumed to accept) the obligation not to kill each other and that creates the right of each member of our society not to be killed by any other member of that society nor by the society itself.

A human right should not be confused with a physical possession; a human right is not a thing you possess like an apple or a house. Nor should it be equated with a human power like the power to think or see or live. Rather, a human right is a relationship between you and all others, that entitles you to certain conduct from every other person and from society. You have the power of life; but the right to your life is created when all others promise not to kill you.

b. Natural or Human Rights as the "Quid Pro Quo" for Natural Duties

Natural rights or human rights are the flip side of the natural duties of the social contract. They are the quid pro quo of the social contract. Natural or

---

[4] *Ibid.*, Quoting from the Information filed against Zenger, p. 63.

human rights are the benefits negotiated by reasonable people and received by each of them in return for their agreement to accept the natural duties imposed by the social contract. Human rights are the consideration for the obligations assumed under that fundamental agreement. When parties enter into a contract, each party becomes obligated to the other and each reciprocally acquires a right to what is promised by the other. When we say that you have a right to life we mean that there is a corresponding duty imposed upon all other persons in our society and upon the society itself not to kill you. Under American ethics each person in the society enjoys natural or human rights that are personal to each individual since each individual has consented (or is assumed to have given consent) to the duties of the social contract and is therefore entitled to these negotiated benefits. Therefore, each person is entitled to the enforcement of these rights by the government against offending members of the society and against an abusive government itself, not only on behalf of the society as a whole but on behalf of each victimized individual member of the society.

c. Human Rights as Inseparable from Natural Duties

The only rights that are natural or human rights are those rights that arise from the acceptance of natural duties, no more and no less. So, to discover a new human right we must first discover a new natural duty which is necessary to a peaceful and just society, general in its application, and accepted by consensus. There can be no human right without the acceptance of a corresponding natural duty. These are not different things but opposite sides of the same relationship.

It is equally true that where human rights are abridged or the benefits of social cooperation are denied, the willingness to observe the basic duties of the society is diminished. In fact, the denial or abridgement of human rights constitutes a breach of the social contract. It is no accident that those in a society who perceive themselves as underprivileged will rebel and commit crimes against those perceived as privileged.

d. Human Rights Are Universal, Inalienable, Indivisible, and Interdependent

Human rights are universal since the reciprocal basic natural duties established by the social contract are general in their application to all people and at all times. Human rights make us human. The manifestation of these duties and rights will vary from civilization to civilization since the degree of knowledge and understanding of these duties and rights will vary and the expression of these duties and rights will be expressed according to each society's history and culture and the sense of justice of different people. The underlying principles, however, are the same everywhere and at all times. Human rights are foreign to no culture and native to all nations. It is the universality of human rights that give them their strength. It endows them with the power to cross any border, climb any wall, defy any force.[5]

We assert that these rights are inalienable, that is, they cannot be taken away or even abridged. Therefore, no government can deny these basic rights to its citizens since the people do not receive these rights from government; these rights precede the formation of government. It is the duty of government to preserve, protect, and defend these rights equally, for all its citizens. Moreover, government has the obligation to protect the rights of visitors, travellers, and resident aliens within its borders and to respect the human rights of the entire human family. Offensive war is immoral and unethical. Defensive war is tolerated only where reasonably necessary for the self-defense of our own country or another innocent country victimized by aggressive war.

Human Rights are indivisible and interdependent. Obviously everything depends upon the right to life. The right to life is inadequate, however, if you are enslaved or falsely imprisoned. And to be free is a cruel sham if you live on the edge of starvation. Human rights need to be enjoyed in their entirety, as an indivisible and interdependent whole, in order to truly live the good life as a human being in a peaceful and just world.

e. Our Objective Ethical Standard

Through the process of self-government, the social contract is expressed in our positive laws. Our federal and state constitutions and laws must conform to the social contract, especially the mandates of our penal codes and legislation establishing political and civil rights. Our personal conduct toward others must conform to the agreements that we have made (or are assumed to have made), directly or through our elected representatives, in our social contract.

The obligations that we accept as a consequence of the natural duties imposed by the social contract and the human rights that are created thereby, constitute the framework of the American ethical system. These duties and rights, which distribute the burdens and benefits of our social cooperation, create the objective ethical standard that constitutes the right in American ethics. All of our subsequent acts must conform to this standard of conduct if we are to consider our later acts as ethical.

Alexis de Tocqueville, a young French aristocrat who toured the United States in the 1830s, wrote the definitive commentary on American society before the Civil War. In *Democracy in America*, he wrote:

THE IDEA OF RIGHTS IN THE UNITED STATES.

No great people without an idea of right—How the idea of right can be given to a people—Respect for right in the United States—Whence it arises.

---

[5] See the speech of Kofi Annan, secretary-general of the United Nations, given on December 10, 1998, the 50th anniversary of the adoption of the Declaration of Universal Human Rights.

I am persuaded that the only means which we possess at the present time of in-culcating the idea of right and of rendering it, as it were, palpable to the senses, is to endow all with the peaceful exercise of certain rights; this is very clearly seen in children, who are men without the strength and the experience of manhood. When a child begins to move in the midst of the objects that surround him, he is instinctively led to appropriate to himself everything that he can lay his hands upon; he has no notion of the property of others; but as he gradually learns the value of things and begins to perceive that he may in his turn be despoiled, he becomes more circumspect, and he ends by respecting those rights in others which he wishes to have respected in himself. The principle which the child derives from the possession of his toys is taught to the man by the objects which he may call his own. In America, the most democratic of nations, those com-plaints against property in general, which are so frequent in Europe, are never heard, because in America there are no paupers. As everyone has property of his own to defend, everyone recognizes the principle upon which he holds it.

The same thing occurs in the political world. In America, the lowest classes have conceived a very high notion of political rights, because they exercise those rights; and they refrain from attacking the rights of others in order that their own may not be violated.[6]

11. THE HISTORICAL DEVELOPMENT OF OUR HUMAN RIGHTS

a. The Rights of Englishmen

The historical development of human rights in American political phi-losophy begins as political rights or procedural safeguards under the British common law. In the Magna Carta or Great Charter (1215), King John granted to the nobility of Britain certain basic political or constitutional rights that were later extended to all freemen. The first and greatest of these was the Writ of Habeas Corpus, "A writ directed to the person detaining another, and com-manding him to produce the body of the prisoner, (or person detained,) with the day and cause of his caption and detention,...to do, submit to, and receive what-soever the judge or court awarding the writ shall consider in that behalf."[7] The English Habeas Corpus Act[8] is justly regarded as the great constitutional guar-antee of personal liberty. This remedy for deliverance from illegal or arbitrary confinement, considered the bulwark of the British common law, was called the "the great writ of liberty."[9]

As we have seen in the chapter on equality, following the dethronement of James II the Constitution Parliament enacted the Bill of Rights (1689) whereby the crown agreed to give up its previous right to suspend laws, erect special courts, keep a standing army, and levy taxes without the consent of

---

[6] Alexis de Tocqueville, *Democracy in America,* vol. 1 (Vintage Classics, A Division of Random House, Inc., New York), pp. 244-5.
[7] 3 Bl. Comm. 131.   [8] 31 Car. II. c. 2, (as amended).
[9] See *Black's Law Dictionary* (West Publishing Co., St. Paul, MN, 1951).

Parliament. The new king and queen, William and Mary, agreed to frequent sessions of Parliament, freedom of speech for Parliamentary debate, freedom of petition, and restrictions against excessive bail and cruel and unusual punishment. The Toleration Act gave some measure of religious freedom but The Act of Settlement required the crown to be Protestant. The important thing to observe here is that all these rights were grants from the crown. Rights were created by abating the prerogatives of the crown.

b. The Virginia Declaration of Rights (1776)

After the publication of *Common Sense* by Thomas Paine in January, 1776, the groundswell toward independence came quickly. That spring George Mason offered to the Virginia legislature the first bill of rights in the colonies. He had taken some of his language from the English Declaration of Rights. His first draft proclaimed:

A DECLARATION OF RIGHTS made by the Representatives of the good people of Virginia, assembled in full and free Convention; which Rights do pertain to them and their posterity, as the Basis and Foundation of Government.

1. That all men are born equally free and independent, and have certain inherent natural rights, of which they cannot, by any compact, deprive or divest their posterity; among which are the enjoyment of life and liberty, with the means of acquiring and possessing property, and pursuing and obtaining happiness and safety.

2. That the power is vested in, and consequently derived from the people; that magistrates are their trustees and servants, and at all times amenable to them.

3. That government is, or ought to be instituted for the common benefit, protection, and security of the people, nation or community. Of all the various modes and forms of government, that is best, which is capable of producing the greatest degree of happiness and safety, and is most effectually secured against the danger of maladministration; and that, whenever any government shall be found inadequate or contrary to these purposes, a majority of the community hath an indubitable, unalienable and indefeasible right to reform, alter or abolish it, in such manner as shall be judged most conducive to the public weal.[10]

Mason's Declaration was far more radical than its parent, which set out simply to reaffirm "ancient rights and Liberties."

c. The Declaration of Independence

North Carolina and Virginia had empowered their delegates to the Continental Congress to vote for a declaration of independence. So it was that, on

---

[10] William H. Gaines, Jr., "Document 6," in *Virginia History in Documents, 1621–1788* (The Virginia State Library, Richmond, Virginia, 1974).

Virginia Declaration of Rights

From the Virginia State Library

June 7, the delegate from Virginia, Richard Henry Lee, offered a resolution that the United Colonies "are and of right ought to be, free and independent States." Jefferson was appointed to a drafting committee and wrote the original draft; the others organized and edited the text.

> Writers forced to complete an assignment under great time pressure often look around for texts they can adapt for their purposes, and Jefferson managed to find two. One was the draft preamble for the Virginia constitution that he had just finished and which was itself based upon the English Declaration of Rights; the other, a preliminary version of the Virginia Declaration of Rights, had been drafted for the convention sitting in Williamsburg by George Mason, an older man whom Jefferson knew and respected.[11]

The committee reported back by the end of June, and on July 2nd and 3rd the Congress did substantial editing. The Declaration did three things: it set forth the basic underlying principles that are the foundation of our government; it cataloged a list of grievances against the king that warranted separation; and it declared separation from the crown. At the time, the only important part to the delegates and the colonists was the operative function that declared independence. Only later did the statement of principles emerge as the standard of justice for our government—a standard, in some cases, yet to be achieved. Thomas Jefferson's famous words, in the Declaration of Independence, succinctly summed up the basic assumptions of American political philosophy and set forth the reason for the existence of governments. But a moral reading of the Declaration immediately shows that with these same words he articulated the basic sense of justice and the fundamental ethical values of the American people; it is not just the united colonies that "are and of right ought to be, free and independent States," but that "all men are created equal." For Jefferson, each person had basic human rights which preceded the formation of government and which could not be taken from any person. Government had the basic duty to protect those rights from violation by other members of the society and from abridgment by the government itself. In Locke, Jefferson found the philosophical rationale for separation from the crown even as Locke's writings had justified the Glorious Revolution almost a century earlier.[12]

---

[11] Maier, *Op. Cit.*, p. 104.

[12] ...Of course, the Declaration of Independence was emphatically not a bill of rights in the American sense, that is a statement of fundamental rights that government must honor and protect... There are, however, good historical reasons why the Declaration of Independence is so easily confused with a bill of rights. After all, the words from its second paragraph that are today remembered beyond all others—"that all men are created equal; that they are endowed by their Creator with certain unalienable rights; that among these are life, liberty, and the pursuit of happiness"—were originally adapted from a draft of the Virginia Declaration of Rights written by George Mason and amended by a committee of the Virginia convention. Maier, *Op. Cit.*, p. 164.

d. The Northwest Ordinance (1787)

The only significant statute adopted by the Congress under the Articles of Confederation was the Ordinance of 1787 that created the Northwest Territorial Government that provided for the addition of three to five states to the Confederation. It provided for a detailed bill of rights for the inhabitants, provided for public education, and prohibited slavery and involuntary servitude in the territory that would later become the states of Ohio, Michigan, Illinois, Indiana, and Wisconsin.

e. The Constitutional Convention (1787)

At the beginning of the constitutional convention, James Madison had proposed attaching a bill of rights to that organic document. However, most of the delegates rejected the idea for two reasons. First, a bill of rights was unnecessary since the powers of the federal government were not plenary but specifically delegated and therefore it could not infringe upon the liberties of the people. Second, most of the states, which had plenary powers, had bills of rights in place, either in their state constitutions or as separate documents.

Alexander Hamilton reminds us, in *The Federalist Papers # 84*,[13] that the Constitution as presented for ratification does contain many provisions protecting natural rights as well as political and civil rights. The rights enumerated in the Constitution include:

1. "The Privilege of the Writ of Habeas Corpus shall not be suspended, unless when in Cases of Rebellion or Invasion the public Safety may require it."[14] This writ is a procedural remedy that is an order from a Judge to a jailor or warden to "produce the body" of the person being imprisoned in order to inquire into the lawfulness of the imprisonment. It was the first great protection against unlawful imprisonment by the king, now incorporated into our basic law as a protection against the new federal government.

2. "No Bill of Attainder.....shall be passed."[15] A Bill of Attainder is defined in *Black's Law Dictionary* as "A legislative act, directed against a designated person, pronouncing him guilty of an alleged crime, (usually treason,) without trial or conviction according to the recognized rules of procedure, and passing sentence of death and attainder upon him."

3. "No ... ex post facto Law shall be passed."[16] An ex post facto law is "A law passed after the occurrence of a fact or commission of an

---

[13] Rossiter, *Op. Cit.*, pp. 510-15.
[14] US Const., Art. I, Sec. 9, Cl. 2.
[15] US Const., Art. I, Sec. 9, Cl. 3.
[16] US Const., Art. I, Sec. 9, Cl. 3.

act, which retrospectively changes the legal consequences or relations of such fact or deed." (See *Black's Law Dictionary*.) It makes an innocent deed a crime after the fact.

4. "The Trial of all Crimes, except in Cases of Impeachment, shall be by Jury; and such Trial shall be held in the State where the said Crimes shall have been committed; but when not committed within any State, the Trial shall be at such Place or Places as the Congress may by Law have directed."[17] The original Constitution did not provide for trial by jury in civil matters.

5. "Treason against the United States, shall consist only in levying War against them, or in adhering to their Enemies, giving them Aid and Comfort. No Person shall be convicted of Treason unless on the testimony of two Witnesses to the same overt Act, or on Confession in open Court."[18] This protection reflected the propensity of the British kings to accuse anyone of treason who disagreed with him.

6. "...no religious Test shall ever be required as a Qualification to any Office or public Trust under the United States."[19] This provision shall be discussed more extensively in the next chapter dealing with Secular ethics, freedom of conscience and religion, and separation of church and state.

7. "No State shall...pass any Bill of Attainder, ex post facto Law, or Law impairing the Obligation of Contracts, or grant any Title of Nobility."[20] The convention imposed some restrictions on the powers of the states, protecting some procedural rights and reserving to the federal government the exclusive power to impair contracts through the bankruptcy laws.

Only three delegates refused to sign the final document, one of whom was George Mason. He protested that:

...There is no Declaration of Rights, and the laws of the general government being paramount to the laws and constitution of the several States, the Declarations of Rights in the separate States are no security. Nor are the people secured even in the enjoyment of the benefit of the common law....

...Under their own construction of the general clause, at the end of enumerated powers, the Congress may grant monopolies in trade and commerce, constitute new crimes, inflict unusual and severe punishments, and extend their powers as far as they shall think proper; so that the State legislatures have no security for the powers now presumed to remain to them, or the people for their rights.

---

[17] US Const., Art. III, Sec. 2, Cl. 3.

[18] US Const., Art. III, Sec. 3, Cl. 1.

[19] US Const., Art. VI, Cl. 3.

[20] US Const., Art. I, Sec. 10, Cl. 1.

There is no declaration of any kind, for preserving the liberty of the press, or the trial by jury in civil causes; nor against the danger of standing armies in time of peace.[21]

f. The Ratification Debate

Those who opposed a strong federal government, for whatever the reason, rallied 'round the failure to adopt a bill of rights as the reason to defeat the proposed Constitution. Those who had championed natural rights, like James Madison, were then in the uncomfortable position of defending the Constitution and insisting that a bill of rights was unnecessary. James Wilson, a delegate from Pennsylvania and a leading member of the Federal Convention, stated at a large public meeting in the yard of Independence Hall on October 6, 1787, that the powers of the proposed federal government were delegated powers and that the people retained power over their natural rights:

> This distinction being recognized, will furnish an answer to those who think the omission of a bill of rights a defect in the proposed constitution; for it would have been superfluous and absurd to have stipulated with a federal body of our own creation, that we should enjoy those privileges of which we are not divested, either by the intention or the act that has brought the body into existence.[22]

He was aptly refuted by "John De Witt," a pseudonym for an unidentified Massachusetts anti-federalist, whose essay appeared in the *Boston American Herald* on October 22 and 27, 1787:

> The people, although fully sensible that they reserved every title of power they did not expressly grant away, yet afraid that the words made use of, to express those rights so granted might convey more than they originally intended, they chose at the same moment to express in different language those rights which the agreement did not include, and which they never designed to part with, endeavoring thereby to prevent any cause for future altercation and the intrusion into society of that doctrine of tacit implication which has been the favorite theme of every tyrant from the origin of all governments to the present day.[23]

During the ratification debate many expressed the idea that the natural rights of the people were not the gift of the king or of Parliament but, as Jefferson had stated so eloquently in the Declaration of Independence, these rights preceded the formation of government and that the purpose of government was to protect these unalienable rights. Political thinking, at the time, asserted not only that our rights preceded the formation of government and that we did not surrender these rights to the king or Parliament or to this new legislature, but that we could not do so for our posterity.

---

[21] Ketcham, *Op. Cit.*, pp. 173-5
[22] Ketcham, *Op. Cit.*, p. 184.
[23] *Ibid.*, pp. 195-7.

In *Federalist Papers, No. 84*, Hamilton urged support for the proposed Constitution notwithstanding the failure to include a Bill of Rights. He justified this omission by noting:

> It has been several times truly remarked that bills of rights are, in their origin, stipulations between kings and their subjects, abridgments of prerogative in favor of privilege, reservations of rights not surrendered to the prince. Such was MAGNA CHARTA, obtained by the barons, sword in hand, from King John. Such were the subsequent confirmations of that charter by subsequent princes. Such was the *Petition of Right* assented to by Charles the First in the beginning of his reign. Such, also, was the Declaration of Rights presented by the Lords and Commons to the Prince of Orange in 1688, and afterward thrown into the form of an act of Parliament called the Bill of Rights. It is evident, therefore, that, according to their primitive signification, they have no application to constitutions, professedly founded upon the power of the people and executed by their immediate representatives and servants. Here, in strictness, the people surrender nothing; and as they retain everything they have no need of particular reservations, "WE, THE PEOPLE of the United States, to secure the blessings of liberty to ourselves and our posterity, do *ordain* and *establish* this Constitution for the United States of America." Here is a better recognition of popular rights than volumes of those aphorisms which make the principal figure in several of our State bills of rights and which would sound much better in a treatise of ethics than in a constitution of government...

> ... I go further and affirm that bills of rights, in the sense and to the extent in which they are contended for, are not only unnecessary in the proposed Constitution but would even be dangerous. They would contain various exceptions to powers which are not granted; and, on this very account, would afford a colorable pretext to claim more than were granted. For why declare that things shall not be done which there is no power to do? Why, for instance, should it be said that the liberty of the press shall not be restrained, when no power is given by which restrictions may be imposed? I will not contend that such a provision would confer a regulating power; but it is evident that it would furnish, to men disposed to usurp, a plausible pretense for claiming that power. They might urge with a semblance of reason that the Constitution ought not to be charged with the absurdity of providing against the abuse of an authority which was not given, and that the provision against restraining the liberty of the press afforded a clear implication that a power to prescribe proper regulations concerning it was intended to be vested in the national government.[24]

The New York convention, however, did not agree and insisted upon a bill of rights. On July 26, 1788, as a part of its instrument of ratification, it declared:

> That all power is originally vested in and consequently derived from the People, and that Government is instituted by them for their common Interest, Protection and Security.

> That the enjoyment of Life, Liberty and the pursuit of Happiness are essential rights which every Government ought to respect and preserve...

---

[24] Rossiter, *Op. Cit.*, pp. 512-4.

Under these impressions, and declaring that these rights aforesaid cannot be abridged or violated, and that the Explanations aforesaid are consistent with the said Constitution,...We the Said Delegates, in the Name and in behalf of the People of the State of New York Do by these present Assent to and Ratify the said Constitution...

The proposed Constitution was narrowly ratified by Virginia on June 26, 1788 (the tenth state to ratify, nine being necessary to adopt the Constitution). However, the following day Virginia urged twenty amendments including:

That there be a Declaration or Bill of Rights asserting and Securing from encroachment the essential and unalienable Rights of the People in some such manner as the following:

First. That there are certain natural rights of which men, when they form a social compact cannot deprive or divest their posterity, among which are the enjoyment of life and liberty, with the means of acquiring, possessing and protecting property, and pursuing and obtaining happiness and safety....[25]

During the debate in Virginia, Madison had a change of heart and agreed that, if elected to the House of Representatives, he would press for an amendment to the new Constitution to add a written bill of rights, as one of the first orders of business. Madison was narrowly elected to the new House of Representatives over James Monroe, upon his commitment to urge a bill of rights upon the new Congress.

g. *The Constitutional Amendments*

True to his word, Madison proposed eight substantive amendments on June 8, 1789, in the First Session of the First Congress.[26] His language draws heavily upon the Bill of Rights of 1688, George Mason's Declaration of Rights, and many of the state resolutions of ratification. These grew to eighteen substantive amendments in the House committee report on July 28 and were debated on and off throughout the summer and early fall of 1789. Finally, on September 28, 1789, Congress approved twelve amendments and these were submitted to the states for ratification. Ten of these amendments were approved by three-quarters of the states with Virginia being the tenth state to ratify. (Ten states were necessary, since there were now fourteen states with the admission of Vermont to statehood.) On December 15, 1791, our Bill of Rights was added to the Constitution.[27] Because of its importance I set forth the Bill of Rights—the first Ten Amendments—in full:

---

[25] Helen E. Veit, Kenneth R. Bowling, and Charlene Bangs Bickford, eds., *Creating the Bill of Rights, The Documentary Record from the First Federal Congress* (The Johns Hopkins University Press, Baltimore and London, 1991), p. 17.

[26] Veit, Bowling, and Bickford, eds., *Op. Cit.*, p. 11 et seq.

[27] USCA, Const., Amend. 1-10, See: Leg. Hist.

AMENDMENT I

Congress shall make no law respecting an establishment of religion, or prohibiting the free exercise thereof; or abridging the freedom of speech, or of the press; or the right of the people peaceably to assemble, and to petition the Government for a redress of grievances.

AMENDMENT II

A well regulated Militia, being necessary to the security of a free State, the right of the people to keep and bear Arms, shall not be infringed.

AMENDMENT III

No Soldier shall, in time of peace be quartered in any house, without the consent of the Owner, nor in time of war, but in a manner to be prescribed by law.

AMENDMENT IV

The right of the people to be secure in their persons, houses, papers, and effects, against unreasonable searches and seizures, shall not be violated, and no Warrants shall issue, but upon probable cause, supported by Oath or affirmation, and particularly describing the place to be searched, and the persons or things to be seized.

AMENDMENT V

No person shall be held to answer for a capital, or otherwise infamous crime, unless on a presentment or indictment of a Grand Jury, except in cases arising in the land or naval forces, or in the Militia, when in actual service in time of War or public danger; nor shall any person be subject for the same offence to be twice put in jeopardy of life or limb; nor shall be compelled in any criminal case to be a witness against himself, nor be deprived of life, liberty, or property, without due process of law; nor shall private property be taken for public use, without just compensation.

AMENDMENT VI

In all criminal prosecutions, the accused shall enjoy the right of a speedy and public trial, by an impartial jury of the State and district wherein the crime shall have been committed, which district shall have been previously ascertained by law, and to be informed of the nature and cause of the accusation; to be confronted with the witnesses against him; to have compulsory process for obtaining witnesses in his favor, and to have the Assistance of Counsel for his defence.

AMENDMENT VII

In Suits at common law, where the value in controversy shall exceed twenty dollars, the right of trial by jury shall be preserved, and no fact tried by a jury, shall be otherwise reexamined in any Court of the United States, than according to the rules of the common law.

AMENDMENT VIII

Excessive bail shall not be required, nor excessive fines imposed, nor cruel and unusual punishment inflicted.

AMENDMENT IX

The enumeration in the Constitution, of certain rights, shall not be construed to deny or disparage others retained by the people.

AMENDMENT X

The powers not delegated to the United States by the Constitution, nor prohibited by it to the States, are reserved to the States respectively, or to the people.[28]

For all the hoopla and high-sounding rhetoric, the Bill of Rights lay dormant for the first 75 years of its existence:

.....In the first century of our nation's existence, the Bill of Rights played a surprisingly trivial role; only once before 1866 was it used by the Supreme Court to invalidate federal action, and that one use was *Dred Scott's* highly implausible and strikingly casual claim that the Fifth Amendment due-process clause invalidated free-soil territory laws like the Northwest Ordinance and the Missouri Compromise. In a review of newspapers published in 1841, Dean Robert Reinstein could find not a single fiftieth anniversary celebration of the Bill of Rights.[29]

Under the discussion on Equality, we discussed the Civil War Amendments that abolished slavery, granted citizenship to the former slaves, provided for equal rights and equal protection of the laws, and gave them the right to vote. We also discussed those later amendments that provided for voting rights for women and young adults and the prohibition of the poll tax. Later Supreme Court cases have interpreted the Fourteenth Amendment as incorporating most of the restrictions on the power of the federal government contained in the Bill of Rights, as restrictions upon state actions, further limiting the power of the states. So today, there is virtually no difference between the federal government's obligation and the states' obligations to respect the rights spelled out in the Federal Constitution.

12. HUMAN RIGHTS AND CONSTITUTIONAL RIGHTS

a. *The Difference between Human Rights, Constitutional Rights, Political Rights, and Civil Rights*

Constitutional rights are those rights found in the federal Constitution. Not all constitutional rights are human rights and not all human rights are spelled out in the Constitution. Witness the Ninth and Tenth Amendments. First Amendment rights and the prohibition against slavery are both human rights and constitutional rights. Most of the other Constitutional rights are procedural devices designed to enhance equality and the franchise and to protect life, liberty, and property. So, for example, the writ of habeas corpus and the right to a trial by a jury of your peers are not natural or human rights; these are procedural safeguards for human rights.

Political rights is a generic term that includes all of those rights that are enjoyed by the citizens of the body politic necessary to implement the political

---

[28] *United States Constitution*, USCA, Const., Amend. 1-10.

[29] Akhil Reed Amar, *The Bill of Rights, Creation and Reconstruction* (Yale University, R.H. Donnelly & Sons Company, Harrisburg, VA, 1998), p.290.

system. Political rights include some constitutional rights such as the right to vote and hold public office as well as federal and state laws that provide for participation in the political process.

Civil rights are not clearly defined; the current popular understanding means those rights derived from the Civil War Amendments. Civil rights include those laws that have abolished apartheid or Jim Crow laws and that promote equality of treatment in employment, public accommodations, transportation, housing, and education among all members of civil society.

b. How Do We Identify Human Rights?

Lawyers will rely upon prior cases, historians will look to our history and culture, and sociologists will explore the new findings of evolutionary psychology to identify and spell out specific individual natural or human rights. But let us take a step back and look at a larger world view. From the perspective of the political philosopher, human rights are those natural rights that flow from the natural duties to which we consent in the social contract. Remember how we arrive at natural duties. A natural duty is one that reasonable persons with equal bargaining power and complete impartiality will unanimously consent to, at all times and in all places, in order to achieve a peaceful and just society. They reach that consensus and become mutually obligated to each other to honor that duty because of the benefit that their enlightened self-interest promotes. From that obligation arises a corresponding natural or human right, individual to every other person in the compact—that is, every person within the society.

Obviously, there are very few human rights—life, liberty, and the pursuit of happiness—but they are basic to our ability to live as human beings. Basic to all is the right to life. Liberty rights include liberty of the body, i.e. freedom from slavery and false imprisonment; they also include liberty of the mind, i.e. freedom of conscience, freedom in our spoken and written communications, and freedom in our association with others. The concept of ordered liberty also includes the right to marry, raise a family, and educate your children according to your best light. The pursuit of happiness includes the right to acquire and own property and the right to a minimum humane standard of living. In recent years, the right of privacy has been added to that short list. In discussing the right of privacy, Mr. Justice Goldberg observed:

....that the concept of liberty protects those personal rights that are fundamental, and not confined to the specific terms of the Bill of Rights...

.....The Ninth Amendment reads, "The enumeration in the Constitution, of certain rights, shall not disparage others retained by the people...."

....In determining which rights are fundamental, judges are not left at large to decide cases in light of their personal and private notions. Rather, they must look to the "traditions and [collective] conscience of our people" to determine whether a principle is "so rooted [there]...as to be ranked as fundamental." The inquiry is whether a right involved "is of such a character that it cannot be denied without violating these 'fundamental principles of liberty and justice which lie at the base of all our civil and political institutions'..."[30]

Mr. Justice Goldberg's meaning of fundamental rights may be broader than our understanding of natural or human rights and probably includes such *fundamental* procedural rights as habeas corpus and trial by jury. It is clear, however, that human rights developed under our consensus parable do meet the "traditions and conscience" test and are included as fundamental rights.

c. Unalienable Rights and Government by the Consent of the Governed

Self-government ultimately boils down to government by the majority of those voting. The issue is whether natural or human rights can be abolished or abridged by a majority in Congress, by a majority vote in a public referendum, or by a super-majority through the process of amending the Constitution. Our philosophy, history, and Supreme Court decisions have consistently held that human rights—including First Amendment rights—are not subject to a majority vote. Unalienable means unalienable.

American political thought and experience after 1776 in fact highlighted a tension built into the Declaration of Independence which proclaimed in one clause that certain rights were "unalienable," and in another that "Governments...derive their just powers from the consent of the governed." Rights to life, liberty, and the pursuit of happiness were not to be submitted to a vote or to depend on the outcome of elections; that is, not even the consent of the governed could legitimately abridge them. But it was nonetheless possible that the people, through their elected representatives, might sanction laws violating "unalienable" rights. Suppose legislatures, state or national, passed laws abridging freedom of the press, or violating liberty of conscience, or permitting default on contracts, as happened in the 1780s. Which principle had priority, that of "consent" or that of "unalienable rights"? Unless it could be assured that all, or at least a majority of the people would always protect "unalienable rights," which few thought likely, the American Revolutionists seemed committed to propositions not always compatible. The Federal Constitution of 1787 was one effort to contain the tension, and the debate over its ratification often revolved around whether the framers had properly adjusted the balance of the two principles. Virtually all the members of the Federal Convention, and both sides in the ratification struggle, sought to fulfill the purposes of the Declaration of Independence to both protect rights and insure government by consent. The key differences arose over which purpose to emphasize and what mechanisms of government best assured some fulfillment of each....[31]

...the federalists still thought of themselves as heirs to the American Revolution and sincere friends of government by consent. To them the ideals of human rights and rule by the people required not suspicion of government but use of it. They were confident that human ingenuity could devise mechanisms that would at once

---

[30] *Griswold v. Connecticut*, 381 US 479, 14 L Ed 2d 510, 516-20, 85 S Ct 1678.
[31] Ketcham, *Op. Cit.*, p. 5.

protect liberty, allow effective government, and rest on the consent of the people…. It was possible both to give sufficient powers to the House of Representatives and to the President, and to guard against the abuse of those powers. It was
only prudent to erect barriers against tendencies toward greed, passion, and self-
ish ambition in any human government, but it was also important to benefit from
wise and good rule….If good government was impossible when "the people"
chose their own rulers, then the very idea of government by consent stood condemned….The federalists believed the new Constitution provided effective resolution of these intricacies.[32]

d. The Supremacy of the Social Contract

There is no power in our government, neither an act of Congress acting
with a majority of both houses and with the consent of the President, nor the
Supreme Court, acting through a majority of its justices, nor any plebiscite of
the whole people—not even a super-majority acting to amend the Constitution—that can abolish or abridge natural or human rights. The natural duties of
the social contract are binding upon our federal and state governments and the
human rights flowing therefrom cannot be taken away in whole or in part. No
amendment to the Constitution could, for example, reinstate slavery or permit
the execution of the mentally ill.

However, Congress and the courts have the power to define those
rights, as in the right to life and capital punishment; describe the outer bounda-
ries of those rights, as with the exercise of free speech and the prohibition
against defamation; and balance one right against another, as in the case of
freedom of public assembly and the needs of public safety. And, of course, as
our knowledge and understanding of human rights develop, we can improve or
expand the scope of existing rights, as with the application of free speech rights to
the internet, and identify or define new human rights, as with the right to privacy.

The supremacy of the social contract applies only to natural or human
rights. Other constitutional rights could be abolished or abridged by constitutional amendment. There is no natural right or human right to the writ of habeas corpus or trial by jury (or other purely procedural remedies) and these
could be abolished by constitutional amendment, however unlikely. But the
Constitution could never abrogate or diminish the underlying substantive rights
and permit or require false imprisonment or the arbitrary execution of innocent
people. Neither the government nor a super-majority of the people have the
right to trample the human rights of any minority.

SUMMARY

The duties imposed and the obligations accepted in American ethics are
based upon mutual agreements required and assumed to be agreed to by every

---

[32] *Ibid.*, p. 15.

member of civil society. Natural rights or human rights are the benefits of the social contract arising from the basic duties imposed by that compact and the obligations of each person to honor those duties. We determine whether a particular right is a human right by first determining whether there is a corresponding basic duty. A basic or natural duty is one that reasonable persons with equal bargaining power and complete impartiality will unanimously consent to, at all times and in all places, in order to achieve a peaceful and just society. From that obligation, required and assumed by every member of civil society, arises the corresponding human right for each person who is a party to the compact.

There are only a few human rights. Basic to all is the right to life. Liberty rights include freedom from slavery and false imprisonment; freedom of conscience, spoken and written communications, and association; and the right to marry and raise and educate a family. The pursuit of happiness includes the right to acquire and own property and includes the right to a minimum humane standard of living. In recent years, the right of privacy has been added to this short list.

Human rights are inseparable from their corresponding basic duties since they are opposite sides of the same relationships. Human rights are universal since the assent of everyone to the corresponding duties is required and assumed. Human rights are inalienable since they are the benefits negotiated for the obligations assumed by each person and to which everyone is entitled. Human rights are indivisible and interdependent. The right to life is basic to all. Other rights are necessary to live as human beings in the fullness of life. Human rights are what make us human. The natural or basic duties imposed by the social contract constitute the right in American ethics and are our objective ethical standard. We assume these obligations out of enlightened self interest and we "...refrain from attacking the rights of others in order that their own may not be violated..."[33]

Historically in America, human rights developed as a mixed bag of natural rights and procedural protections. At first, these were considered as benefits granted by the king in abatement of the king's otherwise absolute authority. With the rise of self government, the people were recognized as the source of all legitimate governmental power and ethical duties.

Because government is not the source of human rights, they can not be diminished, in whole or in part, by a majority vote of the whole people or by their representatives. Not even a constitutional amendment can abolish or abridge human rights since our Constitution, like the organic and ordinary laws of every government and society, must enforce these basic duties and protect the human rights that comprise the social contract.

---

[33] De Tocqueville, *Op. Cit.*, p. 35.

MY PERSONAL OBLIGATION:

Self-Respect

The reason we agree to be obligated to the duties that society imposes upon us is to enjoy the benefits of our social cooperation. Good people do not always get what they deserve. Sometimes they get what they demand. We need to demand to be treated equally and fairly by others in civil society and by the government that is charged with protecting our rights. Standing up for your rights is the beginning of self-respect. If you do not respect yourself, why should you expect anyone else to respect you? Do not be a victim; be a defender of yourself and those dear to you. Have the strength of your convictions and the courage to assert your rights, courteously but firmly!

As a virtuous citizen, keep in mind that while nobody is better than you, neither are you any better than they. Remember that when you protect the rights of others, you also protect your own rights.

MY PERSONAL VIRTUE:

Self-Improvement

The object of learning about ethical values and honoring those obligations and practicing those virtues is to build an ethical center within yourself— an ethical center that is informed, strong, self-confident and courageous. That makes you unbeatable!

When you learn more about your own ethical obligations and rights, you become more sensitive to the values of American ethics and you become a more virtuous citizen. You bring reason to your deliberations and conscious choice to your acts.

When you learn more about the ethical relationships that are the foundation of our social cooperation, you will strive to strengthen those duties and rights for others and build a more law abiding and just community.

As your ethical center matures and strengthens, the relationships in your life with your parents, spouse, children, relatives, personal friends, and business acquaintances will become more reasonable and caring. Everybody wins!

ADDITIONAL READINGS

Ordinance of 1787:[34]
The Northwest Territorial Government
[The Confederate Congress, July 13, 1787]
*An Ordinance for the government of the territory
of the United States northwest of the river Ohio.*

ARTICLE I

No person, demeaning himself in a peaceable and orderly manner, shall ever be molested on account of his mode of worship, or religious sentiments, in the said territories.

ARTICLE II

The inhabitants of the said territory shall always be entitled to the benefits of the writs of habeas corpus, and of the trial by jury; of a proportionate representation of the people in the legislature, and of judicial proceedings according to the course of the common law. All persons shall be bailable, unless for capital offenses, where the proof shall be evident, or the presumption great. All fines shall be moderate; and no cruel or unusual punishments shall be inflicted. No man shall be deprived of his liberty or property, but by the judgment of his peers, or the law of the land, and should the public exigencies make it necessary, for the common preservation, to take any person's property, or to demand his particular services, full compensation shall be made for the same. And, in the just preservation of rights and property, it is understood and declared, that no law ought ever to be made or have force in the said territory, that shall, in any manner whatever, interfere with or affect private contracts, or engagements, bona fide, and without fraud previously formed.

ARTICLE III

Religion, morality, and knowledge being necessary to good government and the happiness of mankind, schools and the means of education shall forever be encouraged. The utmost good faith shall always be observed towards the Indians; their lands and property shall never be taken from them without their consent; and in their property, rights, and liberty they never shall be invaded or disturbed, unless in just and lawful wars authorized by Congress; but laws rounded in justice and humanity shall, from time to time, be made, for preventing wrongs being done to them, and for preserving peace and friendship with them....

---

[34] USCA, Const., Organic Laws, p. 17.
[35] James Alexander, *Op. Cit.*, p. 58 et seq. This pamphlet was written and published by the first attorney for Peter Zenger about a year after the trial. It includes the Information filed by the

ARTICLE VI

There shall be neither slavery nor involuntary servitude in the said territory, otherwise than in the punishment of crimes, whereof the party shall have been duly convicted: Provided always, That any person escaping into the same, from whom labor or service is lawfully claimed in any one of the original States, such fugitive may be lawfully reclaimed, and conveyed to the persons claiming his or her labor or service as aforesaid....

Done by the United States, in Congress assembled, the 13th day of July, in the year of our Lord 1787, and of their sovereignty and independence the twelfth.

LANDMARK CASE #5

The Crown v. John Peter Zenger, (1735)[35]

James Alexander and William Smith had undertaken the defense of John Peter Zenger. They made a motion to disqualify two of the sitting judges and were promptly disbarred. John Chambers was then appointed to defend Zenger. In the meantime, Alexander retained Andrew Hamilton of Philadelphia, reputedly the best lawyer of his day, to assist in the trial. His trial finally began on August 4, 1735.

Although the Sheriff attempted to pack the list of prospective jurors with Cosby supporters, Chambers succeeded in impaneling a fair and impartial jury. The Attorney General read his Information, charging Zenger with printing and publishing two newspaper articles, which were called libels against the Governor and his administration, to which Zenger pleaded "Not Guilty." Then Chambers delivered his opening speech to the jury. All present expected a weak defense of the printer. However, when Chambers had concluded his remarks, Andrew Hamilton rose dramatically from his chair in the New York City Hall courtroom, and announced to the youthful Chief Justice, the honorable James DeLancey, that he would participate in Zenger's defense. An attorney with years of courtroom experience and a well-prepared brief, he spoke with the audacity of one indifferent to the local political contests.

Mr. Hamilton. May it please Your Honor; I am concerned in this cause on the part of Mr. Zenger the Defendant....[I meant to put] Mr. Attorney upon proving that my client printed and published those papers mentioned in the information; yet I cannot think it proper for me (without doing violence to my own principles) to deny the publication of a complaint which I think is the

---

Attorney General, the notes and trial brief of Alexander Hamilton and other attorneys in the case, and the transcript of pre-trial motions and the trial by jury. The work also contains many of the articles published by *The New York Weekly Journal.*

right of every free-born subject to make when the matters so published can be supported with truth; and therefore I'll save Mr. Attorney the trouble of examining his witnesses to that point; and I do (for my client) confess that he both printed and published the two newspapers set forth in the information, and I hope in so doing he has committed no crime.

Mr. Attorney. Then if Your Honor pleases, since Mr. Hamilton has confessed the fact, I think our witnesses may be discharged; we have no further occasion for them....

Indeed sir, as Mr. Hamilton has confessed the printing and publishing these libels, I think the jury must find a verdict for the King; for supposing they were true, the law says that they are not the less libelous for that; nay indeed the law says their being true is an aggravation of the crime.

Mr. Hamilton. Not so neither, Mr. Attorney, there are two words to that bargain. I hope it is not our bare printing and publishing a paper that will make it a libel: You will have something more to do before you make my client a libeler; for the words themselves must be libelous, that is, *false, scandalous, and seditious* or else we are not guilty....(pp. 61-2)

Mr. Attorney. The case before the Court is whether Mr. Zenger is guilty of libeling His Excellency the Governor of New York, and indeed the whole administration of the government. Mr. Hamilton has confessed the printing and publishing, and I think nothing is plainer than that the words in the information are *scandalous, and tend to sedition, and to disquiet the minds of the people of this Province.* And if such papers are not libels, I think it may be said there can be no such thing as a libel.

Mr. Hamilton. May it please Your Honor; I cannot agree with Mr. Attorney: For though I freely acknowledge that there are such things as libels, yet I must insist at the same time that what my client is charged with is not a libel; and I observed just now that Mr. Attorney in defining a libel made use of the words *scandalous, seditious, and tend to disquiet the people*; but (whether with design or not I will not say) he omitted the word *false....*

But we will save Mr. Attorney the trouble of proving a negative, and take the *onus probandi* upon ourselves, and prove those very papers that are called libels to be *true.*

Mr. Chief Justice. You cannot be admitted, Mr. Hamilton, to give the truth of a libel in evidence. A libel is not to be justified; for it is nevertheless a libel that it is *true....*(pp. 68-9)

Mr. Hamilton. Then, gentlemen of the jury, it is to you we must now appeal for witnesses to the truth of the facts we have offered and are denied the liberty to prove; and let it not seem strange that I apply myself to you in this manner, I am warranted so to do both by law and reason. The law supposes you to be summoned *out of the neighborhood where the fact is alleged to be* *committed*; and the reason of your being taken out of the neighborhood is *because you are supposed to have the best knowledge of the fact that is to be tried*. And were you to find a verdict against my client, you must take upon you to say the papers referred to in the information, and which we acknowledge we printed and published, are *false, scandalous and seditious*; but of this I can have no apprehension. You are citizens of New York; you are really what the law supposes you to be, *honest and lawful men*; and therefore in your justice lies our safety. And as we are denied the liberty of giving evidence to prove the truth of what we have published, I will beg leave to lay it down as a standing rule in such cases, *that the suppressing of evidence ought always to be taken for the strongest evidence*; and I hope it will have that weight with you....(p. 75)

...Then it follows that those twelve men must *understand* the words of the information to be *scandalous,* that is to say *false*;...

Mr. Chief Justice. No, Mr. Hamilton; The jury may find that Zenger printed and published those papers, and leave it to the Court to judge whether they are libelous;...

Mr. Hamilton. I know, may it please Your Honor, the jury may do so; but I do likewise know they may do otherwise....(p. 78)

...And has it not often been seen (and I hope it will always be seen) that when the representatives of a free people are by just representations or remonstrances made sensible of the sufferings of their fellow subjects by the abuse of power in the hands of a governor, they have declared (and loudly too) that they were not obliged by any law to support a governor who goes about to destroy a province or colony, or their privileges, which by His Majesty he was appointed, and by the law he is bound to protect and encourage. But I pray it may be considered of what use is this mighty privilege if every man that suffers must be silent? And if a man must be taken up as a libeler for telling his sufferings to his neighbor? (pp. 80-1)

Mr. Chief Justice. Gentlemen of the jury. The great pains Mr. Hamilton has taken to show how little regard juries are to pay to the opinion of the judges, and his insisting so much upon the conduct of some judges in trials of this kind, is done no doubt with a design that you should take but very little notice of what I might say upon this occasion. I shall therefore only observe to you that as the facts or words in the information are confessed: The only thing that can come in question before you is whether the words as set forth in the information make a libel. And that is a matter of law, no doubt, and which you may leave to the Court....(p. 100)

Then the jury withdrew and deliberated for only five minutes. When they returned, the Clerk asked them if they had reached a verdict and whether John Peter Zenger was guilty of seditious libel. They answered, unanimously, by their foreman, Thomas Hunt, Not Guilty! Three huzzas went up in the crowded City Hall. Zenger was discharged the next day.

This trial did not change the laws of libel to make truth a defense to criticism of public officials and provide for effective freedom of the press; that did not happen in New York until 1805. Nor did the trial establish the unfettered right of the jury to determine the guilt or innocence of one accused of libel, again, until 1805. But it was a beginning; the trial highlights the unhappy state of natural and political rights in this country preceding the Revolution and underscores the causes that led up to that separation. It was the memory of this case and others like it that caused the veterans of the Revolution to demand a Federal Bill of Rights including those that would have helped Zenger: freedom of speech and press (First Amendment), the requirement of Grand Jury indictments for serious crimes (Fifth Amendment), the right to a speedy and public trial by an impartial jury (Sixth Amendment), and the right to be released on reasonable bail (Eighth Amendment).

CHAPTER V

Secular Ethics

Freedom of Conscience and Religion

Separation of Church and State

...Whilst we assert for ourselves a freedom to embrace, to profess and to observe the Religion which we believe to be of divine origin, we cannot deny an equal freedom to those whose minds have not yet yielded to the evidence which has convinced us....

—*James Madison*
Memorial and Remonstrance
against Religious Assessments *(1785)*

The Catholic Church became the state religion of the Roman Empire in 313 AD. The concept of heresy—that is, the expression of ideas that are contrary to an established orthodox position—was introduced to this tradition when the Council of Nicaea in 325 AD declared Arius a heretic for holding and teaching that Jesus was only a man and not God. The concept of heresy developed and grew bolder as the temporal power of the Church grew. By the fourteenth century, the fear of witchcraft had spread across Europe like a contagious plague resulting in the torture and death by burning at the stake of thousands of unfortunate women. The fifteenth century brought the Spanish Inquisition. Following the Protestant Revolt in the sixteenth century, the Italian Inquisition began burning heretics such as Brouno. It reached its climax with the trial of Galileo in 1633.

For me, there is no better example of the conditions that prevailed before our Revolution and that cried out for remedy, than the heresy trial of Galileo, held at about the same time that the Puritans were establishing their state religion in Massachusetts Bay colony. Giorgio de Santillana, in his scholarly history, *The Crime of Galileo*, states that Galileo was physically tortured by the orders of the Inquisitors-General—all cardinals of the Church. He describes what befell Galileo following the inquest that had been ordered by the pope:

> On the next day, Wednesday, June 22, 1633, in the morning, Galileo was conducted to the large hall used for such proceedings in the Dominican convent of Santa Maria sopra Minerva, built in the center of Rome out of the ruins of an ancient temple to the Goddess of Wisdom. Clad in the white shirt of penitence, he knelt in the presence of his assembled judges while the sentence was read to him:...

> "...Invoking, therefore, the most holy name of our Lord Jesus Christ and of His most glorious Mother, ever Virgin Mary, by this our final sentence, which sitting in judgment, with the counsel and advice of the Reverend Masters of sacred theology and Doctors of both Laws, our assessors, we deliver in these writings, in the cause and causes at present before us between the Magnificent Carlo Sinceri, Doctor of both Laws, Proctor Fiscal of this Holy Office, of the one part, and you Galileo Galilei, the defendant, here present, examined, tried, and confessed as shown above, of the other part—

> "We say, pronounce, sentence, and declare that you, the said Galileo, by reason of the matters adduced in trial, and by you confessed as above, have rendered yourself in the judgment of this Holy Office vehemently suspected of heresy, namely, of having believed and held the doctrine—which is false and contrary to the sacred and divine Scriptures—that the Sun is the center of the world and does not move from east to west and that the Earth moves and is not the center of the world; and that an opinion may be held and defended as probable after it has been declared and defined to be contrary to the Holy Scripture; and that consequently you have incurred all the censures and penalties imposed and promulgated in the sacred canons and other constitutions, general and particular, against such delinquents. From which we are content that you be absolved, provided that, first, with a sincere heart and unfeigned faith, you abjure, curse, and detest before us the aforesaid errors and heresies and every other error and heresy contrary to the Catholic and Apostolic Roman Church in the form to be prescribed by us for you.

> "And, in order that this your grave and pernicious error and transgression may not remain altogether unpunished and that you may be more cautious in the future and an example to others that they may abstain from similar delinquencies, we ordain that the book of the 'Dialogue of Galileo Galilei' be prohibited by public edict.

> "We condemn you to the formal prison of this Holy Office during our pleasure, and by way of salutary penance we enjoin that for three years to come you repeat once a week the seven penitential Psalms. Reserving to ourselves liberty to moderate, commute, or take off, in whole or in part, the aforesaid penalties and penance...."[1]

---

[1] Giorgio de Santillana, *The Crime of Galileo* (The University of Chicago Press, 1955), pp. 309-10.

On June 30, 1633, Galileo was released in the custody of Archbishop Ascanio Piccolomini in Siena. After five months it was intended that he should go to the Charterhouse of Florence. This was later commuted, and he was allowed to move to his own little farm in Arcetri, where he was to face the remaining eight years of his life, and oncoming blindness, under perpetual house arrest.

The Bill of Rights came about in this historical context making the written statement of protected rights a necessary restraint on the power of government.

13. THE SACRED AND THE SECULAR

American ethics is based upon secular values; that is, the purpose and objective of the rules imposed are for the good of society and not for some otherworld purpose. John Locke had taught that "...the power of civil government relates only to men's civil interests, is confined to the care of the things of this world, and hath nothing to do with the world to come..."[2] The American colonists understood the sacred to be the jurisdiction of the established—the tax supported—church; first the Church of Rome, later the Church of England, and still later the Puritan oligarchy's Congregational Church in New England; the Dutch Reformed Church in New Amsterdam; and the Anglican Church in most of the remaining colonies. The focus of the sacred is the otherworld. Faith in a supernatural God and obedience to His commands, as made manifest by His priesthood, to earn eternal salvation in the afterlife, was the domain of the church. They understood that secular values deal with the needs of the community in this world and that this was the jurisdiction of temporal princes and kings.

It is not that religious values are necessarily different from secular values since many times these values coincide. Most sacred or sectarian values have both a religious purpose as well as a worldly goal. "Remember, keep holy the Sabbath," was, according to the Judeo-Christian tradition, the command of God to honor Him by honoring the Lord's Day. It has the secular benefit of providing one day of rest out of seven, for believers and non-believers alike. When the Jew feeds a hungry man, he may be fulfilling his duty to give charity or perform a mitzvah, the Christian may be caring for Christ, and the Muslim may be honoring Allah's command to care for the poor. But all are providing a temporal benefit to a man who is hungry, thereby promoting social and economic justice, thereby promoting peace in this world. However, it should be remembered that some religious values have no secular purpose, such as the duty of most religions to honor God, and these values cannot become a part of our public morality.

The difference is that religious ethical principles will find their basis or

---

[2] John Locke, *A Letter Concerning Toleration*, in *Great Books of the Western World*, Vol. 35 of Encyclopedia Britannica, ed. Robert Maynard Hutchins (William Benton, Publisher, 1952), p. 4.

authority upon the commandments of God or the teaching of the Bible, the Torah, the Koran, or the commands of a church or sect, while secular ethics will find its justification and authority based on the communitarian needs of the individual and the society as a whole. So, for example, when the New York State Legislature adopted a revised penal code in 1967, forbidding crimes like murder, theft, and perjury, it did not turn to the Ten Commandments or to sacred scripture or to church teaching for its justification. It stated that the general purposes of the statute include "...to proscribe conduct which unjustifiably and inexcusably causes or threatens substantial harm to individuals or public interest..."

Secular values are not anti-religious or irreligious or opposed to sectarian values; they are usually the same values but with a temporal intent or a worldly purpose or objective. Secular values are non-religious values; they are neutral with respect to religion.

We assert that freedom of conscience and religion—the right to choose and act according to each person's religious beliefs or conscientiously held convictions—is a natural or human right. We impose upon our federal and state governments the duty to protect this right for each of us in our pluralistic society. We do this by requiring that government be neutral in matters of religion or conscience when dealing with us as citizens. So, for example, there can be no religious test—a required profession of a sectarian faith or adherence to strictly religious morals, for example—as a qualification to vote or hold public office. There can be no established or official church. No laws are permitted to mandate tax support for the construction or maintenance of churches, schools, or the salaries of clergy or teachers, directly or indirectly. Nor can there be any religious doctrine or orthodoxy established by law, presidential order, or court decision, as governmental policy or to qualify for any benefit, protection, privilege, or immunity provided by law.

> ...If there is any fixed star in our constitutional constellation, it is that no official, high or petty, can prescribe what shall be orthodox in politics, nationalism, religion, or other matters of opinion or force citizens to confess by word or act their faith therein...[3]

To understand how Americans developed from a people ruled by the divine right of kings with the king as the head of the established Church of England to a nation founded on secular values, it is necessary to look at the historical development of freedom of conscience and religion and that uniquely American doctrine of separation of church and state. How we moved from a society of imposed ritual and dogma and enforced orthodoxy to a society where each person's freedom of conscience and religion is respected and protected is one of the great lessons of American history.

---

[3] *West Virginia State Board of Education v. Barnette*, 319 US 624, 87 L Ed 1628 at 1639.

14. THE COLONIAL PERIOD

a. European Heritage

In 1492, when Columbus discovered America, all of Europe, from the Cliffs of Moher on the west coast of Ireland to the far ends of Russia, was Christian, and most of Western Europe was under the spiritual control of the Holy Roman Catholic Church ruled by one absolute monarch—the pope. No one was allowed to profess any other religion or deviate from the official church teaching, except the Jews, who were relegated to ghettos in the emerging cities of Europe, and the Muslims in the Moorish parts of the Iberian peninsula. Orthodoxy was enforced and every diocese had inquisitors assisted by thousands of Dominicans and other priestly officials. Every bishop swore an oath to drive out the heretic and the infidel from his See. The Spanish inquisition was in full swing. The oppression of women suspected of witchcraft was pervasive and terrifying. I personally stood in the torture chamber of the castle of Salzberg in Austria—then a principality ruled by the church—where in the fifteenth century a single bishop put over 300 women to the rack and then to death as witches.

By the time the Separatists (or Pilgrims) set foot on Plymouth Rock in November, 1620, the Protestant Revolt had occurred. The Church of England had been established as the official church of the realm. New dissenters— Puritans (Anglicans who wanted to purify the ritual and the ceremonies of the church), Separatists (those Puritans who wanted to break with the Anglican Church), Presbyterians, Quakers, and Anabaptists—had sprung up. The teachings of John Calvin would have a profound influence upon the political and religious thinking of the United States through these early colonists and their Congregational Church as well as through the Dutch Reformed Church in New York and the Scottish Presbyterians who settled various parts of the new country.

At the same time, great political thinkers who would influence our founding fathers were publishing their writings. Of all modern philosophers, John Locke was the most influential. In his Letter Concerning Toleration,[4] he taught that the magistrate had no authority to rule over souls; that religion must depend on inward conviction, not on external compulsion; and that the rights of conscience in matters of personal religious faith must be treated with respect.

b. New England

i. Massachusetts

It was not the more democratic Separatists who founded the Plymouth colony that set the character of New England but their Puritan neighbors who founded Massachusetts Bay Colony near Boston in 1628–30 and established the purified Anglican Church, a church without bishops, as the state religion.

---

[4] John Locke, *A Letter Concerning Toleration,* in Hutchins, ed., *Op Cit.*, p. 4 et sec.

They established a theocracy where church membership was limited to visible saints according to the Calvinist view of predestination, and the right to vote for officers of the colony was limited to church members. For the first time we see a religious test for the franchise—the right to vote.

Here religion (of an intolerant Calvinistic type) and government were to be closely associated. The church was a carefully selected group of communicants who emphasized their prerogatives and would brook no serious dissent from their duly adopted tenets. This oligarchy would establish a Puritan state church closely related to town government. Following their English tradition, these past dissenters would now take the place of the old Anglican state church to which they had been accustomed in England. They expected the state to support public worship and suppress heresy. They did not wish it to interfere in strictly religious questions but recognized that in matters of church government and ecclesiastical affairs state and church should work together.

In New England, the congregational meetinghouse, the nucleus of every township, was used both for governmental purposes and for religious worship. Furthermore, municipal and certain parochial duties were frequently performed by the same officials. In some cases the minutes of the two organizations were kept in the same book, the facts and votes of both groups being included. Yet, even in Puritan New England, a fairly clear distinction was maintained between the functions of church and state. The elder was not considered eligible for the civil magistracy nor the magistrate for the office of elder.

Although the two functions were considered separate, the church and state were expected to work together and support each other. For example, in 1638, Ann Hutchinson was tried by the General Court of Massachusetts—a civil Court—for heretical and immoral teachings and was banished from the colony. Then she was tried by a church tribunal for breaking ecclesiastical discipline and was excommunicated. She and her family fled to Rhode Island and later moved to New York in the vicinity of Eastchester. She and all of her family were killed by the Indians in 1642, except for one daughter who was ransomed by the Dutch. The Hutchinson River and the Parkway that runs along that river in Westchester County, New York, were both named in her honor.

ii. Connecticut

Thomas Hooker fled religious persecution in England and came to the Massachusetts Bay Colony in 1633. Three years later, he and his congregation migrated to the Connecticut River valley and founded the town of Hartford. Hooker worked for a free church within a free state although he believed in a strong working relationship between the two. His *Fundamental Orders* of 1639[5] provided that civil privilege was not related to church membership ex-

[5] Fundamental Orders of Conn., See: Canon Anson Phelps Stokes and Leo Pfeffer, *Church and State in the United States* (Harper & Row, New York, p. 10, 1964); this work is the source of much of this material and should be referred to for facts not specifically cited.

cept that the governor had to be a member of "some approved congregation."

However, in 1662 the rigidly Puritan settlements along Long Island Sound, led by New Haven, obtained a charter from Charles II absorbing the river colonies and establishing Congregationalism in all of Connecticut. Later, Anglicans, Baptists, and Quakers were allowed to organize but, nevertheless, their members had to pay the tax for the support of the Congregational ministry.

iii. Rhode Island

Roger Williams arrived in Massachusetts Bay Colony in 1630 and was quickly identified by the oligarchy as a dissenter for condemning the Puritan state-church system. Banished in 1635, he founded the colony of Providence and there established the first Baptist church in America. Later, he became a Seeker—a Christian skeptical of divine claims made by all Churches. He asserted that the state had no jurisdiction over one's conscience and that each person must have "soul liberty." His colony became a refuge for victims of religious persecution even Papists and Jews.

In 1644, Williams wrote in his *Bloudy Tenent of Persecution for Cause of Conscience* that:

> God requireth not an *uniformity of Religion* to be enacted [sic] and inforced in any civill State; which inforced uniformity (sooner or later) is the greatest occasion of civill Warre, ravishing of conscience, persecution of Christ Jesus in his servants, and of the hypocrisie and destruction of millions of souls.[6]

That same year, he obtained a charter for the Providence Plantations recognizing only the civil government. In 1647, a civil code was drawn up granting complete liberty of conscience.

In his famous "ship letter," written in 1654, Williams laid down the great principles of church-state relations that have become the foundation of our jurisprudence. He taught that:

a. there is a difference between the sacred and the secular;

b. compulsion may be exercised by officials of the State in the area of the secular but not of the sacred; and

c. where the safety and security of the commonwealth are concerned, religious conscience is not a valid excuse for refusal to obey the lawful commands of the state.[7]

Rhode Island never had an established religion.

c. *The Other Colonies*

Shortly after the founding of the colony at Jamestown in Virginia, the Anglican Church was established and was to be the only Church in the colony.

In the traditional style of establishment, clergy were provided public support in

---

[6] Roger Williams, *Bloudy Tenent of Persecution for Cause of Conscience*, (1644), in *Ibid.*, p. 14.

[7] Roger Williams, *Letter of 1647*; See *Ibid.*, p. 15.

the forms of money or, more often, land and tobacco. "Dale's law" (1610), named after one of the first governors of the colony, required attendance at Anglican worship by all the citizens of the colony, and persistent violation of the law carried the death penalty. There were also laws against blasphemy and criticism of the Anglican Church or any of its particular doctrines. Again, depending on the seriousness of the profanity, penalties could range from mutilation of one's tongue to death.[8]

The Dutch Reformed Church, another Calvinist church, dominated in New Amsterdam but when the English seized that colony in 1664, New York became a royal colony and the Anglican Church was established. Eventually, all the middle and southern colonies established the Anglican Church except Pennsylvania and Delaware. Even Maryland, founded as an asylum for persecuted Roman Catholics by the second Lord Baltimore, Cecil Calvert, himself a Catholic who was quite tolerant toward other Protestant sects, established the Anglican Church after the Glorious Revolution of 1688. While the established Congregational Church in New England tended to dominate the civil governments of those colonies, the Anglican Church tended to be dominated by the governments of those royal and proprietary colonies, where it was established.

All the middle and southern colonies had religious tests for holding public office and some to exercise the franchise. For example, Maryland, in its *Toleration Act of 1649*,[9] provided toleration for all "professing to believe in Jesus Christ"; it also provided that anyone who blasphemed or denied Jesus Christ or the holy Trinity "shall be punished with death and confiscation or forfeiture of all his or her lands." Even Pennsylvania demanded that, as a qualification for office, one believe that God was "the rewarder of good and the punisher of the wicked." The most theological requirement was in Delaware, the only other non-establishment colony, where officeholders had to profess "faith in God the Father, and in Jesus Christ, His only Son, and in the Holy Ghost, One God, blessed forever more."

d. The Road to Religious Freedom

There are many causes that resulted in the prohibition of establishment and the guarantee of religious freedom in the new states and in the Federal Constitution. Before the Revolution, many colonists came to realize that the cause of American democracy and the cause of religious freedom went hand in hand, particularly in those colonies where the Anglican Church was established. After the Revolution every colonial church severed its allegiance to its English or European connection except the Roman Catholic Church. Many later settlers had come seeking religious freedom in the New World and many,

---

[8] Ronald B. Flowers, *The Godless Court?* (Westminster John Knox Press, Louisville, Kentucky, 1994).

[9] "Toleration Act of 1649," in Stokes & Pfeffer, *Op. Cit.*, pp. 11-2.

like the Mennonites, came over in communities so as to have freedom to develop their own religious and social convictions. Many persecuted groups became leaders in opposing official religion. However, I should like to focus on two causes of the move to religious freedom.

i. The Secular Imperative

Many of the American colonists were political liberals and religious non-conformists who brought with them a wide variety of religious sects from England, Scotland, Ireland, Germany, Switzerland, and other parts of Europe. At the beginning of the American Revolution, nine out of the thirteen original colonies had an established church. The colonial population had grown to approximately 4,000,000 inhabitants. Their religious denominations included Congregationalists, Presbyterians, Baptists, and Anglicans, the four largest colonial groups in rank order. There were German sects with Anabaptist backgrounds—the Mennonites, Moravians, and Quakers; and there were Dutch Reformed in New York, as well as Roman Catholics, Methodists (who had split from the Anglicans), and Lutherans. By the close of the Revolution there were about 10,000 Jews who settled principally in Newport, New York City, Philadelphia, and Charleston. In addition, there were the Freemasons, The Society of Ancient Druids (formed by apostate Masons), and the Illuminati of New England and of New York (free thinkers with Masonic ties).

All but the Congregationalists and the Anglicans opposed the establishment of religion and the taxes that supported its churches, ministers, and schools and those laws mandating church attendance and licenses to preach in the various new states. It became very clear, as the new nation struggled to form "a more perfect union," that the only way the members of these various religious groups could unite in forming a federal government was on the basis of religious freedom. Ideology was driven by the need of a pluralistic society to develop a secular—that is, a religiously neutral—state in order to avoid "inforced uniformity [which] (sooner or later) is the greatest occasion of civill Warre." There would be no National Anglican Church nor National Congregational Church. Nor would Christianity be established by the new Federal Constitution.

ii. Low Church Membership

Perhaps the most surprising cause of the surge of religious freedom after the Revolution was the fact that very few colonists were members of any organized religion or sect. John M. Swomley, Jr. discusses myths about religion in colonial America:[10]

> Some religious leaders in America do not like the idea of a secular constitution and a secular state. They advocate a Christian republic in which presumably Jews and other non-Christians would be tolerated.

---

[10] John M. Swomley, Jr., "Toleration Is Not Good Enough," in *Why We Still Need Public Schools* (Prometheus Books, Buffalo, New York, 1992), p. 42.

These religious leaders are responsible for a sixth myth: that early America was a Christian society led by committed pastors and religious leaders. The historical fact is that colonial America was composed largely of people who were not church members, although church members in some colonies were influential enough to persuade colonial governments to provide tax support for their churches. William Warren Sweet in his authoritative book, *The Story of Religions in America*, wrote:

"Up until the third decade of the eighteenth century the lower classes in the American colonies were little influenced by organized religion and only a small percentage of the population were members of the colonial churches...Even in the Puritan colonies only a comparatively small proportion of the total population were members of the church, while in Virginia at the opening of the eighteenth century not more than one in twenty were church members, and the proportion was undoubtedly smaller in the other southern colonies. (William Warren Sweet, *The Story of Religion in America* (New York: Charles Scribner's Sons, 1953), p. 7.)"

By the close of the Revolution, church membership was estimated at no more than one to every eight persons or about 12% of the total population.[11] In comparison with these estimates, in 1990 total church membership in the United States was about 63% of the total population.[12] Clearly, non-churchgoers constituted a large majority of the population at the time that our state and federal constitutions were being formed and quite naturally, they opposed any organic connection between church and state.

e. The Virginia Statute of Religious Freedom of 1786

By the beginning of the Revolution, the Anglican Church was well entrenched in colonial Virginia. Ministers were required to present evidence of ordination by an English bishop and all others could be silenced. Only licensed clergymen could perform marriages. The church had been heavily endowed with land and was supported by the tidewater aristocracy. Taxes were levied to pay for the salaries of Anglican ministers and teachers as well as the construction and maintenance of their churches and schools.

Before the Revolution, Baptists and Presbyterians, who had been coming in large numbers to the Shenandoah Valley, joined forces to challenge the establishment. In particular, they objected to the taxes raised to pay for the salaries of the Anglican clergy and teachers. After the war, they were joined by the Lutherans who pressed for a constitutional statement of religious liberty. Just three weeks before the Declaration of Independence was adopted by the Second Continental Congress, the Virginia Declaration of Rights, authored by George Mason, was adopted. It provided (in part) that "all men are equally

---

[11] See: W. W. Sweet, "Church Membership," *Dictionary of American History*, in Stokes & Pfeffer, *Op. Cit.*, p. 23.
[12] See: "Statistical Abstract of the United States," Table No. 87 in *The American Almanac, 1993–94.*

entitled to the free exercise of religion according to the dictates of conscience."

In 1779, Thomas Jefferson introduced, in the Virginia legislature, his Bill for Establishing Religious Freedom that would forever end the establishment in Virginia. However, it was laid over from session to session since the proposal was so controversial.

In November, 1784, Patrick Henry offered "A Bill for Establishing a Provision for Teachers of the Christian Religion" that read:

> That the people of this Commonwealth, according to their respective abilities, ought to pay a moderate tax or contribution annually, for the support of the Christian religion, or of some Christian church, denomination or communion of Christians, or of some form of Christian worship.[13]

Henry's bill would have the effect of substituting the "Christian religion" as the established church of Virginia. South Carolina had recently done so. In its second constitution (1778), South Carolina declared that "the Christian Protestant religion shall be deemed, and is hereby constituted and declared to be, the established religion of this state." Its action clearly indicated that establishment has become much more than the granting of official status or preference to only one religion. The famed Hanover Presbytery, which had opposed a general tax, would cease to object as long as the revenue was distributed fairly to all denominations. The Presbyterian clergy, Madison remarked acidly, were "as ready to set up an establishment which is to take them in as they were to pull down that which shut them out."[14] (Henry's bill also appears to be an early effort to establish an income tax.) At the request of James Madison, the matter was laid over to the next session, giving time to organize opposition to the Bill.

During the early part of 1785, Madison distributed his famous *Memorial and Remonstrance,* setting forth his cogent defense of freedom of conscience.[15] He asked:

> Who does not see that the same authority which can establish Christianity, in exclusion of all other religions, may establish with the same ease any particular sect of Christians in exclusion of all other sects? That the same authority which can force a citizen to contribute three pence only of his property for the support of only one establishment, may force him to conform to any other establishment in all cases whatsoever?

He continued:

> What influences, in fact, have ecclesiastical establishments had on civil society? In some instances they have been seen to erect a spiritual tyranny on the ruins of civil authority; in many instances they have been seen upholding the thrones of political tyranny; in no instance have they been seen the guardians of the liberties

---

[13] "A Bill for Establishing a Provision for Teachers of the Christian Religion," in Stokes & Pfeffer, *Op. Cit.*, p. 69.   [14] *Ibid.*, p 69.

[15] *Ibid.*, p. 55-60; because of the power of his arguments a copy of the full text is attached as additional reading.

of the people. Rulers who wished to subvert the public liberty may have found an established clergy convenient auxiliaries. A just government, instituted to secure and perpetuate it, needs them not. Such a government will be best supported by protecting every citizen in the enjoyment of his religion with the same equal hand that protects his person and property; neither invading the equal rights of any sect, nor suffering any sect to invade those of another.

In this early document, Madison clearly sets forth the need for a secular state in a pluralistic society. He opposed this bill for the support of the Christian religion or a plural establishment:

Because it will destroy the moderation and harmony which the forbearance of our laws to intermeddle with religion has produced among its several sects. Torrents of blood have been spilt in the world in vain attempts of the secular arm to extinguish religious discord, by proscribing all differences in religious opinions. Time, at length, has revealed the true remedy. Every relaxation of narrow and rigorous policy, wherever it has been tried, has been found to assuage the disease. The American theatre has exhibited proofs, that equal and complete liberty, if it does not wholly eradicate it, sufficiently destroys its malignant influence on the health and prosperity of the state.

He opposed the bill as a violation of their basic law, the Declaration of Rights, passed just nine years earlier:

Because, finally, the equal right of every citizen to the free exercise of his religion, according to the dictates of conscience, is held by the same tenure with all other rights...Either, then, we must say that the will of the legislature is the only measure of their authority, and that, in the plenitude of this authority, they may sweep away all our fundamental rights; or, that they are bound to leave this particular right untouched and sacred: either we must say that they may control the freedom of the press, may abolish the trial by jury, may swallow up the executive and judiciary powers of the state; nay, that they may despoil us of our right of suffrage, and erect themselves into an independent and hereditary assembly: or, we must say that they have no authority to enact into law the bill under consideration.

Madison and other subscribers to this Remonstrance concluded: "...that the general assembly of this commonwealth have no such authority...."

The argument was persuasive. When the General Assembly met in the fall, it received more than a hundred petitions on religion. Only eleven supported the general-assessment plan; many others, with some 11,000 signatures, were copies of the *Memorial and Remonstrance*. Moreover, the Presbyterians, after further reflection, returned to the freedom coalition. Support for a plural establishment had virtually disappeared....[16]

In October 1785, the Assessment Bill was defeated.

Flushed with victory, Madison then called up Jefferson's bill to end the establishment in Virginia. (Jefferson was in Paris at the time, serving as Minis-

---

[16] Merrill D. Peterson, "Jefferson and Religious Freedom," *The Atlantic Monthly*, December, 1994, p. 113.

ter to France.) The great statute declares:

> ...that to compel a man to furnish contributions of money for the propagation of opinions which he disbelieves, is sinful and tyrannical; that even forcing him to support this or that teacher of his own religious persuasion, is depriving him of the comfortable liberty of giving his contributions to the particular pastor whose morals he would make his pattern,...that our civil rights have no dependence on our religious opinions, more than our opinions in physics or geometry; that, therefore the proscribing any citizen as unworthy the public confidence by laying upon him an incapacity of being called to the offices of trust and emolument, unless he profess or renounce this or that religious opinion, is depriving him injuriously of those privileges and advantages to which in common with his fellow citizens he has a natural right;...BE IT THEREFORE ENACTED by the General Assembly that no man shall be compelled to frequent or support any religious worship, place or ministry whatsoever, nor shall be enforced, restrained, molested, or burthened in his body or goods, nor shall otherwise suffer on account of his religious opinions or belief; but that all men shall be free to profess, and by argument to maintain, their opinions in matters of religion, and that the same shall in nowise diminish, enlarge, or affect their civil capacities...."[17]

The Virginia Statute of Religious Freedom was adopted in December, 1785 and signed into law in January, 1786.

> The statute laid the foundation for the unique American tradition of Church-State relations. A few words should be said about some of the most common misconceptions about Jefferson and the statute. To address perhaps the most common fallacy: it is often maintained that nothing in the statute was meant to exclude governmental intrusion in matters of religion as long as the intrusion is on a neutral or non-preferential basis. But that approach is precisely what was rejected in Virginia. And in the statute, after saying it is "sinful and tyrannical" to compel a person to support opinions he does not share, Jefferson went on to declare that even "forcing him to support this or that teacher of his own religious persuasion" is wrong. Present-day neoconservatives and spokesmen for the religious right argue, for essentially political reasons, that a common religion is the necessary glue of the nation, that we began as a Christian people, and that however pluralist we may have become, the survival of the republic rests upon the foundation of Christian or perhaps Judeo-Christian belief. God forbid, they say that the government should regulate our economic behavior, but it ought to regulate moral and religious belief. Again, the whole thrust of Jefferson's philosophy was to reject that position, to reject any idea that a shared community of religious beliefs or of moral values, other than the value of freedom itself, was necessary to society. He sought to raise the republic on the inalienable rights of man, allowing every citizen sovereignty over his own mind and conscience.[18]

Eventually, all the new states would follow Virginia's example. South Carolina abandoned its experiment with a plural establishment in 1790. Con-

---

[17] *The Virginia Statute of Religious Freedom*, in Stokes & Pfeffer, *Op Cit.*, pp. 69-71. A full copy of the statute is attached as additional reading.

[18] Peterson, *Op. Cit.*, p. 122.

necticut terminated tax support for parish churches with its constitution in 1818. Finally, Massachusetts, the original Puritan commonwealth and the home of orthodox Congregationalism, expunged the last vestige of state-supported religion from the United States in 1833.

15. THE CONSTITUTIONAL PERIOD

a. *The Constitutional Convention*

A year and a half after the adoption of the Virginia Statute of Religious Freedom, during the summer of 1787, the Federal Constitution Convention rejected Madison's plea for a federal bill of rights. The delegates believed it either unnecessary or a matter for each state. However, Article VI, Section 3 of the new Constitution did provide that "...no religious Test shall ever be required as a Qualification to any Office or public Trust under the United States." It should be remembered that the Federal Constitution created a government of limited and specifically delegated powers.

"The Constitution," wrote the historian Charles A. Beard, "does not confer upon the federal government any power whatever to deal with religion in any form or manner." James Madison called it "a bill of powers"; he said that "the powers are enumerated and it follows that all that are not granted by the Constitution are retained" by the people. Richard Dobbs Spaight, a delegate from North Carolina to the Constitutional Convention, said about religion: "No power is given to the general government to interfere with it at all. Any act of Congress on this subject would be a usurpation."[19]

During the debate over ratification, the Congregational ministers of New England railed against the proposed Constitution since it did not recognize the existence of God. In fact, nowhere in the document is God mentioned except that it concludes: "Done in Convention by the Unanimous Consent of the States present the Seventeenth Day of September in the Year of Our Lord one thousand seven hundred and Eighty seven and of the Independence of the United States of America the Twelfth."

b. *The First Amendment*

Several of the state conventions, convened to ratify the proposed Constitution, made it clear that they wanted a federal bill of rights. True to this call, James Madison, now a congressman from Virginia, introduced on June 8, 1789, to the First Congress, a series of amendments including the following:

The civil rights of none shall be abridged on account of religious belief or worship, nor shall any national religion be established, nor shall the full and equal rights of conscience be in any manner, or on any pretext, infringed. No State shall violate the equal rights of conscience, or the freedom of the press, or the

---

[19] Swomley, *Op. Cit.*, p. 35.

trial by jury in criminal cases.

During the debate, individual religious liberty was never an issue; rather, the debate focused on the language that would most accurately reflect the intent of the Congress to protect individual freedom of conscience and not merely the freedom of religious sects. However, there was discussion over the nature of establishment.

> By the end of the eighteenth century, the colonial establishments described earlier had changed. None of them was any longer the establishment of a single religious group. No longer was the Anglican Church, the Congregational Church, or any other religious group exclusively established anywhere. As a result of many of the factors described earlier, especially pluralism, all the establishments had become "multiple establishments." By the time the Bill of Rights was ratified in 1791, only six states had any sort of establishment. Of those, three gave government support to Protestantism and three to Christianity—none to a specific denomination...

> ...Thus multiple establishment was the pattern at the time the First Congress was debating the language of the religion provisions of the Bill of Rights.

> Some of the proposals presupposed this multiple-establishment arrangement and wanted to preserve it by prohibiting the government from giving its favor and support to only one denomination. This is known as the "non-preferential" view of establishment: establishment is permitted so long as it is nondiscriminatory, showing no preference between religions. This view is also known as the "accommodationist" approach; the proper relationship between church and state is for the state to accommodate the church.[20]

There were two proposals submitted in the Senate that would have supported this non-preferential view of establishment. One stated that "Congress shall make no law establishing one religious sect or society in preference to others"; the other would require that "Congress shall not make any law infringing the rights of conscience, or establishing any religious sect or society." This view was considered and rejected in favor of what has been described as the separationist or no aid approach. The prevailing view was that religion was wholly exempt from the cognizance of government. Samuel Livermore, congressman from New Hampshire, proposed that "Congress shall make no laws touching religion, or infringing the rights of conscience." His formula would eventually be incorporated into the First Amendment.

In September, 1789, Congress submitted twelve amendments to the Constitution to the several states for their approval. On December 15, 1791, Virginia became the eleventh State to ratify ten of these twelve amendments and this Bill of Rights became a part of our basic law. The very first of these rights contained in the very First Amendment sets forth each individual's constitutionally protected natural right to freedom of conscience with these simple, and majestic words: "Congress shall make no law respecting an establishment

---

[20] Flowers, *Op. Cit.*, p. 17.

of religion, or prohibiting the free exercise thereof;..."

c. Separation of Church and State

In 1802, Thomas Jefferson, then President of the United States, wrote to a committee of Baptists in Connecticut, stating:

> ...Believing with you that religion is a matter which lies solely between man and his God, that he owes account to none other for his faith or his worship, that the legislative powers of government reach actions only, and not opinions, I contemplate with sovereign reverence that act of the whole American people which declared that their legislature should "make no law respecting an establishment of religion, or prohibiting the free exercise thereof," thus building a wall of separation between Church and State.[21]

Thus the commonly held opinion before the American Revolution that civil government could not stand without the prop of a religious establishment, and that the Christian religion would perish if not supported, had been repudiated and replaced by a great new truth.

In 1868, the Fourteenth Amendment was adopted, which provides (in part) that no State shall "...deprive any person of life, liberty, or property, without due process of law;..." In a series of cases beginning in the 1920s, the United States Supreme Court has held that the federal Bill of Rights has been incorporated into the Fourteenth Amendment and has therefore applied these liberties and restrictions to the several states.[22] Today it is clear that, by virtue of the First and Fourteenth Amendments, no state may favor or disparage any religion or interfere with any individual's freedom of conscience.

d. The Great Seal of the United States

Perhaps no other symbol expresses the values of our founding fathers as eloquently as The Great Seal of the United States, found on the back of every dollar bill.[23] Its pictorial vocabulary is little understood today. The face of the Great Seal portrays our national bird, the American bald eagle, holding thirteen arrows—the symbol of war—in one talon and a laurel spray with thirteen leaves—the symbol of peace—in the other. The eagle faces toward peace. In its beak, it holds a banner proclaiming "E pluribus unum"—"One out of many." This refers to the formation of our one nation out of thirteen original colonies. It also alludes to the creation of one pluralistic society out of many peoples from many different lands with many diverse cultures and religious beliefs.

The reverse side of the Great Seal depicts a pyramid with thirteen courses bearing the date 1776 in Latin numerals—MDCCLXXVI—inscribed

---

[21] Stokes & Pfeffer, *Op. Cit.*, p. 53.   [22] *Cantwell v. Connecticut*, 98 U.S. 145, (1940).

[23] See: Joseph Campbell, *The Inner Reaches of Outer Space* (Harper & Row, New York, 1986), pp. 124-9.

Great Seal of the United States

on its foundation. The pyramid represents our newly created nation. At the top of the pyramid is the eye of God—probably the Deist god of nature. Above the pyramid is the inscription "Annuit Coeptis"—"He or It (God or the Eye) has smiled on our undertaking..." (which is adapted from Virgil's *Aeneid*, IX. 625).[24] But what does He smile upon? Below the pyramid another banner proclaims the answer. "Novus Ordo Seclorum"—"A New Secular World Order."

Summary

Freedom of religion and conscience forbids government from requiring what any citizen thinks or believes on any subject. Government may only regulate one's actions and then only where a substantial governmental interest is involved. It may regulate on matters concerning "this world," to promote peace and justice for the commonweal. American ethics is secular since the intent and purpose of its obligations, like those of government, are to promote the good of the community, here and now.

The road from orthodoxy to freedom of religion and conscience was a long and arduous journey that began with Roger Williams in Rhode Island and George Mason, Thomas Jefferson, and James Madison in Virginia. It culminated with the adoption of the First Amendment which requires that "Congress shall make no law respecting an establishment of religion, or prohibiting the free exercise thereof..." That great victory over intolerance was memorialized in the Great Seal of the United States that proclaims our new nation as "A New Secular World Order."

Thomas Jefferson declared that the legislative powers "... of government reach actions only and not opinions..." and hailed the "...wall of separation between Church and State."

Our Personal Obligation:

Tolerance

We impose upon government the duty not to discriminate against any person because of religious affiliation, beliefs, or conscientiously held opinions or convictions. Each of us should gladly accept that duty as our personal obligation to all others in our diverse and pluralistic society. We have an obligation of mutual forbearance in our treatment of others because of their religion or beliefs of conscience. We must be willing to be patient with those with whom we disagree. We must withhold our anger and fear of the stranger, the foreigner, the non-believer, and be willing to live and let live. We need not agree with them; we need not even respect them. However, we must do what we demand of our government; we must never abuse, threaten, intimidate, harass or ridicule another because of religion or opinions of conscience—even as

---

[24] *Ibid.*, p. 125.

we expect the same forbearance from all others. How many times have we bragged, "I can think whatever I want! It's a free country!" Our obligation is to make that boast real for all.

We must never demean the Catholic nun or the Rabbi or the Sunni Muslim or the Hindu or the Buddhist monk for religious garb or long hair. As citizens, we must be neutral in matters of religion and belief and never deny equal employment opportunity, housing, or education to the Jew or the Arab in a Christian business or neighborhood or public school. "...[N]o private person has any right in any manner to prejudice another person in his civil enjoyments because he is of another church or religion. All the rights and franchises that belong to him as a man, or as a denizen, are inviolably to be preserved to him. These are not the business of religion. No violence nor injury is to be offered him, whether he be Christian or Pagan. Nay, we must not content ourselves with the narrow measures of bare justice; charity, bounty, and liberality must be added to it...."[25]

Especially when our religion or opinion constitutes the political majority in the community, we must never allow our enthusiasm to witness, save souls, or convert the unbeliever to our cause, to become so zealous that we would seek to impose our religious values on the minority either through the power of the government or the pressure of society. And finally, as a political majority we have a particular obligation to never seek to have government do what we know it is forbidden to do—pay for our churches, synagogues, temples, schools or the salaries of the clergy or the teachers of religion—directly or indirectly. That is the heart and soul of the establishment of religion.

It is our commitment to religious tolerance and freedom of conscience that has welded America into a strong nation of one people out of many cultures and religions. Our high personal obligation, then, is to be tolerant to all except the intolerant.

OUR PERSONAL VIRTUE:

Sanctuary

The ancient meaning of sanctuary was to give a safe haven within the church sanctuary for a person fleeing justice to allow him or her time to repent his or her crimes. I mean much more than that. I mean that sanctuary demands tolerance for all and that the virtuous citizen will seek to protect the religious freedom of others. I intend sanctuary to be a shield for the innocent victims of racial or religious persecution.

The virtuous citizen would have hidden the Jew, the Catholic dissenter, the Pole, the Czechoslovakian and the downed pilot from the Nazis during the Second World War. The virtuous citizen will protect the black man from the

---

[25] John Locke, *A Letter Concerning Toleration*, in Hutchins, ed., *Op. Cit.*, p. 6.

Ku Klux Klan and the Neo-Nazis. The virtuous citizen will speak out against the persecution of human beings who are homosexual or Muslim or atheist. The virtuous citizen will extend the hand of friendship and make a place at the table for the homeless, the hungry and the despised minority. You need not agree with or even like the person you protect; in fact, the more you disagree or dislike the person you stand up for, the more virtuous the act.

This is a hard virtue to practice since it takes a great deal of courage to stand up to intolerance by your peers. It requires prudence to know when and how to shield the enemies that society creates. It calls for self confidence to demand equal justice and tolerance for those whom society despises. Needless to say, the virtuous citizen will never demonize other human beings but will seek to live in harmony with all.

ADDITIONAL READINGS

To the Honorable the General Assembly
of the Commonwealth of Virginia

A Memorial and Remonstrance
Against Religious Assessments (1785)[26]
by James Madison

We, the subscribers, citizens of the said Commonwealth, having taken into serious consideration, a Bill printed by order of the last Session of General Assembly, entitled "A Bill establishing a provision for Teachers of the Christian Religion" and conceiving that the same, if finally armed with the sanctions of a law, will be a dangerous abuse of power, are bound as faithful members of a free State, to remonstrate against it, and to declare the reasons by which we are determined. We remonstrate against the said Bill,

1. Because we hold it for a fundamental and undeniable truth, "that Religion or the duty which we owe to our Creator and the Manner of discharging it, can be directed only by reason and conviction, not by force or violence." The Religion then of every man must be left to the conviction and conscience of every man; and it is the right of every man to exercise it as these may dictate. This right is in its nature an unalienable right. It is unalienable; because the opinion, of men, depending only on the evidence contemplated by their own minds, cannot follow the dictates of other men: It is unalienable also; because what is here a right towards men, is a duty towards the Creator. It is the duty of every man to render to the Creator such homage, and such only, as he believes to be

---

[26] Stokes & Pfeffer, *Op. Cit.*, pp. 55-60.

acceptable to him. This duty is precedent both in order of time and degree of obligation, to the claims of Civil society. Before any man can be considered as a member of Civil Society, he must be considered as a subject of the Governor of the Universe: And if a member of Civil society, who enters into any subordinate Association, must always do it with a reservation of his duty to the general authority; much more must every man who becomes a member of any particular Civil Society, do it with a saving of his allegiance to the Universal Sovereign. We maintain therefore that in matters of Religion, no man's right is abridged by the institution of Civil Society, and that Religion is wholly exempt from its cognizance. True it is, that no other rule exists, by which any question which may divide a Society, can be ultimately determined, but the will of the majority; but it is also true, that the majority may trespass on the rights of the minority,

2. Because if religion be exempt from the authority of the Society at large, still less can it be subject to that of the Legislative Body. The latter are but the creatures and vicegerents of the former. Their jurisdiction is both derivative and limited: it is limited with regard to the coordinate departments, more necessarily is it limited with regard to the constituents. The preservation of a free government requires not merely, that the metes and bounds which separate each department of power may be invariably maintained; but more especially, that neither of them be suffered to overleap the great Barrier which defends the right of the people. The Rulers who are guilty of such an encroachment, exceed the commission from which they derive their authority, and are Tyrants. The People who submit to it are governed by laws made neither by themselves, nor by an authority derived from them, and are slaves.

3. Because, it is proper to take alarm at the first experiment on our liberties. We hold this prudent jealousy to be the first duty of citizens, and one of [the] noblest characteristics of the late Revolution. The freemen of America did not wait till usurped power had strengthened itself by exercise, and precedents. They saw all the consequences in the principle, and they avoided the consequences by denying the principle. We revere this lesson too much, soon to forget it. Who does not see that the same authority which can establish Christianity, in exclusion of all other Religions, may establish with the same ease any particular sect of Christians in exclusion of all other Sects? That the same authority which can force a citizen to contribute three pence only of his property for the support of any one establishment, may force him to conform to any other establishment in all cases whatsoever?

4. Because, the bill violates that equality which ought to be the basis of every law, and which is more indispensable, in proportion as the validity or expediency of any law is more liable to be impeached. If "all men are by nature equally free and independent," all men are to be considered as entering into society on equal conditions; as relinquishing no more, and therefore retaining no less, one than another, of their natural rights. Above all are they to be con-

sidered as retaining an "equal title to the free exercise of Religion according to the dictates of conscience." Whilst we assert for ourselves a freedom to embrace, to profess and to observe the Religion which we believe to be of divine origin, we cannot deny an equal freedom to those whose minds have not yet yielded to the evidence which has convinced us. If this freedom be abused, it is an offence against God, not against man: To God, therefore, not to men, must an account of it be rendered. As the Bill violates equality by subjecting some to peculiar burdens; so it violates the same principle, by granting to others peculiar exemptions. Are the Quakers and Menonists the only sects who think a compulsive support of their religions unnecessary and unwarrantable? Can their piety alone be intrusted with the care of public worship? Ought their Religions to be endowed above all others, with extraordinary privileges, by which proselytes may be enticed from all others? We think too favorably of the justice and good sense of these denominations, to believe that they either covet preeminencies over their fellow citizens, or that they will be seduced by them, from the common opposition to the measure.

5. Because the bill implies either that the Civil Magistrate is a competent Judge of Religious truth; or that he may employ Religion as an engine of Civil Policy. The first is an arrogant pretension falsified by the contradictory opinions of Rulers in all ages, and throughout the world: The second an unhallowed perversion of the means of salvation.

6. Because the establishment proposed by the Bill is not requisite for the support of the Christian Religion. To say that it is, is a contradiction to the Christian Religion itself; for every page of it disavows a dependence on the powers of this world: it is a contradiction to fact; for it is known that this Religion both existed and flourished, not only without the support of human laws, but in spite of every opposition from them; and not only during the period of miraculous aid, but long after it had been left to its own evidence, and the ordinary care of Providence: Nay, it is a contradiction in terms; for a Religion not invented by human policy, must have pre-existed and been supported, before it was established by human policy. It is moreover to weaken in those who profess this Religion a pious confidence in its innate excellence, and the patronage of its Author; and to foster in those who still reject it, a suspicion that its friends are too conscious of its fallacies, to trust it to its own merits.

7. Because experience witnesseth that ecclesiastical establishments, instead of maintaining the purity and efficacy of Religion, have had a contrary operation. During almost fifteen centuries, has the legal establishment of Christianity been on trial. What have been its fruits? More or less in all places, pride and indolence in the Clergy; ignorance and servility in the laity; in both, superstition, bigotry and persecution. Enquire of the Teachers of Christianity for the ages in which it appeared in its greatest lustre; those of every sect, point to the ages prior to its incorporation with Civil policy. Propose a restoration of this primitive state in which its Teachers depended on the voluntary rewards of their

flocks; many of them predict its downfall. On which side ought their testimony to have greatest weight, when for or when against their interest?

8. Because the establishment in question is not necessary for the support of Civil Government. If it be urged as necessary for the support of Civil Government only as it is a means of supporting Religion, and it be not necessary for the latter purpose, it cannot be necessary for the former. If Religion be not within [the] cognizance of Civil Government, how can its legal establishment be said to be necessary to Civil Government? What influence in fact have ecclesiastical establishments had on Civil Society? In some instances they have been seen to erect a spiritual tyranny on the ruins of Civil authority; in many instances they have been seen upholding the thrones of political tyranny; in no instance have they been seen the guardians of the liberties of the people. Rulers who wished to subvert the public liberty, may have found an established clergy convenient auxiliaries. A just government, instituted to secure and perpetuate it, needs them not. Such a government will be best supported by protecting every citizen in the enjoyment of his Religion with the same equal hand which protects his person and his property; by neither invading the equal rights of any Sect, nor suffering any Sect to invade those of another.

9. Because the proposed establishment is a departure from that generous policy, which, offering an asylum to the persecuted and oppressed of every Nation and Religion, promised a lustre to our country, and an accession to the number of its citizens. What a melancholy mark is the Bill of sudden degeneracy? Instead of holding forth an asylum to the persecuted, it is itself a signal of persecution. It degrades from the equal rank of Citizens all those whose opinions in Religion do not bend to those of the Legislative authority. Distant as it may be, in its present form, from the Inquisition it differs from it only in degree. The one is the first step, the other the last in the career of intolerance. The magnanimous sufferer under this cruel scourge in foreign Regions, must view the Bill as a Beacon on our Coast, warning him to seek some other haven, where liberty and philanthropy in their due extent may offer a more certain repose from his troubles.

10. Because, it will have a like tendency to banish our Citizens. The allurements presented by other situations are every day thinning their number. To superadd a fresh motive to emigration, by revoking the liberty which they now enjoy, would be the same species of folly which has dishonored and depopulated flourishing kingdoms.

11. Because, it will destroy that moderation and harmony which the forbearance of our laws to intermeddle with Religion, has produced amongst its several sects. Torrents of blood have been spilt in the old world by vain attempts of the secular arm to extinguish Religious discord by proscribing all difference in Religious opinions. Time has at length revealed the true remedy. Every relaxation of narrow and rigorous policy, wherever it has been tried, has been found to assuage the disease. The American Theatre has exhibited proofs,

that equal and compleat liberty, if it does not wholly eradicate it, sufficiently destroys its malignant influence on the health and prosperity of the State. If with the salutary effects of this system under our own eyes, we begin to contract the bonds of Religious freedom, we know no name that will too severely reproach our folly. At least let warning be taken at the first fruits of the threatened innovation. The very appearance of the Bill has transformed that "Christian forbearance, love and charity," which of late mutually prevailed, into animosities and jealousies, which may not soon be appeased. What mischiefs may not be dreaded should this enemy to the public quiet be armed with the force of a law?

12. Because, the policy of the bill is adverse to the diffusion of the light of Christianity. The first wish of those who enjoy this precious gift, ought to be that it may be imparted to the whole race of mankind. Compare the number of those who have as yet received it with the number still remaining under the dominion of false Religions; and how small is the former! Does the policy of the Bill tend to lessen the disproportion? No; it at once discourages those who are strangers to the light of [revelation] from coming into the Region of it; and countenances, by example the nations who continue in darkness in shutting out those who might convey it to them. Instead of levelling as far as possible, every obstacle to the victorious progress of truth, the Bill with an ignoble and unchristian timidity would circumscribe it, with a wall of defence, against the encroachments of error.

13. Because attempts to enforce by legal sanctions, acts obnoxious to so great a proportion of Citizens, tend to enervate the laws in general, and to slacken the bands of Society. If it be difficult to execute any law which is not generally deemed necessary or salutary, what must be the case where it is deemed invalid and dangerous? and what may be the effect of so striking an example of impotency in the Government, on its general authority?

14. Because a measure of such singular magnitude and delicacy ought not to be imposed, without the clearest evidence that it is called for by a majority of citizens: and no satisfactory method is yet proposed by which the voice of the majority in this case may be determined, or its influence secured. "The people of the respective counties are indeed requested to signify their opinion respecting the adoption of the Bill to the next session of Assembly." But the representation must be made equal, before the voice either of the Representatives or of the Counties, will be that of the people. Our hope is that neither of the former will, after due consideration espouse the dangerous principle of the Bill. Should the event disappoint us, it will still leave us in full confidence, that a fair appeal to the latter will reverse the sentence against our liberties.

15. Because, finally, "the equal right of every citizen to the free exercise of his Religion according to the dictates of conscience" is held by the same tenure with all our other rights. If we recur to its origin, it is equally the gift of nature; if we weigh its importance, it cannot be less dear to us; if we consult the Decla-

ration of those rights which pertain to the good people of Virginia, as the "basis and foundation of Government," it is enumerated with equal solemnity, or rather studied emphasis.   Either then, we must say, that the will of the Legislature is the only measure of their authority; and that in the plentitude of this authority, they may sweep away all other fundamental rights; or, that they are bound to leave this particular right untouched and sacred: Either we must say, that they may control the freedom of the press, may abolish the trial by jury, may swallow up the Executive and Judiciary Powers of the State; nay that they may despoil us of our very right of suffrage, and erect themselves into an independent and hereditary assembly: or we must say that they have no authority to enact into law the Bill under consideration. We the subscribers say, that the General Assembly of this Commonwealth have no such authority: And that no effort may be omitted on our part against so dangerous an usurpation, we oppose to it, this remonstrance; earnestly praying, as we are in duty bound, that the Supreme Lawgiver of the Universe, by illuminating those to whom it is addressed, may on the one hand, turn their councils from every act which would affront his holy prerogative, or violate the trust committed to them: and on the other, guide them into every measure which may be worthy of his blessing, may redound to their own praise, and may establish more firmly the liberties, the prosperity, and the Happiness of the Commonwealth.

An Act for Establishing Religious Freedom[27]
Passed in the Assembly of Virginia
in the Beginning of the Year 1786
sponsored by Thomas Jefferson

Well aware that Almighty God hath created the mind free; that all attempts to influence it by temporal punishments or burdens, or by civil incapacities, tend only to beget habits of hypocrisy and meanness, and are a departure from the plan of the Holy Author of our religion, who being Lord both of body and mind, yet chose not to propagate it by coercions on either, as was in his Almighty power to do; that the impious presumption of legislators and rulers, civil as well as ecclesiastical, who, being themselves but fallible and uninspired men have assumed dominion over the faith of others, setting up their own opinions and modes of thinking as the only true and infallible, and as such endeavoring to impose them on others, hath established and maintained religions over the greatest part of the world, and through all time; that to compel a man to furnish contributions of money for the propagation of opinions which he disbelieves, is sinful and tyrannical; that even the forcing him to support this or that teacher of his own religious persuasion, is depriving him of the comfortable liberty of

---

[27] Stokes & Pfeffer, *Op. Cit.*, p. 69-71.

giving his contributions to the particular pastor whose morals he would make his pattern, and whose powers he feels most persuasive to righteousness, and is withdrawing from the ministry those temporal rewards, which proceeding from an approbation of their personal conduct, are an additional incitement to earnest and unremitting labors for the instruction of mankind; that our civil rights have no dependence on our religious opinions, more than our opinions in physics or geometry; that, therefore, the proscribing any citizen as unworthy the public confidence by laying upon him an incapacity of being called to the offices of trust and emolument, unless he profess or renounce this or that religious opinion, is depriving him injuriously of those privileges and advantages to which in common with his fellow citizens he has a natural right; that it tends also to corrupt the principles of that very religion it is meant to encourage, by bribing, with a monopoly of worldly honors and emoluments, those who will externally profess and conform to it; that though indeed these are criminal who do not withstand such temptation, yet neither are those innocent who lay the bait in their way; that to suffer the civil magistrate to intrude his powers into the field of opinion and to restrain the profession or propagation of principles, on the supposition of their ill tendency, is a dangerous fallacy, which at once destroys all religious liberty, because he being of course judge of that tendency, will make his opinions the rule of judgment, and approve or condemn the sentiments of others only as they shall square with or differ from his own; that it is time enough for the rightful purposes of civil government, for its offices to interfere when principles break out into overt acts against peace and good order; and finally, that truth is great and will prevail if left to herself, that she is the proper and sufficient antagonist to error, and has nothing to fear from the conflict, unless by human interposition disarmed of her natural weapons, free argument and debate, errors ceasing to be dangerous when it is permitted freely to contradict there.

Be it therefore enacted by the General Assembly, That no man shall be compelled to frequent or support any religious worship, place or ministry whatsoever, nor shall be enforced, restrained, molested, or burthened in his body or goods, nor shall otherwise suffer on account of his religious opinions or belief; but that all men shall be free to profess, and by argument to maintain, their opinions in matters of religion, and that the same shall in nowise diminish, enlarge, or affect their civil capacities.

And though we well know this Assembly, elected by the people for the ordinary purposes of legislation only, have no power to restrain the acts of succeeding assemblies, constituted with the powers equal to our own, and that therefore to declare this act irrevocable, would be of no effect in law, yet we are free to declare, and do declare, that the rights hereby asserted are of the natural rights of mankind, and that if any act shall be hereafter passed to repeal the present or to narrow its operation, such act will be an infringement of natural right.

LANDMARK CASE #6

Wallace v. Jaffree

472 US 38, 86 L Ed 2d 29, 105 S Ct 2479 (1987)

In 1987, the United States Supreme Court was asked whether an Alabama statute that authorized public school teachers to lead "willing students" in a prescribed prayer to "Almighty God... the Creator and Supreme Judge of the world...," was a violation of the First Amendment. In Wallace v. Jaffree, *Mr. Justice Rehnquist, in a dissenting opinion, stated that:*

It would seem from this evidence that the Establishment Clause of the First Amendment had acquired a well-accepted meaning: it forbade establishment of a national religion, and forbade preference among religious sects or denominations...The Establishment Clause did not require government neutrality between religion and irreligion nor did it prohibit the Federal Government from providing nondiscriminatory aid to religion. There is simply no historical foundation for the proposition that the Framers intended to build the "wall of separation" that was constitutionalized in Everson....

But the greatest injury of the "wall" notion is its mischievous diversion of judges from the actual intentions of the drafters of the Bill of Rights. [The Court] is well adapted to adjudicating factual disputes on the basis of testimony presented in court, but no amount of repetition of historical errors in judicial opinions can make the errors true. The "wall of separation between church and State" is a metaphor based on bad history, a metaphor which has proved useless as a guide to judging. It should be frankly and explicitly abandoned....

The State surely has a secular interest in regulating the manner in which public schools are conducted. Nothing in the Establishment Clause of the First Amendment, properly understood, prohibits any such generalized "endorsement" of prayer.

The Supreme Court majority rejected the assertion that the "wall of separation" is "bad history" and again emphasized the neutrality of the government in religious matters; it declared the school prayer statute unconstitutional and concluded that:

Just as the right to speak and the right to refrain from speaking are complementary components of a broader concept of individual freedom of mind, so also the individual's freedom to choose his own creed is the counterpart of his right to refrain from accepting the creed established by the majority. At one time it was thought that this right merely proscribed the preference of one Christian sect over another, but would not require equal respect for the conscience of the infidel, the atheist, or the adherent of a non-Christian faith such as Islam or Judaism. But when the underlying principle has been examined in the crucible of litigation, the Court has unambiguously concluded that the individual freedom of conscience protected by the First Amendment embraces the right to select any religious faith or none at all. This conclusion derives support not only from the interest in respecting the individual's freedom of conscience, but also from the conviction that religious beliefs worthy of respect are the product of free and voluntary choice by the faithful, and from recognition of the fact that the political interest in forestalling intolerance extends beyond intolerance among Christian sects—or even intolerance among "religions"—to encompass intolerance of the disbeliever and the uncertain.

CHAPTER VI

Public Morality and The Right of Privacy

...the very idea that one man may be compelled to hold his life, or the means of living, or any material right essential to the enjoyment of life, at the mere will of another, seems to be intolerable in any country where freedom prevails, as being the essence of slavery itself......
—*Mr. Justice Matthews,* Yick Wo v. Hopkins

In 1880 the City of San Francisco adopted an ordinance forbidding anyone to maintain a laundry in a wooden building without obtaining a license from the board of supervisors. The law conferred upon the supervisors, "...not a discretion to be exercised upon a consideration of the circumstances of each case, but a naked and arbitrary power to give or withhold consent, not only as to places, but as to persons."[1] Over two hundred Chinese applied to continue their businesses. All Chinese applicants were denied; most white applicants were approved. The Chinese sued claiming that they were denied "equal protection of the law."

16. ESTABLISHING PUBLIC MORALITY

a. The Rule of Law

There are no rights that can be protected without rules or laws defining and enforcing our basic duties, our political and social obligations, to each other. In its infancy, human society consisted of small clans or bands that hunted and gathered together and were dominated by the strongest chieftain among them. His will was law and your life could be taken at his whim. In the historical movie *Shaka Zulu*, depicting human society in nineteenth century Africa, the chief asks his British visitors, "Who owns life?" And to prove that, in his tribe, it is he, the chief, who owns the lives of the people, he executes a woman, whom the British doctor had just nursed back to good health, who had done no

---

[1] *Yick Wo v. Hopkins*, 118, U.S. 356; 30 L Ed 220 at 225.

139

wrong, in front of them. Examples abound throughout British history to demonstrate that the kings treated their subjects with arbitrary ruthlessness and murdered innocent victims. For example, and again referring to an historical movie, *Braveheart,* Edward I brutally and arbitrarily murdered whole villages in Scotland, without any color of lawful authority, merely to subdue them.

The history of our federal and state governments, even with our Bill of Rights and an independent judiciary to enforce those rights, exposes arbitrary treatment of some of our people. For example, we tolerated the arbitrary execution of slaves and the lynching of black people even after the prohibition of slavery. The federal government conducted the Tuskegee experiments in the 1930s, injecting black soldiers with syphilis to test the effects of that disease. Our federal government was guilty of the genocide of the Native American after the Civil War. The state of Pennsylvania executed 23 Irish Catholic Molly Maguires, who fought back against the oppressors who subjected them to inhuman conditions in the coal mines of western Pennsylvania. It was the largest public hanging of white people in the history of the United States. After the Second World War, the United States Army ordered American soldiers into the test area during atomic bomb test explosions, to determine the effects of radiation on human beings.

In our century, the butchery of Stalin in Russia, Hitler in Europe, the Japanese in Asia, Mao in China, the Khmer Rouge in Cambodia, the atrocities of Pinochet in Chile and Strasser in Paraguay, and most recently the ethnic cleansing of the former Yugoslavia and the tribal massacres in central Africa, all bear witness to the terrible arbitrary actions of governments toward their people.

How do we create a civil society whose leaders do not act in an arbitrary and capricious manner and whose citizens or subjects live in peace with each other? The creation of a civilized society is, in essence, the creation of laws that spell out the duties and rights of each person, laws that create burdens and benefits for each member of that society. The creation of a civilized society (from a political point of view rather than a cultural or technological perspective) is the implementation of the social contract and the development of the rule of law.

These laws must be created for the common good and must be respected by all others and by the society itself—from the king, president or chairman, to the legislature and the courts. This subjection of the will of the strong to the need for social cooperation for the benefit of the commonweal is the establishment of the rule of law. It is the establishment of a society based on laws not men. John Locke taught that:

.....136. Secondly, the legislative or supreme authority cannot assume to itself a power to rule by extemporary arbitrary decrees, but is bound to dispense justice and decide the rights of the subject by promulgating standing laws and known authorized judges....

137...For all the power the government has, being only for the good of the society, as it ought not to be arbitrary and at pleasure, so it ought to be exercised by
established and promulgated laws, that both the people may know their duty, and
be safe and secure within the limits of the law, and the rulers, too, kept within
their due bounds, and not be tempted by the power they have in their hands....[2]

The duty we impose upon society and our leaders is not to be arbitrary
or capricious in its dealings with the people within its jurisdiction. Society and
its leaders may not act:

1. in a criminal or tyrannical manner toward any of their people by com-
    mitting acts of murder, genocide, arrest, imprisonment without
    cause, torture, or other similar conduct that violates fundamental
    human rights;

2. to impose a duty or deny a benefit, without pre-established laws de-
    fining that burden or benefit; the ancient common law rule is that
    there is no offence without a law.[3]

3. to create laws that are substantively unfair;

4. by the arbitrary or capricious application or administration of laws
    that are fair.

But for there to be laws there must be a government to make and enforce those laws. Thomas Jefferson proclaimed in the Declaration of Independence "...That to secure these rights, Governments are instituted among men,
deriving their just power from the consent of the governed...." The establishment of the rule of law is the fundamental mandate of government. The establishment of the rule of law is the mechanism by which the society establishes
the burdens and benefits, duties and rights, for all the members of the society.
The establishment of the rule of law is the means by which we implement the
social contract and define our public morality. The rule of law is what makes
society civilized.

American ethics protects the right of each person to fair and equal treatment
by the government and its officials by requiring that each person be treated with
"due process" of law. In our federal system, the Constitution forbids arbitrary
and capricious conduct by the Federal government. The Fifth Amendment
declares that "No person shall be...deprived of life, liberty or property,
without due process of law;...." And the Fourteenth Amendment continues

---

[2] John Locke, *Concerning Civil Government, Second Essay,* in *Great Books of the Western
World,* Encyclopedia Brittanica, ed. Robert Maynard Hutchins (William Benton, Publisher,
Chicago, 1952), pp. 56-7.

[3] However, under international law, the rule of law will not require specific pre-existing laws before bringing to justice those who control the law-making machinery of their government and
who commit heinous crimes against their people or their neighbors that violate basic human
rights.

"...nor shall any State deprive any person of life, liberty, or property, without due process of law; nor deny to any person within its jurisdiction the equal protection of the laws...." Due process means that laws must pre-exist the conduct complained of and must be specific in describing what is forbidden. Due process means that laws must be fair, that they are made for the common good and not some private interest, and that they burden or benefit all equally. And due process means that fair laws must be fairly and equally administered.

> The framers of the Constitution knew, and we should not forget today, that there is no more effective practical guaranty against arbitrary and unreasonable government than to require that the principles of law which officials would impose upon a minority must be imposed generally. Conversely, nothing opens the door to arbitrary action so effectively as to allow those officials to pick and choose only a few to whom they will apply legislation and thus to escape the political retribution that might be visited upon them if larger numbers were affected. Courts can take no better measure to assure that laws will be just than to require that laws be equal in operation.[4]

The rule of law is the prerequisite for rational people agreeing to cooperate with each other. It is what makes civil society civil. Without the rule of law, society reverts to anarchy and the rule of the strong.

b. The Role of Government

But what rules should we impose? What laws should we enforce? What is the role or purpose of government? When we reduce government to its essential mission, the role or purpose of government is to implement the social contract, define our public ethical values, and enforce our public morality. Ethics provides the rules that we live by; to be moral is to obey those rules.[5] American ethics provides the rules for our public lives to guide the virtuous citizen. Public morality is obedience to those rules made for the public good. The laws that we adopt are those that promote our public morality, the values of American ethics according to our standard of justice, those that provide for the peace and security of our society with equal justice for all. Our private ethical, philosophical or religious values provide the sectarian rules for our private lives; our private morality is obedience to those ethical, philosophical or religious sectarian mandates.

The people, through their elected representatives, define America's public ethical values and enforce our public morality, the morality that binds us

---

[4] Mr. Justice Jackson concurring in *Railway Express Agency v. New York*, 336 US 106, 112-3, 93 L Ed 533, 540, 69 S Ct 463 (1949).

[5] "Moral Law" is defined as "The law of conscience; the aggregate of those rules and principles of ethics which relate to right and wrong conduct and prescribe the standards to which the actions of men should conform in their dealings with each other." *Moore v. Strickling*, 46 W. Va. 515, 33 S.E. 274, 50 L.R.A. 279, *Black's Law Dictionary*.

all, through the power of the legislature, to define what conduct constitutes a crime. In our federal system, the general power to define what conduct is a criminal offense is vested in the legislatures of the several states, although Congress can establish crimes that are "necessary and proper" to the execution of its delegated powers. The police power, as it is called, is the broad, inherent power of the legislature to regulate our conduct to promote the peace, safety, health, education, general welfare, and public morals of the community. ("Public morals" should not be confused with "public morality"—that is, a general obedience to law; here, "public morals" refers to particular laws that enforce our public mores or community standards of decency—such as regulating the sale or use of liquor, forbidding houses of prostitution, or forbidding the sale of child pornography.) The police power rests upon necessity and the right of self-protection.

> ...the state may interfere wherever the public interests demand it and in this particular a large discretion is necessarily vested in the legislature to determine, not only what the interests of the public require, but what measures are necessary for the protection of such interests. To justify the state in thus interposing its authority in behalf of the public, it must appear, first, that the interests of the public generally, as distinguished from those of a particular class, require such interference; and, second, that the means are reasonably necessary for the accomplishment of the purpose, and not unduly oppressive upon individuals.[6]

"...A crime may be defined to be any act done in violation of those duties which an individual owes to the community, and for the breach of which the law has provided that the offender shall make satisfaction to the public...."[7] The legislature may:

> ...enact all laws it may deem expedient for the protection of public and private rights and the preventions and punishment of public wrongs. Thus, the legislature may make acts criminal which were previously innocent and ordain punishment in future cases where before none could have been inflicted. However, the state legislature may not declare an act to be criminal which, by its nature, is and must under all circumstances be innocent. Nor may the legislature, in defining crimes or in declaring the punishment therefor, take away or impair any inalienable right secured by the Constitution;...[8]

Conduct such as murder, assault, rape, theft, arson, and perjury will be readily agreed to be a violation of our ethical values which have a public purpose. Some crimes that prohibit conduct of a more private nature, including adultery, fornication, and sodomy by consenting adults, are still on the books in many states. These are the crimes against public morals and reflect a time when our public morality was imbued with the religious values of the established churches.

---

[6] *Lawton v. Steele*, 152 U.S. 133, 137, 38 L Ed 385, 388. (1894).
[7] *Black's Law Dictionary* (West Publishing Co., St. Paul, MN).
[8] NY Jur. 2nd Criminal Law, Sec. 3340.

Although most governments assert that their law-making authority is plenary or absolute in its scope, governments are not free to make any law they wish on any subject however whimsical. Every federal and state law must be founded on some substantial governmental interest. In recent years, every law adopted by Congress and the state legislatures began with findings of fact that establish some community need, a statement of purpose or intent, and a statement of how this community need will be met by the legislation, in order to establish legislative intent and identify the governmental interest involved. The intent and purpose of all legislation and the governmental interest involved must be secular in nature. The public morality that our government enforces implements our secular ethical values. Freedom of conscience forbids government from establishing laws that mandate any form of ideology or prescribed orthodoxy as public policy. The government cannot tell you what to think or believe on any subject. The government may only regulate your actions, not your beliefs or opinions, and then only when it establishes a substantial governmental interest such as public health, public safety, public welfare, or some other secular community need.

c. Religious Values and Public Morality

> ...[T]hey say that by history and practice of our people we were intended to be—and should be—a Christian country in law.
>
> But where would that leave the nonbelievers? And whose Christianity would be law, yours or mine?
>
> This "Christian nation" argument should concern—even frighten—two groups: non-Christians and thinking Christians.
>
> —Mario Cuomo, Governor of New York
> Speech at the University of Notre Dame
> September 13, 1984

American ethics is based on secular values. How then, do our diverse religious values become a part of our public morality? Mario Cuomo's speech to the Department of Theology at the University of Notre Dame in 1984, at the height of the abortion debate, is perhaps the finest commentary on public morality and political philosophy since Lincoln's speeches opposing slavery during the Lincoln-Douglas debates in 1858. He states with great persuasive power that:

> Almost all Americans accept some religious values as a part of our public life. We are a religious people, many of us descended from ancestors who came here expressly to live their religious faith free from coercion or repression. But we are also a people of many religions, with no established church, who hold different beliefs on many matters.
>
> Our public morality, then—the moral standards we maintain for everyone, not

just the ones we insist on in our private lives—depends on a consensus view of right and wrong. The values derived from religious belief will not—and should not—be accepted as part of the public morality unless they are shared by the pluralistic community at large, by consensus.

That values happen to be religious values does not deny them acceptability as a part of this consensus. But it does not require their acceptability, either.

The agnostics who joined the civil rights struggle were not deterred because that crusade's values had been nurtured and sustained in black Christian churches. Those on the political left are not perturbed today by the religious basis of the clergy and lay people who join them in the protest against the arms race and hunger and exploitation.

The arguments start when religious values are used to support positions which would impose on other people restrictions they find unacceptable. Some people do object to Catholic demands for an end to abortion, seeing it as a violation of the separation of church and state. And some others, while they have no compunction about invoking the authority of the Catholic bishops in regard to birth control and abortion, might reject out of hand their teaching on war and peace and social policy.

Ultimately, therefore, the question whether or not we admit religious values into our public affairs is too broad to yield a single answer. Yes, we create our public morality through consensus and in this country that consensus reflects to some extent religious values of a great majority of Americans. But no, all religiously based values don't have an a priori place in our public morality.

The community must decide if what is being proposed would be better left to private discretion than public policy, whether it restricts freedoms, and if so to what end, to whose benefit, whether it will produce a good or bad result, whether overall it will help the community or merely divide it.[9]

Religious values, by their nature, divide us into sects. What then, will build the consensus of "the pluralistic community at large" necessary to transform religious values into "the moral standards we maintain for everyone..."?

A religious value can become a standard of public morality only if it is secularized. It is only by defining a religious value in terms of the needs of this world that we are able to build the consensus necessary to impose that duty on all in the community. The religious duty to obey God or Allah and obey His commandment "Thou shalt not kill," becomes the secular duty of the virtuous citizen not to kill each other, to promote peace and justice for the commonweal. The duty to care for the poor for the greater honor and glory of God becomes the duty of the virtuous citizen to promote economic justice in this world. Holy days become holidays. Secular values unite us since their purpose is to enhance the common good, the good of all. Secular values are the communitarian

---

[9] Mario Cuomo, *Religious Belief and Public Morality, A Catholic Governor's Perspective*, A Speech delivered in 1984 at Notre Dame, in Mario Cuomo, *More Than Words* (St. Martins Press, New York) pp. 38-9.

values that we share in common, that obligate and benefit us all.

This does not mean that we do not esteem religious values as individuals. We may still do good works to honor God or Allah or because we want to go to heaven or reach Nirvana. But the religious motives and objectives are personal to each individual. Public morality cannot be based on or motivated by strictly religious or sectarian values and objectives. Conduct cannot be criminalized that violates only a religious value but violates no commonly shared communitarian value or objective. The common law maxim is that there is no rule without a fault. Without a consensus regarding a fault there can be no crime.

ADDITIONAL READINGS

Religious Belief and Public Morality
A Catholic Governor's Perspective
September 13, 1984
University of Notre Dame
by Mario Cuomo, Governor of New York

The Catholic church is my spiritual home. My heart is there, and my hope.

There is, of course, more to being a Catholic than a sense of spiritual and emotional resonances. Catholicism is a religion of the head as well as the heart, and to be a Catholic is to say, " I believe," to the essential core of dogmas that distinguishes our faith.

The acceptance of this faith requires a lifelong struggle to understand it more fully and to live it more truly, to translate truth into experience, to practice as well as to believe. That's not easy: applying religious belief to everyday life often presents difficult challenges.

It's always been that way. It certainly is today. The America of the late twentieth century is a consumer society, filled with endless distractions, where faith is more often dismissed than challenged, where the ethnic and other loyalties that once fastened us to our religion seem to be weakening.

In addition to all the weaknesses, dilemmas, and temptations that impede every pilgrim's progress, the Catholic who holds political office in a pluralistic democracy—who is elected to serve Jews and Muslims, atheists and Protestants, as well as Catholics—bears special responsibility. He or she undertakes to help create conditions under which all can live with a maximum of dignity and with a reasonable degree of freedom; where everyone who chooses may hold beliefs different from specifically Catholic ones, sometimes contradictory to them, where the laws protect people's right to divorce, to use birth control, and even to choose abortion.

In fact, Catholic public officials take an oath to preserve the Constitution that guarantees this freedom. And they do so gladly. Not because they love what others do with their freedom, but because they realize that in guaranteeing freedom for all, they guarantee our right to be Catholics: our right to pray, to use the sacraments, to refuse birth control devices, to reject abortion, not to divorce and remarry if we believe it to be wrong.

The Catholic public official lives the political truth most Catholics through most of American history have accepted and insisted on: the truth that to assure our freedom we must allow others the same freedom, even if occasionally it produces conduct by them which we would hold to be sinful.

Protect my right to be a Catholic by preserving your right to believe as a Jew, a Protestant, or nonbeliever, or as anything else you choose.

We know that the price of seeking to force our beliefs on others is that they might someday force theirs on us.

This freedom is the fundamental strength of our unique experiment in government. In the complex interplay of forces and considerations that go into the making of our laws and policies, its preservation must be a pervasive and dominant concern.

But insistence on freedom is easier to accept as a general proposition than in its applications to specific situations. There are other valid general principles firmly embedded in our Constitution, which, operating at the same time, create interesting and occasionally troubling problems. Thus the same amendment of the Constitution that forbids the establishment of a state church affirms my legal right to argue that my religious belief would serve well as an article of our universal public morality. I may use the prescribed processes of government— the legislative and executive and judicial processes to convince my fellow citizens, Jews and Protestants and Buddhists and nonbelievers, that what I propose is as beneficial for them as I believe it is for me, that it is not just parochial or narrowly sectarian but fulfills a human desire for order, peace, justice, kindness, love, any of the values most of us agree are desirable even apart from their specific religious base or context.

I am free to argue for a governmental policy for a nuclear freeze not just to avoid sin, but because I think my democracy should regard it as a desirable goal.

I can, if I wish, argue that the state should not fund the use of contraceptive devices not because the pope demands it, but because I think that the whole community, for the good of the whole community, ...should not sever sex from an openness to the creation of life.

And surely I can, if so inclined, demand some kind of law against abortion not because my bishops say it is wrong, but because I think that the whole community, regardless of its religious beliefs, should agree on the importance of protecting life—including life in the womb, which is at the very least potentially human and should not be extinguished casually.

No law prevents us from advocating any of these things: I am free to do so. So are the bishops. And so is Reverend Falwell.

In fact, the Constitution guarantees my right to try. And theirs. And his.

But should I? Is it helpful? Is it essential to human dignity? Does it promote harmony and understanding? Or does it divide us so fundamentally that it threatens our ability to function as a pluralistic community?

When should I argue to make my religious value your morality? My rule of conduct your limitation?

What are the rules and policies that should influence the exercise of this right to argue and promote?

I believe I have a salvific mission as a Catholic. Does that mean I am in conscience required to do everything I can as governor to translate all my religious values into the laws and regulations of the state of New York or the United States? Or be branded a hypocrite if I don't?

As a Catholic, I respect the teaching authority of the bishops.

But must I agree with everything in the bishops' pastoral letter on peace and fight to include it in party platforms?

And will I have to do the same for the forthcoming pastoral on economics even if I am an unrepentant supply-sider?

Must I, having heard the pope renew the church's ban on birth control devices, veto the funding of contraceptive programs for non-Catholics or dissenting Catholics in my state?

I accept the church's teaching on abortion. Must I insist you do? By law? By denying you Medicaid funding? By a constitutional amendment? If so, which one? Would that be the best way to avoid abortions or to prevent them?

These are only some of the questions for Catholics. People with other religious beliefs face similar problems....

I think it's already apparent that a good part of this nation understands—if only instinctively—that anything which seems to suggest that God favors a political party or the establishment of a state church is wrong and dangerous.

Way down deep the American people are afraid of an entangling relationship between formal religions—or whole bodies of religious belief—and government. Apart from constitutional law and religious doctrine, there is a sense that tells us it's wrong to presume to speak for God or to claim God's sanction of our particular legislation and his rejection of all other positions. Most of us are offended when we see religion being trivialized by its appearance in political throwaway pamphlets.

The American people need no course in philosophy or political science or church history to know that God should not be made into a celestial party chairman.

To most of us, the manipulative invoking of religion to advance a politician or a party is frightening and divisive. The American people will tolerate religious leaders taking positions for or against candidates, although I think the

Catholic bishops are right in avoiding that position. But the American people are leery about large religious organizations, powerful churches, or synagogue groups engaging in such activities—again, not as a matter of law or doctrine, but because our innate wisdom and democratic instinct teaches us these things are dangerous.

LANDMARK CASE # 7

Yick Wo v. Hopkins
118, U.S. 356; 30 L Ed 220 at 226-8.

Mr. Justice Matthews. The Fourteenth Amendment to the Constitution is not confined to the protection of citizens. It says: "Nor shall any State deprive any person of life, liberty, or property without due process of law; nor deny any person within its jurisdiction the equal protection of the laws." These provisions are universal in their application, to all persons within the territorial jurisdiction, without regard to any differences of race, of color, or of nationality; and the equal protection of the laws is a pledge of the protection of equal laws. It is accordingly enacted by Section 1977 of the Revised Statutes, that "All persons within the jurisdiction of the United States shall have the same right in every State and Territory to make and enforce contracts, to sue, be parties, give evidence, and to the full and equal benefit of all laws and proceedings for the security of persons and property as is enjoyed by white citizens, and shall be subject to like punishments, pains, penalties, taxes, licenses and exactions of every kind, and no other." The questions we have to consider and decide in these cases, therefore, are to be treated as involving the rights of every citizen of the United States equally with those of the strangers and aliens who now invoke the jurisdiction of the court.

When we consider the nature and theory of our institutions of government, the principles upon which they are supposed to rest, and review the history of their development, we are constrained to conclude that they do not mean to leave room for the play and action of purely personal and arbitrary power. Sovereignty itself is, of course, not subject to law, for it is the author and source of law; but in our system, while sovereign powers are delegated to the agencies of government, sovereignty itself remains with the people, by whom and for whom all government exists and acts. And the law is the definition and limitation of power. It is, indeed, quite true, that there must always be lodged somewhere and in some person or body, the authority of final decision; and, in many cases of mere administration the responsibility is purely political, no appeal lying except to the ultimate tribunal of the public judgment, exercised either in the pressure of opinion or by means of the suffrage. But the fundamental rights to life, liberty, and the pursuit of happiness, considered as individual possessions, are secured by those maxims of constitutional law which are the monuments showing the victorious progress of the race in securing to men the blessings of civilization under the reign of just and equal laws, so that, in the famous language of the Massachusetts Bill of Rights, the government of the Commonwealth "may be a government of laws and not of men." For, the very idea that one man may be compelled to hold his life, or the means of living, or any material right essential to the enjoyment of life, at the mere will of another, seems to be intolerable in any country where freedom prevails, as being the essence of slavery itself....

...Though the law itself be fair on its face and impartial in appearance, yet, if it is applied and administered by public authority with an evil eye and an unequal hand, so as practically to make unjust and illegal discriminations between persons in similar circumstances, material to their rights, the denial of equal justice is still within the prohibition of the Constitution....

...No reason whatever, except the will of the supervisors, is assigned why they should not be permitted to carry on, in the accustomed manner, their harmless and useful occupation, on which they depend for a livelihood. And while this consent of the supervisors is withheld from them and from two hundred others who have also petitioned, all of whom happened to be Chinese subjects, eighty others, not Chinese subjects, are permitted to carry on the same business under similar conditions. The fact of this discrimination is admitted. No reason for it is shown, and the conclusion cannot be resisted, that no reason for it exists except hostility to the race and nationality to which the petitioners belong, and which in the eye of the law is not justified. The discrimination is therefore illegal, and the public administration which enforces it is a denial of the equal protection of the laws and a violation of the Fourteenth Amendment of the Constitution. The imprisonment of the petitioners is therefore illegal, and they must be discharged.

17. LIMITING THE ROLE OF GOVERNMENT AND THE SCOPE OF PUBLIC MORALITY

a. Constitutional Limitations

> *...the concept of liberty protects those personal rights that are fundamental, and not confined to the specific terms of the Bill of Rights...*
> —*Mr. Justice Goldberg,*
> Griswold v. Connecticut

This section deals with the protection of those personal rights that the "traditions and collective conscience of our people" rank as fundamental.[10] We will explore the extent to which government may regulate our personal conduct in the exercise of these rights. When we limit the power or the role of government we deny government the right to enforce public morality in the excluded area of personal conduct.

The Bill of Rights is intended to limit the power of the federal and state governments to make or enforce laws that violate protected constitutional rights. So, for example, neither could enact a law requiring a particular religious belief or the prior censorship of a book or newspaper or permit the execution of a person without a trial or one not proved guilty of a capital offense or the arbitrary taking of the life of a mentally handicapped person. But these are limitations upon the abusive acts of the government. In this discussion, we are searching for the limits of the *role or purpose* of government.

There is no specific statement in the Constitution or any of our founding state papers that defines the limits of the jurisdiction of government qua government—federal or state. Nor has Congress or the Supreme Court defined the outer boundary of the rightful exercise of the police power. However, the Ninth Amendment (and the Tenth Amendment) recognizes that there are "other rights retained by the people."

> ...the great Federalist leader James Wilson reminded the Pennsylvania ratifying convention that "supreme...power *remains* in the people"—a point that he formulated a bit later as follows: The people "never part with the whole" of their "original power" and "they *retain* the right of recalling what they part with... [T]he citizens of the United States may always say, WE *reserve* the right to do what we please...."

> In short, conventional wisdom today misses the close triangular interrelation among the Preamble and the Ninth and Tenth Amendments. The Ninth Amendment is said to be about unenumerated individual rights, like personal privacy; the Tenth about federalism; and the Preamble about something else entirely. But look again at these texts. All are at their core about popular sovereignty. All, indeed, explicitly invoke "the people." In the Preamble, "We the people...*do*" exercise our right and power of popular sovereignty, and in the Ninth and Tenth "the people" expressly "retain" and "reserve" our "right" and "power" to do it again.[11]

Our search, then, is for that area of our life that has been retained by the people, that has not been ceded over to the state. What is the human conduct over which the state has no jurisdiction?

Why is this important? The extent of the jurisdiction of the government determines the extent to which government can interfere with our private lives. For example, can the government make it a crime to smoke in the privacy

---

[10] *Griswold v. Connecticut*, supra.

[11] Amar, *Op. Cit.*, pp. 121-2.

of your own home? Can the state require seat belts for your baby's high-chair or forbid you to educate your children according to your best light? The outer boundary of the police power determines the area of your life where you are entitled to be let alone.

b. John Stuart Mill and Individual Liberty

John Stuart Mill was a nineteenth century British philosopher and member of Parliament who has influenced American political thought after the 1860s. His treatise, *On Liberty*, published in 1859, was a powerful argument for limiting the role of government to the regulation of *social* conduct. He denied government any jurisdiction over *personal* conduct.

> .....the sole end for which mankind are warranted, individually or collectively, in interfering with the liberty of action of any of their number, is self-protection. That the only purpose for which power can be rightfully exercised over any member of a civilized community, against his will, is to prevent harm to others. His own good, either physical or moral, is not a sufficient warrant. He cannot rightfully be compelled to do or forbear because it will be better for him to do so, because it will make him happy, because, in the opinion of others, to do so would be wise, or even right. Here are good reasons for remonstration with him, or reasoning with him, or persuading him, or entreating him, but not for compelling him, or visiting him with any evil in case he do otherwise. To justify that, the conduct from which it is desired to deter him must be calculated to produce evil to some one else. The only part of the conduct of any one, for which he is amenable to society, is that which concerns others. In the part which merely concerns himself, his independence is, of right, absolute. Over himself, over his own body and mind, the individual is sovereign.[12]

However, the American courts have rejected Mill's doctrine in a number of cases. In a Supreme Court case involving the viewing of obscene movies in an adult theater the high court said; "Our Constitution establishes a broad range of conditions on the exercise of power by the States, but for us to say that our Constitution incorporates the proposition that conduct involving consenting adults only is always beyond state regulation, is a step we are unable to take."[13] The Court noted that laws forbidding prostitution, suicide, voluntary self-mutilation, brutalizing bare fist prize fights, dueling, bigamy, adultery, fornication, white slavery and gambling, to list only some examples, have all been upheld even when cutting into the freedom to associate by consenting adults.

In a New York case that challenged the mandatory use of seat belts, the

---

[12] John Stuart Mill, *On Liberty*, in *Great Books of the Western World*, Vol. 43 of Encyclopedia Britannica, ed. Robert Maynard Hutchins, (William Benton, Publisher, Chicago, IL), p. 271.

[13] *Paris Adult Theatre v. Slaton*, 413 US 49, 37 L Ed 2d 446, 463, 93 S Ct 2628, (1973), citing J. Mill, *On Liberty*, 13 (1955 ed.).

trial court said, in upholding the law:

> The United States Supreme Court has rejected the Mill's maxim as a measure of State legislative power....Ultimately, all social legislation affects someone's "freedom"; competing interests have to be carefully weighed and a reasonable and rational relationship to the purpose for which the police power has been exercised must be demonstrated. Plaintiff view this statute as a confrontation between the right of the individual to determine his own fate and the power of the State to interfere with his determination....

> This Court must determine whether a law compelling motorists to use a seat belt advances the State's interest in protecting the health, safety and welfare of its citizens. Legislation tending to promote this interest is a proper exercise of the State's police power. An appropriate test, then, for any legislation which mandates public conduct and restricts individual choice should measure a statute in light of its reasonable and rational relationship to the purpose for which the law was enacted.

> Numerous studies, both here and abroad, have demonstrated that the use of seat belts does significantly lower, not only mortality rates, but the severity of injuries in automobile crashes....

> The State has a compelling interest in saving lives (the ultimate goal in the promotion of health and safety), but in addition to this, the State has an interest in promoting the welfare of its citizens. The cost to society of the results of death or severe injuries is enormous. The long-term care, often extending to lifetime care, of paraplegics, quadraplegics and patients on life-support systems devolves on the State....[14]

The Court concluded that "...the showing of harm to the individual was a basis upon which the protection to personal autonomy might be infringed."

The North Carolina Supreme Court reached the same conclusion in a similar case involving the mandatory use of motorcycle helmets:

> Death on the highway can no longer be considered as a personal and individual tragedy alone. The mounting carnage has long since reached proportions of a public disaster. Legislation reasonably designed to reduce the toll may for that reason alone be sufficiently imbued with the public interest to meet the constitutional test required for a valid exercise of the State's police power.[15]

In the last analysis the Mill's assertion that the individual is not accountable to society for his or her actions, insofar as these acts affect no one but himself, has been rejected by American courts as too extreme. Mill's idea of harm to others meant only immediate and substantial *physical* injury. He ignored the emotional harm caused to loved ones by a self-abuser or the financial damage done to society by one who will need extended medical care caused by self-regulating negligence. In truth, there is very little human conduct that affects no one else, either directly or indirectly, especially when we consider those who love us.

---

[14] *Wells v. The State of New York, et ano,* —NY Misc. 2nd—, (1985).

[15] *State v. Anderson,* N.C. app. 1968, 164 S. E. 2d 48, 50, affd. 166 S. E. 2d 49.

c. The Right of Privacy

> *...The makers of our Constitution undertook to secure conditions favorable to the pursuit of happiness.... They conferred, as against the Government, the right to be let alone—the most comprehensive of rights and the right most valued by civilized men....*
>
> —*Mr. Justice Brandeis*[16]

In 1958 the legislature of the State of Connecticut made it a crime for anyone, married or unmarried, adult or child, to use contraceptives:

> Any person who uses any drug, medicinal article or instrument for the purpose of preventing conception shall be fined not less than fifty dollars or imprisoned not less than sixty days nor more than one year or both fined and imprisoned.[17]

It was also a crime to help couples to use contraceptives. Estelle T. Griswold was the executive director of the Planned Parenthood League of Connecticut and Dr. Buxton was a professor at Yale Medical School and the medical director for the league. They gave information, instruction and medical advice to married couples to help them plan their families. They were arrested, tried for violating the statute, found guilty and fined $100 each. They appealed their convictions, eventually to the Supreme Court.

When our Constitution was written, a zone of privacy was recognized regarding certain rights set forth in the Bill of Rights. The Third Amendment guarantees the sanctity and the privacy of the home: "No soldier shall...be quartered in any house..." without the consent of the owner. The Fourth Amendment protects the privacy of one's self and home as well as one's personal effects, papers, and documents by forbidding unreasonable search and seizure. The Fifth Amendment right against self-incrimination recognizes the zone of privacy in one's private thoughts, beliefs, and knowledge.

In the 1960s, the high court expanded our understanding of the zone of privacy to mean that the First Amendment right of assembly included the right to associate privately. So, for example, the State of Alabama could not require the NAACP to turn over its membership lists to the state.[18] And the right of conscience includes the right to educate one's children as one chooses.[19]

In 1965, the Supreme Court recognized a general right of privacy. It was the first time that privacy was extended to a right not specifically enumerated in the Constitution or the Bill of Rights—the right to marry. The Griswold case placed the privacy of the marital relationship beyond the control of the government.

---

[16] *Dissenting in Olmstead v. United States*, 277 US 438, 478, 72 L Ed 944, 956.

[17] Gen. Stat. of Conn. (1958 rev., Sec. 54-195.)

[18] *NAACP v. Alabama*, 357 US 449, 462, 2 L Ed 2d 1488,1499, 78 S Ct 1163.

[19] *Pierce v. Society of Sisters*, 268 US 51, 69 L Ed 1070, 45 S Ct 571. Other cases are cited in the Griswold case.

The present case, then, concerns a relationship lying within the zone of privacy created by several fundamental constitutional guarantees. And it concerns a law which, in forbidding the *use* of contraceptives rather than regulating their manufacture or sale, seeks to achieve its goals by means having a maximum destructive impact upon that relationship. Such a law can not stand in light of the familiar principle, so often applied by this Court, that a "governmental purpose to control or prevent activities constitutionally subject to state regulation may not be achieved by means which sweep unnecessarily broadly and thereby invade the area of protected freedoms." Would we allow the police to search the sacred precincts of marital bedrooms for telltale signs of the use of contraceptives? The very idea is repulsive to the notions of privacy surrounding the marriage relationship.

We deal with a right of privacy older that the Bill of Rights—older than our political parties, older than our school system. Marriage is a coming together for better or for worse, hopefully enduring, and intimate to the degree of being sacred. It is an association that promotes a way of life, not causes; a harmony in living, not political faiths; a bilateral loyalty, not commercial or social projects. Yet it is an association for as noble a purpose as any involved in our prior decisions.[20]

Following the Griswold case, a number of state statutes forbidding the sale or distribution of contraceptive devices were struck down. A Massachusetts statute made it a crime for anyone to "...give away...any drug, medicine, instrument or article whatever for the prevention of conception...,"[21] except for a physician or a pharmacist prescribing or dispensing such drugs or articles to married persons. William R. Baird delivered a lecture to a group of students at Boston University on contraception and overpopulation, during which he demonstrated a number of various contraceptive devices. He urged them to petition the legislature to change this law. At the end of the lecture he invited the students to take the contraceptives he used in his demonstration and he gave a young woman (presumed to be an unmarried adult) a package of vaginal foam. He was arrested and convicted of violating the statute; he appealed, ultimately to the Supreme Court. In overturning the statute, Mr. Justice Brennan said:

If under Griswold the distribution of contraceptives to married persons cannot be prohibited, a ban on distribution to unmarried persons would be equally impermissible. It is true that in Griswold the right of privacy in question inhered in the marital relationship. Yet the marital couple is not an independent entity with a mind and heart of its own, but an association of two individuals each with a separate intellectual and emotional makeup. If the right of privacy means anything, it is the right of the *individual*, married or single, to be free from unwarranted governmental intrusion into matters so fundamentally affecting a person as the decision whether to bear or beget a child.[22]

---

[20] *Griswold v. Connecticut*, 381 US 479, 14 L Ed 2d 510, 85 S Ct 1678, (1965).

[21] Mass. Gen. L. Ann. c. 272, Par. 21 & 21A.

[22] *Eisenstadt v. Baird*, 405 US 438, 31 L Ed 2d 349, 362, 92 S Ct 1029, (1972).

In January, 1973 the Supreme Court decided *Roe v. Wade*, one of the most important cases of our time. Texas had made it a crime to have an abortion except to save the life of the mother. "Jane Roe," an unwed mother, sued the state for violating her right of privacy claiming that "the woman's right [to control her own body] is absolute and that she is entitled to terminate her pregnancy at whatever time, in whatever way, and for whatever reason she alone chooses..."[23] (p.153.) This case is mentioned here to help understand the concept of the Right of Privacy and the limitations on governmental power over the conduct of a pregnant woman. On the issue of privacy, the Court said:

> The Constitution does not explicitly mention any right of privacy....[T]he Court has recognized that a right of personal privacy, or a guarantee of certain areas or zones of privacy, does exist under the Constitution....These decisions make it clear that only personal rights that can be deemed "fundamental" or "implicit in the concept of ordered liberty," are included in this guarantee of personal privacy. They also make it clear that the right has some extension to activities relating to marriage, procreation, contraception, family relationships, and child rearing and education.

> The right of privacy whether it be founded in the Fourteenth Amendment's concept of personal liberty and restrictions upon state action, as we feel it is, or, ...in the Ninth Amendment's reservation of rights to the people, is broad enough to encompass a woman's decision whether or not to terminate her pregnancy. The detriment that the State would impose upon the pregnant woman by denying this choice altogether is apparent. Specific and direct harm medically diagnosable even in early pregnancy may be involved. Maternity, or additional offspring, may force upon the woman a distressful life and future. Psychological harm may be imminent. Mental and physical health may be taxed by child care. There is also the distress, for all concerned, associated with the unwanted child, and there is the problem of bringing a child into a family already unable, psychologically and otherwise, to care for it. In other cases, as in this one, the additional difficulties and continuing stigma of unwed motherhood may be involved. All these are factors the woman and her responsible physician necessarily will consider in consultation....

> The Court's decision recognizing a right of privacy also acknowledge that some state regulation in areas protected by that right is appropriate. As noted above, a State may properly assert important interest in safeguarding health, in maintaining medical standards, and in protecting potential life. At some point in pregnancy, these respective interests become sufficiently compelling to sustain regulation of the factors that govern the abortion decision. The privacy right involved, therefore, cannot be said to be absolute. In fact, it is not clear to us that the claim asserted by some [friends of the Court] that one has an unlimited right to do with one's body as one pleases bears a close relationship to the right of privacy previously articulated in the Court's decisions. The Court has refused to recognize an unlimited right of this kind in the past.

---

[23] *Roe v. Wade*, 410 US 113, 35 L Ed 2d 147, 93 S Ct 705 (1973); see pages 152-5 for the quotes in this section.

We, therefore, conclude that the right of personal privacy includes the abortion decision, but that this right is not unqualified and must be considered against important state interest in regulation....

Where certain "fundamental rights" are involved, the Court has held that regulation limiting these rights may be justified only by a "compelling state interest," and that legislative enactments must be narrowly drawn to express only the legitimate state interests at stake.

In later cases the Court established some limits on the privacy right. In 1973, in a case where the state of Georgia made it a crime to view obscene movies in an adult theater, the Supreme Court limited the right of privacy to private acts and private relationships.

.....The Civil Rights Act of 1964 specifically defines motion-picture houses and theaters as places of "public accommodation" covered by the Act as operations affecting commerce.

Our prior decisions recognizing a right of privacy guaranteed by the Fourteenth Amendment included "only personal rights that can be deemed 'fundamental' or 'implicit in the concept of ordered liberty.'" The privacy right encompasses and protects the personal intimacies of the home, the family, marriage, motherhood, procreation, and child rearing. Nothing, however, in this Court's decisions intimates that there is any "fundamental" privacy right "implicit in the concept of ordered liberty" to watch obscene movies in places of public accommodation.[24]

The Court concluded that the protection afforded by an earlier case,[25] where the Court held that one may view or read obscene material in the privacy of one's own home, is restricted to a place, the home.

.....In contrast, the constitutionally protected privacy of family, marriage, motherhood, procreation, and child rearing is not just concerned with a particular place, but with a protected intimate relationship. Such protected privacy extends to the doctor's office, the hospital, the hotel room, or as otherwise required to safeguard the right to intimacy involved. Obviously, there is no necessary or legitimate expectation of privacy which would extend to marital intercourse on a street corner or a theater stage.

In recent years, state courts have been more willing than the United States Supreme Court to expand the right of privacy to encompass additional fundamental rights. New York State had made consensual sodomy by unmarried people, a crime:

A person is guilty of consensual sodomy when he engages in deviant sexual intercourse with another person.

.....Deviant sexual intercourse means sexual conduct between persons not married to each other consisting of contact between the penis and the anus, the mouth and the penis, or the mouth and the vulva.[26]

---

[24] *Paris Adult Theatre I, v. Slaton,* 413 US 49, 37 L Ed 2d 46, 93 S Ct 2628 (1973).

[25] *Stanley v. Georgia,* 394 US 557, 22 L Ed 2d 542, 89 S Ct 1243, (1969).

[26] NY Penal Law 130.00 & 130.38.

Several defendants, male and female, had been convicted of this crime, one committed at home and another in a vehicle. On appeal, the New York Court of Appeals overturned this statute as a violation of the right of privacy. The People had contended "that a prohibition against consensual sodomy will prevent physical harm which might otherwise befall the participants, will uphold public morality and will protect the institution of marriage":

.....Commendable though these objectives clearly are, there is nothing on which to base a conclusion that they are achieved by Section 130.38 of the Penal Law. No showing has been made...that physical injury is a common or even occasional consequence of the prohibited conduct.

....Any purported justification for the consensual sodomy statute in terms of upholding public morality is belied by the position reflected in the *Eisenstadt* decision in which the court carefully distinguished between public dissemination of what might have been considered inimical to public morality and individual recourse to the same material out of the public arena in the sanctum of the private home. There is a distinction between public and private morality and the private morality of an individual is not synonymous with nor necessarily will have effect on what is known as public morality. So here, the People have failed to demonstrate how government interference with the practice of personal choice in matters of intimate sexual behavior out of view of the public and with no commercial component will serve to advance the cause of public morality or do anything other than restrict individual conduct and impose a concept of private morality chosen by the State.

[In a footnote, the Court added:]....We express no view as to any theological, moral or psychological evaluation of consensual sodomy. These are aspects of the issue on which informed, competent authorities and individuals may and do differ.....It is not the function of the Penal Law in our governmental policy to provide either a medium for the articulation or the apparatus for the intended enforcement of moral or theological values. Thus, it has been deemed irrelevant by the United States Supreme Court that the purchase and use of contraceptives by unmarried persons would arouse moral indignation among broad segments of our community or that the viewing of pornographic materials even within the privacy of one's home would not evoke general approbation. We are not unmindful of the sensibilities of many persons who are deeply persuaded that consensual sodomy is evil and should be prohibited. That is not the issue before us. The issue before us is whether, assuming that at least at present it is the will of the community (as expressed in legislative enactment) to prohibit consensual sodomy, the Federal Constitution permits recourse to the sanctions of the criminal law for the achievement of that objective. The community and its members are entirely free to employ theological teaching, moral suasion, parental advice, psychological and psychiatric counseling and other noncoercive means to condemn the practice of consensual sodomy. The narrow question before us is whether the Federal Constitution permits the use of the criminal law for that purpose.[27]

---

[27] *People v. Onofre*, 51 NY 2d 476, 434 N.Y.S. 2d 947.

The Court concluded that the Penal Law could not be used to enforce the state's view of morality where there was no compelling public interest. Many states, most recently the state of Georgia, have overturned similar statutes forbidding sodomy (and oral sex) by consenting adults as a violation of the right of privacy. I have not attempted to explore all the cases that deal with the right of privacy but to set forth a few examples that describe what privacy means.

We say that the right of privacy is the right to be let alone; but let alone to do what? The fundamental personal rights that are implicit in the concept of ordered liberty include the constitutional guarantees against the quartering of soldiers and unreasonable search and seizure of our person, home, and personal effects. We have the right to be let alone to enjoy our property—our homes and personal effects, to be let alone in our thoughts and knowledge, and to be let alone with the people with whom we associate. The right to marry and raise a family includes a zone of privacy that protects the personal intimacies inherent in the home and family relationships. This encompasses the marital relationship including the nature of the sexual relations between husband and wife, contraception, motherhood, procreation, the abortion decision, child rearing, and education. The zone of privacy for freedom of expression includes the right to read or view pornographic material in the privacy of one's home. And the privacy zone of the right of assembly includes the right of private association and the development of friendships and relationships with whomever you wish. It also includes the right to engage in heterosexual and homosexual intimacies outside the public view. In essence, the courts are telling us that there are fundamental personal rights that have a zone of privacy, an area of conduct, that the government may not invade.

However, none of these privacy rights are absolute; there are limits to the right to exercise fundamental rights in private. The state has a legitimate interest in promoting the public health, safety, education, peace, morals, and general welfare of the community. Where there is a compelling need to protect the public interest, the state may criminalize private acts exercising fundamental rights. However, where there is no compelling need to invade one's privacy, private acts and decisions that involve the exercise of fundamental rights are none of society's business and the individual has the right to be let alone.

d. The Boundary between Constitutional Democracy and Ordered Liberty

So what then is the outer limit on the exercise of the police power by the state? We don't know, exactly. Privacy is not a right that stands by itself; it is a means by which we enhance and protect other fundamental rights by creating a zone of privacy for those rights, where the state may not enter.

An overview of the privacy cases suggests that the general right of privacy is becoming the boundary between our notion of constitutional democracy and ordered liberty. Constitutional democracy is government that is not arbitrary, that governs by the rule of law and that enforces public morality only to the extent required by the public need. Ordered liberty is the freedom to exercise fundamental rights, without government restraint, in private matters that do not involve the public in any serious or compelling way. The Constitution protects our rights and liberties from abusive governmental acts. The general right of privacy expands that protection by defining and limiting the role or purpose of government. It divides our lives into a public area where the government may define American ethics and enforce public morality, and a private area where government may not go.

Since the Griswold case in 1965, the general right of privacy has focused on our public morals (not to be confused with our public morality) and has become the right that defines our public mores and community standards of decency. In the process, these cases have defined and protected our private morality from government interference. The cases invoking the general right of privacy, federal and state, are striking down laws that violate fundamental rights and do not show a substantial or compelling governmental interest or public purpose. Many of these laws are the holdovers from the age of established Puritanism. Some are new laws that reflect the misplaced attempt by overzealous believers to impose their views of faith and morals upon nonbelievers by the use of the coercive power of government. Many of these people are well intentioned, but misunderstand the secular nature of American ethics and would have the government "...restrict individual conduct and impose a concept of private morality chosen by the State."[28]

The regulation of private conduct, according to the principles of American ethics, is left to each individual's conscience guided by his/her religious, philisophical, or ethical values. It is in this private realm that "Over himself, over his body and mind, the individual is sovereign."[29]

LANDMARK CASE # 8

Griswold v. State of Connecticut
381 US 479, 14 L Ed 2d 510, 85 S Ct 1678 (1965)

In his concurring opinion, Mr. Justice Goldberg emphasizes the importance of the Ninth Amendment in recognizing fundamental rights that are not in the Constitution or the Bill of Rights.

---

[28] *People v. Onofre*, supra.
[29] Mill, *Op. Cit.*, p. 271.

Mr. Justice Goldberg, whom the Chief Justice and Mr. Justice Brennan join, concurring:

I agree with the Court that Connecticut's birth-control law unconstitutionally intrudes upon the marital privacy, and I join in its opinion and judgment. Although I have not accepted the view that "due process" as used in the Fourteenth Amendment incorporates all of the first eight Amendments, I do agree that the concept of liberty protects those personal rights that are fundamental, and is not confined to the specific terms of the Bill of Rights. My conclusion that the concept of liberty is not so restricted and that it embraces the right of marital privacy though that right is not mentioned explicitly in the Constitution is supported both by numerous decisions of this Court, referred to in the Court's opinion, and by the language and history of the Ninth Amendment.

...I add these words to emphasize the relevance of that Amendment to the Court's holding.

The Court stated many years ago that the Due Process Clause protects those liberties that are "so rooted in the traditions and conscience of our people as to be ranked as fundamental." In *Gitlow v. New York*, the Court said:

"For present purposes we may and do assume that freedom of speech and of the press—which are protected by the First Amendment from abridgment by Congress—are among the fundamental personal rights and 'liberties' protected by the due process clause of the Fourteenth Amendment from impairment by the States."

And, in *Meyer v. Nebraska*, the Court, referring to the Fourteenth Amendment, stated:

"While this Court has not attempted to define with exactness the liberty thus guaranteed, the term has received much consideration and some of the included things have been definitely stated. Without doubt, it denotes not merely freedom from bodily restraint but also [for example,] the right...to marry, establish a home and bring up children.

This Court, in a series of decisions, has held that the Fourteenth Amendment absorbs and applies to the States those specifics of the first eight amendments which express fundamental personal rights. The language and history of the Ninth Amendment reveal that the Framers of the Constitution believed that there are additional fundamental rights, protected from governmental infringement, which exist alongside those fundamental rights specifically mentioned in the first eight constitutional amendments.

The Ninth Amendment reads, "The enumeration in the Constitution, of certain rights, shall not be construed to deny or disparage others retained by the people." The Amendment is almost entirely the work of James Madison. It was introduced in Congress by him and passed the House and Senate with little or no debate and virtually no change in language. It was proffered to quiet expressed fears that a bill of specifically enumerated rights could not be sufficiently broad to cover all essential rights and that the specific mention of certain rights would be interpreted as a denial that others were protected.

In presenting the proposed Amendment, Madison said:

"It has been objected also against a bill of rights, that, by enumerating particular exceptions to the grant of power, it would disparage those rights which were not placed in that enumeration; and it might follow by implication, that those rights which were not singled out, were intended to be assigned into the hands of the General Government, and were consequently insecure. This is one of the most plausible arguments I have ever heard urged against the admission of a bill of rights into this system; but, I conceive, that it may be guarded against. I have attempted it, as gentlemen may see by turning to the last clause of the fourth resolution [the Ninth Amendment] ." I Annals of Congress 439 (Gales and Seaton ed 1834).

Mr. Justice Story wrote of this argument against a bill of rights and the meaning of the Ninth Amendment:

"In regard to...[a] suggestion, that the affirmance of certain rights might disparage others, or might lead to argumentative implications in favor of other powers, it might be sufficient to say that such a course of reasoning could never be sustained upon any solid basis....But a conclusive answer is, that such an attempt may be interdicted (as it has been) by a positive declaration in such a bill of rights that the enumeration of certain rights shall not be construed to deny or disparage others retained by the people." II Story, Commentaries on the Constitution of the United States 626-7 (5th ed 1891).

He further stated, referring to the Ninth Amendment:

"This clause was manifestly introduced to prevent any perverse or ingenious misapplication of the well known maxim, that an affirmation in particular cases implies a negation in all others; and, e converso, that a negation in particular cases implies an affirmation in all others." Id. at 651.

These statements of Madison and Story make clear that the Framers did not intend that the first eight amendments be construed to exhaust the basic and fundamental rights which the Constitution guaranteed to the people.

While this Court has had little occasion to interpret the Ninth Amendment "[i]t cannot be presumed that any clause in the constitution is intended to be without effect." In interpreting the Constitution, "real effect should be given to all the words it uses." The Ninth Amendment to the Constitution may be regarded by some as a recent discovery and may be forgotten by others, but since 1791 it has been a basic part of the Constitution which we are sworn to uphold. To hold that a right so basic and fundamental and so deep-rooted in our society as the right of privacy in marriage may be infringed because that right is not guaranteed in so many words by the first eight amendments to the Constitution is to ignore the Ninth Amendment and to give it no effect whatsoever. Moreover, a judicial construction that this fundamental right is not protected by the Constitution because it is not mentioned in explicit terms by one of the first eight amendments or elsewhere in the Constitution would violate the Ninth Amendment, which specifically states that "[t]he enumeration in the Constitution, of certain rights, shall not be construed to deny or disparage others retained by the people."

...the Ninth Amendment shows a belief of the Constitution's authors that fundamental rights exist that are not expressly enumerated in the first eight amendments and an intent that the list of rights included there not be deemed exhaustive. As any student of this Court's opinions knows, this Court has held, often unanimously, that the Fifth and Fourteenth Amendments protect certain fundamental personal liberties from abridgment by the Federal Government or the States. The Ninth Amendment simply shows the intent of the Constitution's authors that other fundamental personal rights should not be denied such protection or disparaged in any other way simply because they are not specifically listed in the first eight constitutional amendments. I do not see how this broadens the authority of the Court; rather it serves to support what this Court has been doing in protecting fundamental rights.

In sum, the Ninth Amendment simply lends strong support to the view that the "liberty" protected by the Fifth and Fourteenth Amendments from infringement by the Federal Government or the States is not restricted to rights specifically mentioned in the first eight amendments. In determining which rights are fundamental, judges are not left at large to decide cases in light of their personal and private notions. Rather, they must look to the "traditions and [collective] conscience of our people" to determine whether a principle is "so rooted [there]...as to be ranked as fundamental."

The inquiry is whether a right involved "is of such a character that it cannot be denied without violating those fundamental principles of liberty and justice which lie at the base of all our civil and political institutions."..."Liberty also gains content from the emanations of...specific [constitutional] guarantees" and "from experience with the requirements of a free society."

I agree fully with the Court that, applying these tests, the right of privacy is a fundamental personal right, emanating "from the totality of the constitutional scheme under which we live." Mr. Justice Brandeis, dissenting in *Olmstead v. United* comprehensively summarized the principles underlying the Constitution's guarantees of privacy:

"The protection guaranteed by the [Fourth and Fifth] Amendments is much broader in scope. The makers of our Constitution undertook to secure conditions favorable to the pursuit of happiness. They recognized the significance of man's spiritual nature, of his feelings and of his intellect. They knew that only a part of the pain, pleasure and satisfactions of life are to be found in material things. They sought to protect Americans in their beliefs, their thoughts, their emotions and their sensations. They conferred as against the Government, the right to be let alone—the most comprehensive of rights and the right most valued by civilized men."

The Connecticut statutes here involved deal with a particularly important and sensitive area of privacy—that of the marital relation and the marital home. This Court recognized in *Meyer v. Nebraska*, that the right "to marry, establish a home and bring up children" was an essential part of the liberty guaranteed by the Fourteenth Amendment. In *Pierce v. Society of Sisters* the Court held unconstitutional an Oregon Act which forbade parents from sending their children to private schools because such an act "unreasonably interferes with the liberty of parents and guardians to direct the upbringing and education of children under their control." As this Court said in *Prince v. Massachusetts*, the *Meyer* and *Pierce* decisions "have respected the private realm of family life which the state cannot enter."

.....Of this whole private realm of family life it is difficult to imagine what is more private or more intimate than a husband and wife's marital relations."

18. TEACHING THE VIRTUOUS CITIZEN

> .....*The process of educating our youth for citizenship in public schools is not confined to books, the curriculum, and the civics class; schools must teach by example the shared values of a civilized social order. Consciously or otherwise, teachers—and indeed the older students—demonstrate the appropriate form of civil discourse and political expression by their conduct and deportment in and out of class...*
>
> —*Chief Justice Berger*[30]

> .....*As long as you think of basic moral values as having to be taught to children, you will end up focusing on the particular culturally bound rules of behavior that children learn in each society. Once you consider that the function of value concepts is to regulate social behavior and that children develop moral concepts by having to get along with other people, you will see how the development of value concepts can be a universally common experience.*
>
> —*Reimer, Paolitto and Hersh*
> Promoting Moral Growth

---

[30] *Bethel School Dist. No. 403 v. Fraser*, 478 US 675, 92 L Ed 2d 549, 558, 106 S Ct 3159, (1986).

a. The Need to Teach American Ethics

Teaching secular ethics in the public schools does not violate the prohibition against separation of church and state. In fact, it is the duty of a democratic state to provide basic literacy and training in our ethical obligations to our children and to all our citizens. And this training should be more than an education in the penal code, but instead a more comprehensive education in our history, political philosophy and the encouragement to strive for the ideals and virtues that enrich our community.

> The role and purpose of the American public school system were well described by two historians, who state: "[P]ublic education must prepare pupils for citizenship in the Republic... It must inculcate the values in themselves conducive to happiness and as indispensable to the practice of self-government in the community and the nation." ...[W]e echoed the essence of this statement of the objectives of public education as the "inculcation of fundamental values necessary to the maintenance of a democratic political system."

> These fundamental values of "habits and manners of civility" essential to a democratic society must, of course, include tolerance of divergent political and religious views, even when the views expressed may be unpopular. But these "fundamental values" must also take into account consideration of the sensibilities of others, and in the case of a school, the sensibilities of fellow students. The undoubted freedom to advocate unpopular and controversial views in schools and classrooms must be balanced against the society's countervailing interest in teaching students the boundaries of socially appropriate behavior. Even the most heated political discourse in a democratic society requires consideration for the personal sensibilities of the others participants and audiences.[31]

As of this writing, 28 states are receiving federal assistance for values projects and a number of states have enacted laws requiring public school districts to teach character development or citizenship training. Some have detailed the specific values that they wished taught. Most respect the secular nature of American ethics.

b. The Process of Moral Development

I have said that the essence of our personal code of morality is our explicit consent to the duties of the social contract, to make explicit the consent that is assumed and imputed. Understanding and affirming the social contract is a process of moral development. Moral development is not preaching at offenders telling them what society demands of them. While education in ethical values is important, real moral growth and socialization is a function of intellectual and emotional maturity.

Jean Piaget, the Geneva-born biologist and child psychologist, began studying children in the 1920s and 1930s, to understand how children orient

---

[31] Ibid, Bethel School District No. 403 v. Fraser, at 557.

themselves to the social world. He presented a *developmental* concept of human intelligence, describing how the learning and reasoning processes (as well as feelings), which underlie intelligence in the individual, develop from one chronological period to the next. It soon became clear to Piaget that the fundamental differences in the way children reason are age-related. He established that moral development is not merely the teaching of children to obey society's moral rules and to dedicate themselves to the good of the society. He held that moral growth is a function of the development of the child's physical and intellectual capacities. His main assumption was that thought process and feelings develop on a parallel track and that moral judgment represents a naturally developing learning process.[32]

> ...Piaget's response takes us to the core of what is meant in this theory by moral development. The six-year-old's respect for law is based on a very partial, egocentric understanding of rules. As a child who is first consciously entering the world of social interaction, the six-year-old is most aware of the presence of authorities (usually adults), who insist on his following the rules. He does not know why they so insist, but only that he had better listen or else. He imagines that the authorities' rules are fixed, for he cannot put himself in their place and understand the process by which they made their decisions. Nor can he step outside his own role and view his actions from the perspective of others. Thus he believes he is faithfully following the rules even when he is not, and imagines terrible consequences were he to deviate from their rulings. Understandably, Piaget calls this the stage of unilateral (one-sided) respect.
>
> As the child gains greater experience in interacting with others, particularly with his peers, his understanding of rules changes. Involved in joint pursuits, peers more easily communicate their intentions to one another and can see one another as people who make decisions. They develop a feeling of equality and an understanding that the other person acts and thinks very much as they do. This sense of sharedness, based on the ability to coordinate thoughts and actions, matures into a moral concept of cooperation. Rules emerge as agreements made to ensure that everyone will act in similar ways. Respect for rules is mutual rather than unilateral: one respects rules because others do and because one wants to participate equally in the joint activities of the group....[33]

Lawrence Kohlberg, an American psychologist and a professor at Harvard University, continued the work of Piaget in the 1950s. He moved from the age-related moral development theories of Piaget to an understanding of the ability of children to make moral judgments at various age levels. His main contribution has been to apply this concept of stage to the development of moral judgment. He has shown that, from middle childhood to adulthood, there

---

[32] Jean Piaget, *The Moral Judgment of the Child* (The Free Press, A Division of MacMillian Publishing Co., Inc., New York, 1965), p. 315.

[33] Joseph Reimer, Diana Pritchard Paolitto and Richard H. Hersh, *Promoting Moral Growth* (Waveland Press, Inc., Prospect Heights, Illinois, 1990), pp. 40-2.

are six stages in the development of moral judgment.[34] He defines moral judge-ments as "...the weighing of claims of others against one's own..." The exercise of moral judgment is a cognitive process that allows us to reflect on our values and order them in a logical hierarchy.

In our society, the ability to develop formal or abstract logic typically begins during middle adolescence. Not all adolescents or adults reach this stage. A recent study in California of a large sample of adolescents and adults showed that only about half had reached the stage of basic abstract logic.

Kohlberg's theory of moral development and moral education grows out of, and depends on, his empirical delineation of the stages of moral judg-ment. The six stages of moral judgment are outlined in Table 1 below.[35]

> The three levels broadly define the scope of moral development as described by Kohlberg. The first level most often characterizes children's moral reasoning; still, many adolescents and some adults may persist in its use. The second level usually arises early in adolescence, comes into fuller prominence later in adoles-cence, and remains the dominant form of thinking among most adults. The third level is the least common. If it arises at all, it does so during early adulthood; it characterizes the reasoning of only a minority of adults.[36]

Kohlberg defines moral development in terms of movement through the stages, and moral education in terms of stimulating such movement. In order to understand and affirm the social contract, it is necessary for us to move to Level III—the principled stage of moral development. This book is not just to explain ethics from the vantage point of an American but for all of us to reaffirm and strengthen the commitments that we have made to each other in our most fundamental agreement and to encourage habits of virtue among us. If we are to build a stronger, more peaceful and just society, each of us must honor the equality of all others in their fundamental humanity. We must be tolerant with those with whom we disagree. All of us, especially the rich, need to share, out of our abundance, with those in need. The under-privileged must not use their need as an excuse for crime. In our more perfect world, the virtuous citizen would promote political, social, and economic justice and would work to reduce crime by promoting respect for the mutual obligations of the social contract.

The value of the work of Piaget and Kohlberg to our discussion is that they bring a different perspective to our analysis of how moral or ethical obli-gations arise and how mutual social agreements come into existence. Their teachings are useful in understanding how the average person in any society will assume and accept the agreements made by those reasonable persons. The clinical approach does clearly establish the social nature of human beings and

---

[34] *Ibid.*, p. 51-2.

[35] *Ibid.* p.57

[36] *Ibid.* p. 64-5.

Table I
The Six Stages of Moral Judgement

Level and Stage	Content of Stage		Social Perspectives of Stage
	What Is Right	Reasons for Doing Right	
Level 1: Preconventional Stage 1: Heteronomous morality	Sticking to rules backed by punishment; obedience for its own sake; avoiding physical damage to persons and property.	Avoidance of punishment; superior power of authorities.	*Egocentric point of view.* Doesn't consider the interests of others or recognize that they differ from the actor's; doesn't relate two points of view. Actions considered physically rather than in terms of psychological interests of others. Confusion of authority's perspective with one's own.
Stage 2: Individualism, Instrumental purpose, and Exchange	Following rules only when in one's immediate interest; acting to meet one's own interests and needs and letting others do the same. Right is also what is fair or what is an equal exchange, deal, agreement.	To serve one's own needs or interest in a world where one has to recognize that other people also have interests.	*Concrete individualist perspective.* Aware that everybody has interests to pursue and that these can conflict; right is relative (in the concrete individualistic sense).

Level and Stage	What Is Right	Reasons for Doing Right	Social Perspectives of Stage
Level II: Conventional Stage 3: Mutual interpersonal expectations, Relationships, and Interpersonal conformity	Living up to what is expected by people close to you or what people generally expect of a good son, brother, friends, etc. "Being good" is important and means having good motives, showing concern for others. It also means keeping mutual relationships such as trust, loyalty, respect, and gratitude.	The need to be a good person in your own eyes and those of others; caring for others; belief in the Golden Rule; desire to maintain rules and authority that support stereotypical good behavior.	*Perspective of the individual in relationships with other individuals.* Aware of shared feelings, agreements, and expectations which take primacy over individual interests. Relates points of view through the concrete Golden Rule, putting oneself in the other guy's shoes. Does not yet consider generalized system perspective.
Stage 4: Social system and conscience	Fulfilling duties to which you have agreed; laws to be upheld except in extreme cases where they conflict with other fixed social duties. Right is also contributing to the society, group, or institution.	To keep the institution going as a whole and avoid a breakdown in the system "if everyone did it"; imperative of conscience to meet one's defined obligations. (Easily confused with Stage 3 belief in rules and authority.)	*Differentiates societal point of view from interpersonal agreement or motives.* Takes the point of view of the system that defines roles and rules; considers individual relations in terms of place in the system.

Level and Stage	What Is Right	Reasons for Doing Right	Social Perspectives of Stage
Level III: Postconventional, or Principled Stage 5: Social contract or utility and Individual rights	Being aware that people hold a variety of values and opinions and that most of their values and rules are relative to their group. Relative rules usually upheld in the interest of impartiality and because they are the social contract. Some nonrelative values and rights (e.g. life and liberty) must be upheld in any society and regardless of majority opinion.	A sense of obligation to law because of one's social contract to make and abide by laws for the welfare of all and for the protection of all people's rights. A feeling of contractual commitment, freely entered upon, to family, friendship, trust, and work obligations. Concern that laws and duties be based on rational calculation of overall utility, "the greatest good for the greatest number."	*Prior-to-society perspective.* Rational individual aware of values and rights prior to social attachments and contracts. Integrates perspectives by formal mechanisms of agreement, contract, objective impartiality, and due process. Considers moral and legal points of view; recognizes that they sometimes conflict and finds it difficult to integrate them.
Stage 6: Universal ethical principles	Following self-chosen ethical principles. Particular laws or social agreements usually valid because they rest on such principles; when laws violate these principles, one acts in accordance with principle. Principles are universal principles of justice: equality of human rights and respect for the dignity of human beings as individuals.	The belief as a rational person in the validity of universal moral principles and a sense of personal commitment to them.	*Perspective of a moral point of view from which social arrangements derive.* Perspective is that of a rational individual recognizing the nature of morality or the fact that persons are ends in themselves and must be friends as such.

Source: Lawrence Kohlberg, "Moral Stages and Moralization: The Cognitive-Developmental Approach," in *Moral Development and Behavior: Theory, Research and Social Issues*, ed. Thomas Lickona (New York: Holt, Rinehart and Winston, 1976), pp. 34-5.

identifies some basic cross-cultural social agreements that have historically developed and that, in fact, exist everywhere.

c. Affirming the Social Contract

I have said that the Social Contract is an *assumed contract* whose duties are imputed to each member of society. An assumed contract is not an agreement to which you have given your actual consent. It does not become an ethical act unless and until these duties are, consciously and knowingly, accepted as personal obligations. I offer the following affirmation to serve that purpose:

I, _____, hereby do solemnly affirm the social contract and promise to honor my obligations to protect and defend the human rights of all others. I expect and demand that all others protect and defend my rights as a human being. I make these duties, which the law imposes upon me, my personal obligations.

I acknowledge my obligations to:

deal in good faith with others;

respect others as equal human beings;

keep my promises;

respect myself;

be tolerant toward others' beliefs; and

be reciprocal in my relationships with others.

I make this promise voluntarily and in good faith with the knowledge and understanding of my obligations to others to act for the public good where I live and work and learn and play.

SUMMARY

Basic or natural duties cannot be enforced nor human rights protected without the establishment of rules that implement the burdens and benefits of the social contract. The rule of law means that we have a society of laws not men. The rule of law is what makes society civilized. Society and its leaders may not:

1. act in a criminal or tyrannical manner toward any of their people by committing acts of murder, genocide, arrest, imprisonment without cause, torture, or other similar conduct that violates fundamental human rights;

2. impose a duty or deny a benefit, without pre-established laws defining

that burden; the ancient common law rule is that there is no offence without a law.

3. create laws that are substantively unfair;

4. act in an arbitrary or capricious manner in the application or administration of laws that are fair.

In order that there might be rules, there must be a government to make and enforce just laws. In American society these laws must be developed for the common good according to our standard of justice. American ethics requires that each person be treated with due process of law, meaning that each person must be treated equally and fairly regarding life, liberty, and property.

The fundamental role of government is to implement the basic or natural duties and protect the human rights contained in the social contract. By making certain conduct criminal, we define our public ethical values and enforce our public morality, the morality that binds us all. Police power rests upon necessity and self-protection. Government cannot tell you what to think or believe on any subject. Government may only regulate your actions and then only when it establishes a substantial governmental interest such as public health, public safety, public welfare, or some other secular community need.

Some religious values find their way into our public ethics and become a part of our public morality. In our time, Mario Cuomo observed that religious values become a part of our public morality only when those values are adopted by consensus of all the people. We would add that this consensus is built by transforming religious values with otherworld objectives into secular values that focus on the needs of the community, here and now.

The role of government and therefore the scope of public morality is limited by the restrictions that the Constitution places upon the federal and state governments. With respect to the federal government the people have retained rights that they have not ceded to that government.

Although our law protects individual liberty, American ethics is not libertarian to the extent that John Stuart Mill would have allowed any individual conduct that did not *physically* harm another. American ethics recognizes that self-regulating or self-destructive behavior does hurt society economically because of publicly supported medical and hospital costs. Those close to a person injured or deceased through their own recklessness suffer great emotional and psychological pain and injury. American ethics recognizes that the state may interfere to protect you from yourself in many circumstances.

However, when you exercise a fundamental right such as freedom of conscience, expression, association, or the right to marry and raise a family according to your best lights, you have a right to privacy in the exercise of those rights. The government has no jurisdiction over that private conduct unless it can show a compelling state interest such as a serious danger to national security or the public health.

The general right of privacy, which includes not only constitutionally protected rights but other human rights as well, has become the line of demarcation or the boundary line between the role of government as a constitutional democracy and the ordered liberty of the people to do as they wish without government interference in their private lives.

It is our obligation to teach secular ethical values in our public schools to develop virtuous citizens who know their obligations to each other and to society and to encourage virtuous conduct that manifests our care for each other. We need to develop the social skill of reciprocity in order to understand the point of view of another, to be able to deal with all others as equals, and to be tolerant of those with whom we disagree.

The essence of my code of personal morality is my explicit consent to the duties of the social contract and my intention to make those duties my personal obligation and commitment to others—to act for the public good where I live, work, learn, and play.

MY PERSONAL OBLIGATION:

Reciprocity

Professor Kohlberg observes that the development of moral judgment depends upon the one's ability to stand in the shoes of another—"...[T]he capacity 'to react to the other as someone like the self and to react to the self's behavior in the role of the other.' The ability to take the role of another person is a social skill that develops gradually from about the age of six and proves to be a turning point in the development of moral judgment...."[37] It is that skill that enables one to effectively negotiate with another. The ability to reach that point in the development of moral judgment is dependent upon the child developing concrete operational thinking—that is, the ability to see logical relationships between physical things and eventually social relationships.[38]

Reciprocity is not like other duties that are enforced by law; rather it is a skill that you, as a virtuous citizen, must learn and utilize if you are to develop your capacity to make mature moral judgements. If you, the virtuous citizen, are to move from the child-like ethics of obedience to rules, to the adult ethics of mutual agreement and self-imposed mutual obligations, you need to develop the social skill of reciprocity, the ability to stand in the shoes of one with whom you disagree and see things from the point of view of your adversary. This does not mean that you abandon your heartfelt convictions but it does mean that you can role play and gain a deeper understanding of the needs and the perspective of the other person. Only then do you learn how to com-

---

[37] *Ibid.* p. 49.
[38] See: *Ibid.* pp. 50-1.

promise on those things where there is common ground without violating core values. Only then can you make rules that concern the public good—rules that can legitimately claim the obedience of all.

MY PERSONAL VIRTUE:
Open-Mindedness

The dictionary defines "open-mindedness" as being "receptive to arguments or ideas—unprejudiced...."[39] The virtuous citizen is open to the opinions and ideas of one with whom you disagree. In the exercise of good faith and a high degree of intellectual honesty, the virtuous citizen is willing to be persuaded by reasonable argument based upon credible evidence. The virtuous citizen is not dogmatic or opinionated but is open to the rule of reason.

ADDITIONAL READING

Promoting Moral Growth[40]
by Joseph Reimer, Diana Pritchard Paolitto and Richard H. Hersh
Chapter 4:
Kohlberg's Theory of Moral Development and Moral Education

Question 1:

How can Kohlberg claim that there is one sequence of stages that accurately describes the moral reasoning of all people? Doesn't he know that values differ from person to person and from society to society?

Kohlberg is certainly aware of cultural relativity. He knows that different societies have different values and socialize their children to follow their society's values. Yet he defends the claim for the existence of a single sequence of stages of moral judgment on both philosophic and psychological grounds.

Kohlberg begins his argument by asking: What are the real differences in moral values from society to society? If we take as an example the value of human life and the concomitant prohibition from the taking of innocent life, how much cultural variation is evident? We see that some societies practice human sacrifice, patricide, or infanticide—all of which are outlawed as murder in Western societies. Within our own society, debates over abortion and eutha-

---

[39] *Webster's New Collegiate Dictionary* (G. & C. Merriam Company, Springfield, Massachusetts, 1977).
[40] Reimer, Paolitto & Hersh, *Op. Cit.*, pp. 283-6.

nasia reflect serious differences of moral opinion on the value of life.

Despite these obvious cultural differences, Kohlberg argues that there is a common recognition of the value of life and a common concern for preserving human life. If a nomadic people set out for a new camp and leave behind some of their weaker members to die, it is not because they are indifferent to the value of life. Quite the opposite. They perceive that the lives of all tribal members might be in danger, and so they decide to leave behind the few. Faced with a similar choice, most Western people would also sacrifice the few to save the many. They might disagree on the criteria for choosing whom to sacrifice, but that disagreement would presuppose a common adherence to the basic value of human life.

The value of human life is one of ten basic moral values that Kohlberg believes are common to all human societies:

The Ten Universal Moral Issues

1. Laws and rules

2. Conscience

3. Personal roles of affection

4. Authority

5. Civil rights

6. Contract, trust, and justice in exchange

7. Punishment

8. The value of life

9. Property rights and values

10. Truth

One may disagree with the particular values Kohlberg has chosen as being universal, but it would seem hard to deny that some values or moral institutions are universally common, even though the practices associated with these values may vary radically in different societies.

Even if we accept the hypothesized existence of some universally accepted basic moral values, how would their existence substantiate the claim of one universal sequence of moral stages? Kohlberg's reasoning at this point is complex. He does not believe that these universal values are directly taught to children. Rather, the basic values are embodied in common social institutions such as the family, the legal system, and the economy. All societies have family units in which personal roles of affection are embodied, economic systems in which rules of fair exchange are formalized, legal systems in which the value of law is upheld, and so forth. Children in every society are exposed to, and taught to participate in, these institutions. Yet children begin learning the basic values before participating in the institutions in which these values are embodied. A child does not, for example, have to go to court to begin thinking about the value of laws and rules; he does not have to enter the market to begin thinking about the value of fair exchange. The rudimentary experience of these values already has taken place within the house and the peer group. The values arise out of the child's experience of interacting with adults and peers, and operate as conceptual modes for regulating social interaction.

This last point is a crucial one for understanding Kohlberg's position. As long as you think of basic moral values as having to be taught to children, you will end up focusing on the particular culturally bound rules of behavior that children learn in each society. Once you consider that the function of value concepts is to regulate social behavior and that children develop moral concepts by having to get along with other people, you will see how the development of value concepts can be a universally common experience.

Children in our society play baseball; children in Europe and Latin America play soccer; children in other societies play other organized games. No matter what game is being played, to play the game, children have to agree on certain rules and follow them. Similarly, children in our society exchange baseball cards; children in Switzerland exchange marbles; children elsewhere exchange other objects of value. Regardless of what objects are being exchanged, if the exchange is to take place amicably, the children have to develop a concept of fair exchange and stick to it. In any of these cases, children develop the moral concept by engaging in activity and regulating their behavior according to the concept involved.

A stage of moral judgment represents prescribed modes of deciding how one ought to interact with others in conflict situations. Whether a society teaches children rules about crossing streets or swimming in lagoons, if a child is to distinguish between what he may do and what he must do, he has to develop a concept of rules as obligatory. Given children's common cognitive limitations (as detailed in Piaget's work) and their commonly limited social experience (involving role taking and participating in social institutions), Kohlberg assumes that they also have limited modes of judgment available to them for resolving moral conflict. Children aged six to seven develop a concept of rules as absolute and of punishment as inevitably following the breaking of rules. Usually by age ten children have also developed the mode of reciprocity and the concept of fair exchange. These commonly available modes of judgment are what universally constitute the first two stages of moral judgment. As children gain more experience within social institutions and learn to take the role of the community, they develop modes of judgment that universally characterize the conventional stages of moral judgment.

Glossary of Terms

The words and phrases defined here are not necessarily dictionary definitions. Rather, these terms are defined in the way that they are used in this book. Ordinary words and phrases are not included; only those more technical terms that are drawn from ethics, philosophy or law are defined.

A priori Relating to or devised by reasoning from self-evident propositions; presupposed by experience.

Accidental human characteristic Human characteristics arising from extrinsic causes; human characteristics that are not essential to the definition of the human being, such as sex, race, wealth, or social status. See: essential human characteristic.

Agreement An oral or written promise between two or more people regarding future conduct; a mutual commitment or obligation as to a course of action; harmony of opinion or action; a meeting of the minds; when legally binding, a contract. See: contract, social contract.

American ethics The public morality of the American people.

Annuit coeptis The inscription on the back of The Great Seal of the United States; He or It (God or the Eye) has smiled on our undertaking. See: novus ordo seclorum.

Bad, evil Subjectively, not good in the short term. See: good, right, wrong.

Bill of attainder Special act of the legislature inflicting capital punishment for treason or other felonies without a trial and conviction in the ordinary course of judicial proceedings.

Body politic A group of persons organized under a single governmental authority; a people considered a collective unit.

Citizen A native or naturalized person who is a member of the civil state, who owes allegiance to the United States and the state wherein he or she resides and who is entitled to the enjoyment of political rights and privileges as well as the protection of human and civil rights; an American national. See: political rights, virtuous citizen, human being, person.

Civil rights The rights derived from the Civil War Amendments, the Thirteenth, Fourteenth and Fifteenth Amendments to the Constitution;   includes those laws that have abolished apartheid or Jim Crow laws in this country and that promote equality of treatment in employment, public accommodations, transportation, housing, and education, among all members of civil society. See: human or natural rights, political rights, economic rights, constitutional rights.

Common good, public good Refers to laws enacted for the benefit of everyone in the society.

Common law The body of law developed in England primarily from judicial decisions based on custom and precedent, unwritten in statute or code and constituting the basis of the English legal system and the federal and state legal systems, except for Louisiana whose legal system is based upon the Napoleonic Code. See: statutory law.

Commonweal The general welfare.

Condition Precedent A condition that must be satisfied for a contract or agreement to come into existence.

Constitution The US Constitution; the organic and fundamental written law of the United States establishing the character and conception of the federal government and the relationship to state governments, laying the basic principals to which its internal life is to be conformed, organizing the government and regulating, distributing and limiting the functions of its various departments and agencies, and prescribing the extent and the manner of the exercise of sovereign power; the written implementation of some basic provisions of the social contract. See: law, positive law.

Constitutional rights Human rights, political rights, and civil rights found in the US Constitution.

Constitutional democracy Self-government that is not arbitrary, that governs by the rule of law, i.e., a government of laws not of men, which enforces public morality only to the extent required by the public need and which honors the Constitution as the supreme law of the land. See: ordered liberty.

Contract A legally enforceable agreement or mutual promise between two or more persons to do or not to do a particular thing. See: agreement, social contract, quid pro quo.

Conscience One's understanding of what is objectively right and wrong and that which prompts one to choose what is right and avoid what is wrong. See: right, wrong.

Consensus Group solidarity in sentiment and belief; general agreement; the judgement arrived at by most of those concerned without any reasonable or significant opposition.

Crime Any act done in violation of those duties that an individual owes to the community, specified in criminal codes, for which there is a penalty; an unethical act; it is an injury to the people as a whole and not just to the victim. See: tort, unethical.

Determinism The school of psychology that holds that acts of the will are determined by antecedent causes. See: free choice, free will, responsibility.

Due process Laws and procedures that are fair and reasonable and equally benefit or burden all in society.

Duty A rule imposed by a lawgiver for which obedience is demanded and enforced. See: natural duties, obligation, virtue.

Economic rights The right to a fair share of the economic benefits of social cooperation; the right to a minimum humane standard of living, including adequate nutritious food, adequate shelter and clothing, elementary education to the level of basic literacy, and basic health care, for yourself and your family. See: human or natural rights, political rights, civil rights, constitutional rights.

Essential human characteristic Human characteristics arising from intrinsic causes; human characteristics that are essential to the definition of the human being, such as the capacity to think and reason and the power of free will. See: accidental human characteristic.

Established church, single establishment A single church recognized by law as the official church of a nation and supported by civil authority. See: established religion, multiple or plural establishment.

Established religion, multiple or plural establishment Where the construction and maintenance of churches, schools and the salaries of the clergy and teachers of organized religious bodies are paid for by general taxation; generally, tax support is given to favored religious groups while others are tolerated and allowed to exist; it is also known as non-preferential establishment and accomodationist establishment. See: separationist or "no aid" approach.

Ethics The study of ideal personal conduct; the continuing search for pragmatic principles of social interaction that create a peaceful and just society. See: natural duties, political philosophy.

Ethical Conduct that is right. See: right, moral.

Ethical center Your innermost contemplative self where ethical principles and standards exist, where moral judgements and decisions are made that determine what kind of a person you are.

Ex post facto A law that makes an innocent deed a crime retroactively.

Franchise The right to vote in public elections. See: political rights.

Free choice, free will The power of human beings to choose between alternatives or to act with a specific intent so that the choice and action are to a certain extent creatively determined by the conscious subject; to choose between right and wrong conduct or to choose to act with right or wrong intent without instinctual compulsion, random chance, or causal effect. See: responsibility, determinism.

Good The perceived immediate benefit to the individual. In this book this subjective good may be wrongful, unethical and criminal conduct. See: right, wrong, bad, evil.

Habeas corpus, the writ of A court order directed to the person detaining another, and commanding him to produce the body of the prisoner (or person detained) before the court; an ancient protection against arbitrary imprisonment.

Human being A rational animal, i.e., the last of the five great apes that is social, has the capacity to think and reason and the power of free will; a member of the species *Homo sapiens, sapiens*; See: person.

Human rights, natural rights The relationships that arise from our nature as human beings that entitle everyone to certain conduct from all others; the benefits or the quid pro quo for honoring the natural duties of the social contract. See: natural duties, social contract, quid pro quo.

Immoral unethical; choosing and doing wrong.

Inchoate Duty Imperfect; partial; unfinished; begun but not completed.

Justice giving to each his or her due. See: sense or standard of justice.

Law, positive law Man-made statutes that constitute the written embodiment of the social contract, especially natural duties. In our federal system, laws refer to statutes passed by Congress or the state legislatures that must conform to the provisions of the US Constitution i.e. these laws must not be unconstitutional. See: Constitution.

Laws of Nature The Enlightenment concept of natural law; the physical laws of nature discovered by Isaac Newton and Galileo that were thought to include laws governing social interaction in the state of nature before the formation of governments. See: natural law.

Malum in se Conduct that is wrong in itself, such as murder.

Malum prohibitum Conduct that is not wrong in itself but is prohibited for the good order of society, such as the establishment of traffic regulations.

Moral, morality To follow the dictates of a rightly formed conscience; to act ethically; ethics establishes the rules of ideal conduct, morality is to honor those rules; in this book to be ethical and to be moral, are interchangeable terms. See: ethics, public morality.

Natural duties The necessary rules of social conduct for human beings to live together in groups with peace and justice. See: duty, obligation, virtue.

Natural Law The theories developed by Aristotle, the Romans and later Aquinas, claiming there are laws of God arising from the nature of human beings, that can be discovered by reason, that are binding on all people, the highest embodiment of which is the Ten Commandments. See: laws of nature.

Novus ordo seclorum The inscription on the back of the Great Seal of the United States under the pyramid; A New Secular World Order. See: annuit coeptis.

Obligation The explicit assumption of, acceptance of, and personal commitment to honor the natural duties of the social contract.

Onus probandi The burden of proof.

Ordered liberty The freedom to exercise fundamental rights without governmental restraint, in private matters that do not involve the public in any serious way. See: constitutional democracy.

Person A member of society entitled to the protection of his or her human and civil rights by the government. See: human being, citizen.

Police power The general power of the state to define and enforce public morality through the power of the legislature to define what constitutes a crime; the broad inherent power of the legislature to regulate our conduct to promote the peace, safety, health, education, general welfare, and public morals of the community.

Political philosophy The study of the ideal social organization that examines monarchy, aristocracy, democracy, socialism, and communism as models of social and political organization; the social science that sets forth the rules and principles for a community that promotes peace and justice among its people; See: ethics, natural duties.

Political rights The rights of citizens, such as the right to vote and hold public office. See: citizen, human or natural rights, constitutional rights, civil rights, economic rights.

Procedural law Laws that effectuate substantive rights. For example, the writ of habeas corpus is a procedural remedy that protects one from arbitrary arrest and unlawful imprisonment. See: substantive law.

Public morality Honoring the natural duties of the social contract; that conduct and relationships that the government may regulate through the criminal law; the rules that constitute American ethics. See: American ethics, natural duties, secular values.

Public mores, public morals Particular laws that enforce community standards of decency such as laws that regulate the distribution, sale and use of alcoholic beverages, forbidding houses of prostitution, forbidding the sale of child pornography, or prohibiting public nudity.

Quid pro quo Something for something; something given in exchange for something received; the benefit of a contract. See: contract, social contract, human rights.

Responsibility The duty to choose what is right and avoid what is wrong. See: free choice, free will.

Right The objective good; conduct that promotes a peaceful and just society. See: good, bad, evil, wrong.

Rule of law Government by pre-existing fair and equal laws, not the arbitrary rule of men.

Rule of reason Conduct that is guided by ethical principles, not the use of force.

Sectarian, sacred or religious values Duties commanded by God, Allah, the

Bible, the Torah, the Koran, or some other sacred scripture; otherworld values that promote service and honor to a deity or that are motivated by the desire to go to heaven, reach nirvana, and avoid hell. See: secular values.

Secular values The commonly shared community values of this world that promote peace and justice in society for the commonweal. See: sectarian, sacred or religious values.

Sense or standard of justice How equally society distributes the benefits and the burdens of social cooperation.

Separationist or "no aid" approach Strict separation of church and state. See: established religion, multiple or plural establishment.

Statutory law Laws made by a legislature, not by a king or the courts. See: common law.

Substantive law Law that declares human rights, creates, defines and regulates political and civil rights. See: procedural law.

Super majority A majority of more than half plus one of those voting; for example, an amendment to the Federal Constitution requires a proposal by two-thirds of both houses of Congress or by two-thirds of the legislatures of the several states and the ratification or approval of the proposed amendment by three-fourths of all state legislatures or state constitutional conventions.

Tort An injury to an individual, not the people as a whole, for which the victim is entitled to money damages. In this book a tort, such as wrongful death, is not treated as unethical, although where there is a corresponding crime such as murder, that is an unethical act.

Unethical Criminal conduct. See: crime.

Virtue Ethical and altruistic conduct for the greater good of the community beyond what the law requires.

Virtuous citizen The term of art used by the Founding Fathers to describe every member of society, not just citizens, who were well informed, obeyed the law, and performed altruistic conduct to promote the commonweal.

Wrong the objective bad or evil; unethical conduct; criminal conduct that injures the people as a whole. See: right, good, bad, evil.

Index